W9-BIV-665

Date: 2/8/21

**943.087 BLA
Black, Monica,
A demon-haunted land :
witches, wonder doctors, and**

ALSO BY MONICA BLACK

Death in Berlin: From Weimar to Divided Germany

A DEMON-HAUNTED LAND

A DEMON-HAUNTED LAND

WITCHES, WONDER DOCTORS, AND THE GHOSTS OF THE PAST IN POST-WWII GERMANY

MONICA BLACK

METROPOLITAN BOOKS   HENRY HOLT AND COMPANY   NEW YORK

Metropolitan Books
Henry Holt and Company
Publishers since 1866
120 Broadway
New York, New York 10271
www.henryholt.com

Metropolitan Books® and ⛰® are registered trademarks of
Macmillan Publishing Group, LLC.

Library of Congress Cataloging-in-Publication data

Names: Black, Monica, 1968– author.
Title: A demon-haunted land : witches, wonder doctors, and the ghosts of the past in
    post-WWII Germany / Monica Black.
Other titles: Witches, wonder doctors, and the ghosts of the past in post-WWII Germany
Description: First edition. | New York, New York : Metropolitan Books, Henry Holt and
    Company, [2020] | Includes bibliographical references and index.
Identifiers: LCCN 2019052302 (print) | LCCN 2019052303 (ebook) |
    ISBN 9781250225672 (hardcover) | ISBN 9781250225665 (ebook)
Subjects: LCSH: Germany—Social conditions—1945–1955. | National
    socialism—Psychological aspects. | Occultism—Germany—History—20th
    century. | Healers—Germany (West)—Biography. | World War,
    1939–1945—Germany—Psychological aspects. | World War, 1939–1945—Moral
    and ethical aspects—Germany. | Spiritual healing—Germany—History—20th century. |
    Psychic trauma—Germany. | Germany (West)—Moral conditions.
Classification: LCC DD257.2 .B54 2020 (print) | LCC DD257.2 (ebook) |
    DDC 133.40943/09044—dc23
LC record available at https://lccn.loc.gov/2019052302
LC ebook record available at https://lccn.loc.gov/2019052303

Our books may be purchased in bulk for promotional, educational, or business use. Please
contact your local bookseller or the Macmillan Corporate and Premium Sales Department at
(800) 221-7945, extension 5442, or by e-mail at MacmillanSpecialMarkets@macmillan.com.

First Edition 2020

Designed by Kelly S. Too

Printed in the United States of America

1 3 5 7 9 10 8 6 4 2

For Nikki, my sister

In the closed domain of a diabolical discourse, anxiety, revenge, and hatred are indeed given free rein . . . but above all they are displaced, enclosed . . . masked, subjugated.

—Michel de Certeau, *The Possession at Loudun*

CONTENTS

A DEMON-HAUNTED LAND

INTRODUCTION

Frau N. and her family hailed from a village in Franconia, in southern Germany. Her father was known as a *Braucher*, a person with certain healing powers. As much as locals relied on those who possessed such powers, communities like Frau N.'s often regarded healers with ambivalence, even mistrust. After all, might not someone able to use magic to take sickness away also be able to bring it? When Frau N.'s father died a difficult death, many of their neighbors were confirmed in their suspicion that he had been in league with sinister powers, and now the community adopted this unease toward Frau N. herself. She was also said to hold herself aloof, generally "swimming against the stream," and orienting herself too much toward "the better sort."

Frau N.'s real trouble started, though, when Herr C. arrived in the village. He claimed to have healing knowledge, and said he could establish the sources of illness by reading signs—bits of bread, charcoal, and broom straws floating in water. He became active in the village, performing magical tasks. He claimed to possess powers of sympathetic magic and to command magnetic forces. He also began circulating rumors about N., saying he had seen her through a window reading a book that contained spells and charms. This meant that she worked for the Devil, C. claimed, whereas he worked for God.

Herr C. drank, worked little, and neglected his large family. The community did not think very highly of him. Nonetheless, when two middle-aged villagers suddenly died, the rumors already circulating about Frau N. got worse. She was suspected of having had a hand in their deaths. When the local pastor's child abruptly lost his appetite, that was also laid at N.'s feet, as was the death of a hog. C. began to predict that the children of the family who had owned the pig would themselves fall ill and become lame. To avoid this curse, he directed their mother to collect the children's urine; he wanted to spray it on N.'s house as a defense against her evildoing. He also predicted that N. would come on three occasions to the family and ask to borrow things; they must not loan anything out. If all his instructions were followed to the letter, N. would have no more power over the family, C. said.

The family rejected Herr C.'s help but remained filled with concern. He had succeeded in creating a climate of great fear in the community. The smallest events in the village began to be interpreted as the result of witchcraft. Children were forbidden to eat anything Frau N. cooked or to accept gifts from her. If she brought flowers to a wedding, they were tossed out. If she gave someone a potted plant, it was dug up by the roots.

Finally, N. had no recourse but to take C. to court. He was found guilty of defamation and given a light jail term. After that, rumors about N. may still have been whispered but were no longer spoken aloud.[1]

. . .

When I first read about N. and C., their story sounded to me—until that surprise twist at the end—like something that might have taken place in early modern Europe. But then there is that jarring about-face: Frau N., the one persecuted and defamed, goes to court to make it stop. The accuser, Herr C., is sanctioned and sentenced to jail. Such an outcome would hardly have been likely in, say, the sixteenth or seventeenth century, when a single accusation of witchcraft could lead to large-scale juridical and clerical investigations. Torture of suspects would often turn up further witches. Executions and burnings, on quite a number of occasions, were the result.

But the story of Frau N. and Herr C. did not transpire in the sixteenth or seventeenth century. It happened just after the Second World War, in the newly created Federal Republic of Germany. For a period of time after the Third Reich's horrors, after the Holocaust and the bloodiest and most nihilistic conflict in human history, witches—men and women believed to personify and to be in league with evil—appeared to have been loosed on the land. Between roughly 1947 and 1965, scores of "witchcraft trials"—so dubbed by the press—took place all around the country, from Catholic Bavaria in the south to Protestant Schleswig-Holstein in the north. They happened in rural villages like Frau N.'s, but also in small towns and big cities.

At its most basic level, an accusation of witchcraft in postwar Germany was an imputation of covert evildoing, an allegation of malevolent conspiracy. Indeed, the question of evil seemed to haunt postwar imaginations and the lives of many ordinary citizens after Nazism, and witches were only one of its many manifestations. In the archives I found sources in which people talk of being pursued by devils and hiring exorcists. I learned about a wildly popular healer who claimed the ability to identify the good and the wicked, to heal the former and cast out the latter. I located court and police records describing prayer circles whose members convened to combat demonic infection. I read about people making mass pilgrimages to holy sites in search of spiritual cures and redemption. In newspaper clippings, I discovered end-of-days rumors prophesying doom for the wicked and salvation for the innocent.

To appreciate how witchcraft and other fantasies about evil can help us understand West Germany's early years requires thinking about witchcraft differently than we are often accustomed to doing. Unlike the witch scares of the sixteenth and seventeenth centuries, postwar West German witchcraft accusations did not involve having sex with the Devil, flying around at night, levitating, or being able to fall down a flight of stairs without injury. The repertoire no longer included succubi and incubi or the witches' Sabbath.[2] The story of N. and C. and many others like it were more pedestrian and not especially fantastic. Though the accusations imputed magical evildoing, they principally involved ordinary suspicion, jealousy, and mistrust. But as petty as they might have seemed to outsiders, these episodes were mortally serious, existentially serious, because they dealt with good and evil, sickness and health.

Beliefs in witches, demons, and magical healing are not simply vestiges of a "premodern" world, static and timeless, handed down unchanged from generation to generation. They have unique cultures and histories that change over time. But they also have common traits across eras and geography. Almost anyone who lived through the 1980s in the United States, for example, will remember the nationwide obsession with alleged satanic cults of ritual child abusers. While different in most particulars from the episodes this book discusses, that obsession nonetheless shares certain motifs with them: the accusations generally flared up in close relationships, among families and caregivers and neighbors. The allegations carried more than a whiff of not just interpersonal conflict but also cultural malaise and anxiety. In the same way, post–World War II German fantasies about witchcraft can help us understand the society in which they festered. Why did fears of covert malevolence, spiritual damage, and the possibility of cosmic punishment erupt when they did? What should we make of the fact that certain kinds of evil appeared to gain traction *after* Nazism?

. . .

Every moment in time contains an unfathomably vast, kaleidoscopic array of variables that influence the direction and character of historical change in entirely unpredictable ways. It is a truism, in that sense, that every historical moment is unique. But the immediate post–World War II period was unique in a more radical way. That war still stuns us into silence. The scope of the disaster Nazi Germany unleashed on the world, so overwhelming as to defy understanding, recalibrated everything.[3] In its capacity to make a mockery both of ordinary, everyday forms of knowledge and of expert wisdom, the war posed an anthropological shock—a shock to humanity as such—casting the basic knowability of the world into doubt.[4] The ingenuity for destruction and cruelty demonstrated in World War II upended much that had seemed apparent or graspable about human behavior, inspiring the work of social scientists for decades to come.[5] The very means by which the war was fought—genocide, massacres of civilians, mass population transfers, death squads and death camps, medical torture, mass rapes, mass starvation of prisoners of war, aerial bombardment, atomic weapons—obliterated taken-for-granted distinctions not only between soldier and civilian, home and battlefront, but also between the real and the incomprehensible. Who could have believed, before the Nazis created them, industrial complexes designed for no other purpose than the production and destruction of corpses?[6]

When the twentieth century began, airplanes had not yet been invented. Few could have envisioned back then that within decades whole cities could be flattened from the air. Few could have imagined that a single bomb could destroy all life in a city and vaporize human bodies, leaving behind only ghostly traces of formerly living beings—or that people could be left "neither dead nor alive," as took place at Hiroshima, "like walking ghosts."[7] Science fiction became science reality. German philosopher and physician Karl Jaspers, who had opposed the Nazis, hoped to redeem science after the war, in the aftermath of the atomic bomb and Nazi medical experimentation. But even he admitted in 1950 that the "human condition throughout the millennia appears relatively stable in comparison with the impetuous movement that has now caught up mankind as a result of science and technology, and is driving it no one knows where."[8]

In defeated Germany, the problem of how to know the world was especially grave. The country itself did not even survive the war as an intact state, if a "state" means a sovereign entity with its own government, bureaucracy, and army, its own national economy and treaties and trade agreements. Germany no longer had the right to issue currency or even put up street signs.[9] Many traditional sites of authority— the military, the press, universities, the medical establishment—were deeply morally compromised or had been abolished by the Allied armies now occupying the country. The British, French, Soviets, and Americans carved up former Germany into four military occupation zones. The British and Americans merged their zones to create Bizonia, taking effect in January 1947. When the French joined them in 1949, Trizonia was born. The place even had an unofficial national anthem, "We Are the Natives of Trizonia"—a big hit at carnival time, since, like the German government and army, the German national anthem had also been banned.[10] The Allies had talked extensively about dismantling the country's industrial apparatus altogether, of closing down its mines and crippling its heavy industry, the source of its outsized military capacity.[11] Germany, it was felt, could safely make clocks and toys and beer but not guns.

A general sense of indeterminacy hung over former Germany—and not just because its government had been decapitated, its powerful economy reduced to barter, its administration of public life controlled almost completely by foreign armies. Things people felt even more directly in their daily lives had all changed. Words and ideas, symbols and forms of greeting, even gestures that Germans freely used one day became taboo the next. Almost literally, the ground had shifted beneath everyone's feet: in summer 1945, the Allies conferenced at Potsdam and agreed to redraw the map of Europe, stripping Germany of its territories east of the Oder and Neisse Rivers. In the ensuing whirlwind, between twelve and fourteen million Germans from various parts of Eastern Europe, some from communities that had existed since the Middle Ages, fled or were expelled, sometimes with great violence, from their towns and villages, and forced onto the roads.[12] Will-Erich Peuckert, a folklorist, fled his native Silesia as a refugee. After the collapse of his country and his experience of flight, he found, "rational and causal thinking" were "no longer sufficient" to do his work as a scholar. He wondered whether this was because "our empire shattered and we stood mired in darkness, and nothing mattered anymore but just to harvest the grain."[13]

Millions were dead. Millions were missing and lost, never to return. Millions more remained imprisoned in POW camps all over the world. Millions had lost everything for a cause few could even seem to remember having supported. "Suddenly, we had to recognize," recalled one man, "that everything we had done, often with great enthusiasm or out of a sense of duty—everything had been in vain."[14] Defeat and occupation and loss only compounded the need for answers. What had caused defeat? Who was to blame?

Social alienation and dislocation had become increasingly acute even before the war ended. In 1945, a report from the SD (the *Sicherheitsdienst*, the intelligence division of the *Schutzstaffel*, or SS) described feelings among the people "of mourning, despondency, bitterness, and a rising fury," growing out of the "deepest disappointment for having misplaced one's trust." Such feelings were most pronounced, the report observed, "among those who have known nothing in this war but sacrifice and work."[15] By the war's last months, Germans were fighting not only the Allied armies on their own soil but sometimes also each other. Some 300,000 or more non-Jewish Germans were put to death by the regime for treason, deserting the front lines, or showing signs of defeatism. Those who chose to leave the fight sometimes wound up hanging from the end of a rope with a sign around their necks pronouncing them cowards.[16] Such acts of "local justice," especially those meted out in small localities and urban neighborhoods, could hardly have been forgotten after the war, even if the resentments found no ready outlet.[17]

Imagine living in a small town where your family doctor after the war is the same one who had recommended to the Nazi state that you be sterilized. Such scores could never be settled; such losses would go unredeemed.[18] For many people, daily life was blighted by fraud and betrayal. Lying awake at night, people wondered what had become of their loved ones who vanished during the war. Some remembered seeing their Jewish neighbors carried away, and even if they did not fully comprehend what was happening then, they did later. Some families had adopted children during the war; orphans, they were told, maybe from Poland or Czechoslovakia. But surely some asked themselves, in a dark moment, who their child's parents had been and what happened to them. During the war, people bought goods at open-air urban markets, items that had been stolen from Jews expelled to their deaths in Eastern Europe—tableware, books, coats, furniture. Germans ate and drank from china and glassware that had belonged to their neighbors and wore their clothing and sat at their dinner tables.[19]

German is famous for its expressive vocabulary. *Schicksalsgemeinschaft* was a term used during the war to describe a community supposedly bound together by a shared experience of fate. Consensus among historians now holds that it was more an invention of Nazi propaganda than anything else.[20] Certainly after 1945, German society evinced nothing like a coherent sense of communal and mutual experience, but rather shattered trust and dissolved moral bonds. In the Third Reich, denunciation had been a way of life. Citizens were encouraged to betray to the state anyone whom they suspected of the slightest disloyalty, sending many to concentration camps and often to their deaths.[21] A person could be reported to the Gestapo for something as seemingly minor as listening to foreign radio. The memory of these experiences, for betrayer and betrayed, did not quickly dissipate. Alexander Mitscherlich, a psychiatrist who would later become one of the Federal Republic's most prominent and respected social critics, described a "chill" that had "befallen the relationships of men among one another"—one that defied understanding. It was "on a cosmic scale," he wrote, "like a shift in the climate."[22] A 1949 public opinion poll asked Germans whether most people could be trusted. Nine out of ten said no.[23]

A great deal of what we know about the world comes to us secondhand, from parents and friends, teachers and the media; we take much of it on faith. For example, as the historian of science Steven Shapin says, we might "know" the composition of DNA without ever having independently verified it. In this sense, knowledge and trust are linked. "Knowing things" requires trusting other people as mutual witnesses to a shared reality, and trusting in the institutions that supply information that shapes everyday existence. Society itself could be reasonably described as nothing more or less than a system of commonly held beliefs about how the world works, beliefs that undergird and lend sense and continuity to our daily lives.[24] Yet trust is never a given, never axiomatic: it is historically specific, constituted in different ways under varying circumstances.[25]

In Germany after World War II, even the most basic facts of daily life could not always be easily or definitively substantiated. Up to 1948 at least, the black market reigned, and food was often found to be adulterated.[26] Was this coffee or chicory? Flour or starch? Down to the simplest questions, things were not quite what they seemed. For years after the war, there were official documents that still referenced the "German Reich," or whose authors appeared unsure about whether pieces of Germany ceded to Poland still belonged to the "empire."[27] Moral confusion produced a desire to "treat facts as if they were mere opinions."[28] And, as the novelist W. G. Sebald reflected, a "tacit agreement, equally binding on everyone," made discussing "the true state of material and moral ruin in which the country found itself" quite simply taboo.[29]

Some basic truths were too toxic even to acknowledge, let alone discuss. The philosopher Hans Jonas escaped Nazi Germany as a young man in 1933 and went to Palestine, where he joined the Jewish Brigade. His mother stayed behind in Mönchengladbach, the family's Rhineland hometown. She was murdered at Auschwitz. When Jonas came back in 1945, he visited his family home on Mozartstraße. He spoke to the new owner. "And how's your mother?" the man asked.

Jonas said she had been killed. "Killed? Who would have killed her?" asked the man, dubious. "People don't do that to an old lady." "She was killed at Auschwitz," Jonas told the man. "No, that can't be true," the man replied. "Come on, now! You mustn't believe everything you hear!" He put his arm around Jonas. "But what you're saying about killing and gas chambers—those are just atrocity stories." Then the man saw Jonas looking at the beautiful desk that had belonged to his father. "Do you want it? Do you want to take it with you?" Revolted by the man, Jonas said no and quickly left.[30]

Some people found their wartime experiences so overwhelming that they could not connect their own thoughts and feelings even to those with whom they had shared them. The novelist Hans Erich Nossack witnessed the Allied firebombing of Hamburg, his home city, in 1943. Afterward, he found that "people who lived together in the same house and ate at the same table breathed the air of completely separate worlds. . . . They spoke the same language, but what they meant by their words were entirely different realities."[31] Heinrich Böll's 1953 novel *And Never Said a Word* features a character named Fred Bogner who can hardly relate to anyone from his prewar, pre-soldier life. He is so mortified by his poverty and inability to cope that he has left the home he shared with his wife, Käte, and their children. He spends his days drinking and visiting cemeteries, finding comfort among the dead, and attending funeral masses for people he never knew. Sometimes he is invited out to lunch by their families, whom he finds easier to talk to than almost anyone he knows.[32]

. . .

When World War II came to an end, Germany lay in ruins. Entire cities had been shattered by bombs and artillery, expanses of land left bare where every tree had been cut down for fuel, parts of the country practically erased. More lasting than the physical devastation, however, and even greater than the stigma of defeat and occupation, was the moral ruination. Germany in 1945 was a global pariah, responsible for crimes that beggared imagination. Yet within a short time, occupied Trizonia became the Federal Republic of Germany, or West Germany. It was integrated into the Cold War's Western alliance, had an economy unrivaled in Europe, and was seeing its bomb-flattened cities rapidly rebuilt for a good life of consumerist plenty. History, which is often thought to move glacially, has in its annals not many shifts of fortune as sudden as this. And in this dramatic transformation lie questions at once rich and unsettling.

For quite some time, scholars wrote the Federal Republic's history as a success story.[33] They described its fundamental conservatism, but also its stability, and the establishment of a constitutional republic under the cautious leadership of Chancellor Konrad Adenauer. Historians emphasized the "economic miracle" of the 1950s and '60s and highlighted the combination of full-bore capitalist enterprise and a powerful social welfare state—the "social market economy"—that produced nearly unparalleled consumer affluence for West German citizens. The historiography accentuated the country's integration into the Cold War West, telling a story about the hard work of rebuilding and the gradual achievement of economic power and "normalization" after the devastations of war. This narrative remains implicit in accounts of the immediate postwar period. "With every passing year," one historian writes, "German lives inched further toward . . . the stability and predictability of a civilian life."[34]

It is an appealing story. And it's one a lot of West Germans wanted to see themselves in after the war, after the trauma of defeat and foreign occupation. A new, national self-image was under development in the Federal Republic's early decades, one based not on fantasies of racial superiority and indomitable military prowess but on technical skill, discipline, and hard work. That narrative was reassuring, too, no doubt, because its concreteness and orderliness and reasonableness contrasted so sharply with the magical thinking of the Third Reich. Gone was its myth-ridden leader cult, its blood-and-soil mysticism.

Such master narratives offer coherence, but they also smooth out the rough spots. As insightful critics have noted, the early Federal Republic was a little like a film noir—a genre popularized in the Hollywood of the 1930s and '40s but rooted aesthetically in German expressionism. Noir plays with depths and surfaces, shadow and light, emphasizing that what we see is not necessarily all there is to know, and that a shiny veneer can conceal something considerably less appealing. Just below the surface of West Germany, moving murkily in the near depths, was the ever-present memory of the war and crimes that had led to the state's creation in the first place.[35] What's more, the surreally abrupt shift that had taken place—from murderous dictatorship to democracy, from wholesale theft and mass death to "normal life"—relied extensively on the integration of Nazi perpetrators into society. Largely shielded from prosecution, many of them found promising new métiers amidst changed economic and political realities. Many professions, from government, law, and police to medicine and education, remained packed with former Nazis.

The dissonant contradictions of that transition—such as it was—cannot be accounted for in the bland terms of unemployment statistics and GDP.[36] Appreciating the noirish qualities of early West German history requires an openness to other realities. As one scholar notes, the literature of this period speaks of "magical eyeglasses, limping prophets, martial toys, games and sports, powerful engines, robots and hydrogen bombs, abortion, suicide, genocide and the death of God."[37] Such artifacts fit together only incongruously, brandishing jagged edges. Period newspapers reveal similarly sharp juxtapositions: an advertisement for laundry soap starring a perfectly coiffured, wasp-waisted hausfrau wearing a crisp, white apron appears alongside a story about unmarked mass graves just discovered in a local park.

On one level, it seemed to even the keenest observers after World War II that Germans remained remarkably unchanged by their recent history. Most famous of these commentators was the German-Jewish philosopher Hannah Arendt, who fled her homeland in 1933 but returned from her new home in the United States to visit in 1949.

The country seemed to go on as though nothing much had happened. Nowhere else in devastated Europe was the nightmare of the recent years "less felt and less talked about than in Germany," Arendt wrote. She described an indifferent, emotionless population inscrutably sending each other postcards of a destroyed and vanished past, of historic sights and national treasures that bombs had blown away. She wondered whether postwar German "heartlessness" signified "a half-conscious refusal to yield to grief or a genuine inability to feel."[38] It was as though, after the war ended, Germans just dusted themselves off, began picking up the rubble piece by piece, and started rebuilding. What, if anything, most people felt or thought about what had just happened—the collapse of their country in defeat, its occupation by foreign armies, their participation or complicity in the most heinous crimes—these remained largely opaque, shrouded in silence. While Germans did talk, obsessively, about their own losses in the war, there were many other things they simply did not discuss, at least not publicly: allegiances to the former regime, participation in antisemitic persecution and looting, genocide, war crimes.

The German philosopher Hermann Lübbe famously (and controversially) argued that silence about Nazi crimes was crucial to making a new country out of an old one, a "social-psychological and politically necessary medium to change our postwar population into the citizenry of the Federal Republic of Germany."[39] Silence was what allowed a society riven by the knowledge that it contained all sorts of people—those who had worked to support the Nazis, those who had actively opposed them, and everyone in between—to rebuild a country together. People kept quiet for the sake of reintegration.[40]

It sounds almost harmonious. It was not, this book argues. Silence about what was euphemistically called "the most recent past" was pervasive, but far from perfect. No one forgot the demons Nazism had unleashed: they just didn't talk about them, or they talked about them only in highly coded, ritualized ways.[41] The past often slipped into view, like a ghost that wants to remind the living that its work on earth is not done.

. . .

Silence—even an imperfect one—can make things hard for historians. Our work relies heavily on words, ideally words neatly collected and easily accessible. But a great deal of human experience transpires outside of words, or goes unrecorded. And in some cases silence itself becomes a form of evidence. While implicit codes restricted how people talked about the Nazi era, and neither high crimes nor misdemeanors were discussed in any detail, the past could and did percolate to the surface in out-of-the-way settings and unexpected forms. Even as things began to look smoother and more put-back-together—like a crisp, white apron—the past pierced the present again and again.

Ultimately this book tells the story of a society that collapsed morally and materially, and then had to begin the process of remaking itself. The old values—those that made National Socialism possible in the first place—became outwardly taboo, but they did not vanish. Culture—understood here in terms of the ideas that groups of people impose upon the world and that form the deep structure of their understanding of how it works—transforms only gradually. Circumstances have to change, and new ideas need time to take hold: new ways of living and being and acting, new manners and morals, even new ways of rearing future generations.[42] At least initially, German reconstruction in its many guises took place under the powerful gaze of outsiders, the victorious Allies, who played a considerable role in shaping the discourse and disseminating novel ways of thinking, not to mention administering all kinds of basic, everyday procedures. At the same time, many of the functionaries of the old order quickly returned to positions of power and influence. The old values did not truly depart. A new world had to be created amidst them.

To understand something about how one type of society began the process of becoming a very different one, this book looks at two distinctive but related forms of postwar haunting. One plagued individuals, beleaguered souls who sought spiritual respite—who wanted to be healed, transformed, or redeemed. Another took hold of whole communities, where seething social resentments were sublimated into fears of witches.

Evidence of the first kind of haunting emerged already at the tail end of the war, when apocalyptic rumors took flight, spreading fears not just of generic catastrophe, but, more specifically, of cosmic judgment and divine wrath. Subsiding with the war's end, the rumors came rushing back four years later. A holy man materialized out of nowhere and began curing the sick. This healer, Bruno Gröning, would be embraced by enormous numbers of people who believed he was a new messiah, the architect of their deliverance, even as he castigated those he called "the evil ones," whom he deemed too wicked to cure. While Gröning was not the only postwar healer with a mass following, he was far and away the most famous, and the enormous cache of files related to him in various German archives provides an incomparable perspective on postwar culture and the anxieties of an era. Those anxieties were equally on display in other scenes the book describes, too: amidst the thousands of sightings of the Virgin Mary in Catholic regions of West Germany, within homespun prayer groups performing exorcisms, and among the audiences that came to hear traveling evangelists preach an eye for an eye.

Gröning's obsession with evil hints at the second kind of haunting, one that consumed entire districts or villages. Starting in the early 1950s, newspaper headlines from north to south began to register, with increasing frequency, cases of neighbors accusing each other of witchcraft, as with the story of Frau N. and Herr C. The best-documented example we have of this phenomenon left behind a huge collection of sources—possibly the only richly narrative sources still in existence concerning the witchcraft scare of that era. These divulge hidden complexities of the early post-Nazi moment and get us down in the weeds of postwar social relationships in a way that few contemporary documents can.

Across the modern period, historians have scrupulously chronicled

the strong interest that millions of Germans, across various sociological divides, demonstrated in supernatural beliefs and practices
of many kinds. Urban and rural, men and women, well-heeled and
working-class—all kinds of people exhibited an appetite for astrol-
ogy, parapsychology, séances, palm reading, spiritualism, telepathy,
and divining, as well as occult movements like Ariosophy and The-
osophy.[43] Germany's highly diverse medical landscape had also long
allowed traditions of folk and magical healing to flourish alongside
what, until the revelations of physicians' crimes at Nuremberg, was
the world's vanguard medical culture.

But there was something quite particular about the kinds of mass
supernatural events that took place in Germany after World War II,
so many of which focused suspiciously on sin and guilt, healing and
redemption. Why did so many of the scenes this book reconstructs
and recounts turn on questions of good and evil, innocence and guilt,
sickness and healing? This is a deeply *historical* question, a question
of "why this place?" and "why now?" With their powerful folk-
religious overtones of spiritual damage and spiritual cleansing, these
phenomena were expressions of social harm unique to Germany's
postwar era. They were rooted in terrors, forms of guilt and shame,
responsibility and mistrust and loss that marked post-Nazi life. They
are evidence of a void—at once moral, social, and epistemic—that
defeat and collapse and an Allied-superintended confrontation with
mass murder opened up.

Looking through the prism of the mostly unremembered scenes
and events this book describes, one perceives things that have often
remained occluded: fears of spiritual defilement, toxic mistrust, and
a malaise that permeated daily life. Beneath the affectless behavior
that Arendt observed lay anxieties that didn't even have names, and
these churned away throughout the 1950s against the backdrop of
consumerist forgetfulness. In the immediate shadow of the Holocaust, defeat in World War II, and the tension of the early Cold War
decades, West Germans quietly nursed various wounds and pricks of
conscience. Corruption laced many relationships, and a fundamental

estrangement among people lingered on, even as reconstruction pro-
ceeded and the roads were repaved and the shops and schools and
squares again bustled with life and enterprise. The scenes this book
describes offer a view into that otherwise inaccessible existential and
spiritual territory.[44] They are a portal onto a demon-haunted land.

1

READING SIGNS

In the sixteenth and seventeenth centuries, the Calvinist region around the city of Lemgo, between the Teutoburg Forest and the Weser River, in what is today the state of North Rhine–Westphalia, was a hotbed of witch persecution. During four successive waves between 1561 and 1681, more than two hundred Lemgoers were executed as witches.[1] Most were women, many of them elderly.[2] By cleansing their communities of witches, people believed, they were subverting the Devil's intentions, exposing his clandestine conspirators, and eradicating evil. To unmask witches was to do God's will.

Over subsequent centuries, this aspect of the city's past became an increasingly uncomfortable memory for locals. Marianne Weber, feminist author and spouse of the sociologist Max Weber, went to school in Lemgo as a girl in the 1880s. The city's reputation as a "witches nest," she recalled, was "a disgrace!"[3]

Half a century later, with the Nazis in power, Lemgo's recently refurbished hometown museum opened, and with it a new exhibit on the witch-hunting era. Displaying interrogators' torture instruments, like thumb screws and "Spanish boots" used to crush the calves of suspects, the museum portrayed the persecutions as "the unfortunate consequences of the dark ages." In a speech he gave to commemorate the 1937 opening, Mayor Wilhelm Gräfer addressed the era of the witch hunt as a "somber chapter in the history of our city," one that represented "an entirely inexplicable distortion of the German mentality, spirit, and essence."[4]

Many citizens shared the confidence Gräfer expressed. With the coming of the Third Reich, they felt, a new era had dawned. The unenlightened bad old days were gone. A journalist who saw the Lemgo museum exhibit felt his heart fill with a "deep gratitude . . . that fate has bestowed upon us happier times—times which not only pass sentence upon the tortures of the witch persecutions, but which guarantee and secure all German racial comrades' right to live." The witch-hunting era seemed so remote, so safely tucked away behind museum glass, that in June 1939, when a festive regional parade was organized, members of Lemgo's local chapter of the National Socialist League of German Girls dressed up as witches to lead guests to their seats.[5]

Only seven months earlier, in November 1938, the pogroms of Kristallnacht had taken place all across the country. In large cities and small towns, Germans had torched synagogues, smashed the windows of Jewish-owned shops, and physically attacked and murdered Jews. Residents of Lemgo, too, destroyed the local synagogue, breaking its windows and setting fire to the ruins in broad daylight. The photography studio of Erich Katzenstein, a Jewish Lemgoer, was likewise smashed, and two Jewish cemeteries were vandalized.[6]

Just as fantasies about witches had gained such cultural authority in sixteenth- and seventeenth-century Lemgo that they led to waves of executions, fantasies about an all-powerful Jewish enemy bent on destroying Germany steadily accrued validity among Germans over the course of the 1930s. When war came, these fictions became the explanation for why fighting was an existential necessity. After 1943, as the war turned increasingly deadly inside Germany itself, all kinds of chimeras became steadily more compelling. Premonitions, rumors, and legends gained tremendous, predictive power. Word of mouth, speculation, and whispers achieved epistemological sovereignty. People read signs to comprehend what was to them incomprehensible, even unthinkable: that they were losing the war.

. . .

In Lemgo, as across Germany, Jewish life had become ever more precarious in the years after Kristallnacht. Jews had lived in Lemgo since the fourteenth century. In 1900, at the community's peak, 111 of 8,184 Lemgoers were Jews.[7] By 1942, only 22 remained, many of them elderly.[8] Then, in late July that year, a large number of townspeople gathered in the market square to watch the last of their Jewish neighbors assemble for deportation.

What went through the minds of those who gathered to witness this expulsion? At least some, we know, found the proceedings disturbing and worse—dangerous. They warned that the "German nation should expect God's punishment" for treating old people that way, people who "could not hurt a fly."[9] It was not a popular point of view, but once voiced, it could not be unheard. It was there, it had been said. Later on, when everyone knew exactly what fate met Lemgo's Jews, surely someone remembered having heard it. Or having said it.

Most Germans remained largely indifferent to their Jewish neighbors' persecution. But there were those for whom the way the war was being carried out—a merciless, apocalyptic campaign that swept even the elderly into its vortex—presented dangers associated not just with violence and guns and falling bombs but *spiritual* dangers. During the catastrophic later stages of World War II, some wondered whether they were seeing divine punishment. "Germans mixed anxieties about their culpability with a sense of their own victimhood," writes the historian Nicholas Stargardt.[10] People found themselves listening to all available hypotheses, sorting through a variety of possible outcomes. Nearly everyone got into the business of predicting the future and became adept in reading signs.

A pattern of engaging in interpretive speculation, driven by fear and self-pity, emerged with particular force after what Stargardt sees as the turning point of Germany's war: the firebombing of Hamburg. Over a week's time in late summer 1943, British and American bombers assaulted the city from the air. Thirty-four thousand people were killed and much of Germany's second-largest city burned to the ground. The Allies called the campaign Operation Gomorrah, after the impenitent city razed by God in Genesis. The name was surely intended to telegraph something more than just a message about destructive capacity alone. "Gomorrah" was a claim about whose side God was on. It was prophecy. On some level, the Allies understood how to weaponize spiritual anxiety, understood that the war they were fighting was capable of provoking ancient fears of vengeful gods. "Our home town is dying," a pastor told his congregation after Hamburg's bombing. "Should we accuse the Royal Air Force?" No, he concluded; it was not just the enemy's hand at work here, it was "His hand!"[11]

Signs, the pastor clearly understood, have to be read. They are oblique; they require deciphering. As the war dragged on, auguries of every kind began to mount up. Some Germans drew explicit connections between Hamburg's bombing and the persecution of the Jews. The Nazi state actually encouraged this interpretation—a version of it, anyway. To stiffen the country's resolve, Propaganda Minister Joseph Goebbels floated the idea that Allied bombs were "Jewish retribution": that Jewish influence had been brought to bear in Washington and London to destroy Germany. But after Hamburg, this idea took on a life of its own. All over the country, Germans whispered that it was revenge for Kristallnacht. Mammoth concrete bunkers had been built in many cities, including Hamburg, on top of sites where synagogues once stood. This made the bombs look, to growing numbers of people, like God's vengeance.[12]

Hoping to brighten the national mood, Goebbels promised miracles, including "wonder weapons" that would turn the war's tide. He had his staff type up and send anonymously, through the mail, prophecies that predicted Germany's final triumph.[13] Old legends and bits of folklore began to circulate, depicting a luminous, greater German Reich, represented as a great bird sheltering chicks—a surreal image of benevolence in the midst of a war of annihilation.[14] Popular songs with titles like "Things Will Go On" and "It's Not the End of the World" filled the airwaves, calling for endurance. Others—"Don't Worry About It," "I Know Some Day a Miracle Will Come," and "Buy Yourself a Colorful Balloon"—pretended the troubles away.[15] But still the bombs continued to fall, and the front moved closer and closer. As the end approached, there was no halting the flood tide of rumors proliferating across every part of the Reich.

So people did what human beings have long done when faced with a void of understanding: they scanned nature for portents. They searched for evidence of judgment, favor, or punishment, trying to make sense of the world crashing in around them. In fall 1944, in the Sudetenland, people reported an enormous cloud of smoke in the eastern sky, and a bloody fist, shaking threateningly.[16] In Lower Silesia, people saw the sun "dance" and look as though, at any moment, it would collide with the earth. Those who witnessed it believed that the world would soon "sink in flames and death."[17] A fiery sword materialized over the Bohemian Forest.[18] Someone witnessed an immense cross in the heavens, with the full moon at its center.[19] In Friesoythe, in Lower Saxony, a local man with the gift of second sight had a vision: his whole town consumed in flames.[20]

Such apocalypticism was not unwarranted. Adolf Hitler refused to allow a repeat of what had happened in 1918, when World War I ended in what many Germans considered a dishonorable capitulation. The Nazi leadership committed itself to fighting on until the absolute end, come what may. "Warfare was continued," historian Richard Bessel writes, "not out of any strategic considerations, but for its own sake."[21] Teenage boys were sent to fight with little training, and old men and youths were handed antitank weapons with which they were expected to defend the homeland. Soldiers were driven into suicidal battles in which they could not hope to prevail. By autumn 1944, five thousand German soldiers were dying each day at the Eastern Front.[22]

In the single month of January 1945, 450,000 Wehrmacht soldiers died, many more deaths than either the United States or the United Kingdom sustained in the entirety of the war.[23]

And the longer the German army fought to maintain increasingly desperate positions, the more fatally exposed civilians became to the fighting. By spring 1945, an estimated nineteen million people either had been evacuated from the cities to the countryside to escape the bombs or had fled westward ahead of the Soviets now occupying eastern German territories.[24] Many were women who trekked on foot, dragging all their worldly possessions behind them, sometimes with children in tow. They had nowhere to stay, little to eat, and were utterly vulnerable to violence at the hands of locals and invading military. With German air defenses weakened, the Allied bombing of the cities became more intense and deadlier. The air raids could now reach the country's south and east, which had until then been regarded as fairly safe. In February 1945, up to 25,000 people were killed in Dresden in a single night of bombing. Afterward, there was nothing to do but pile the bodies onto metal grates, douse them with fuel, and set them alight. They burned for days.[25]

As the Red Army advanced from the east, visions of Soviet vengeance—retribution for the brutal, annihilationist policies the Nazis had pursued against the Soviet Union—inspired particular anxiety. People took "to attempting, convulsively, to calm themselves, by thinking that maybe the end will not be so bad." These observations, written by an anonymous intelligence agent in the SD in March 1945, are especially striking. A "people of 80 million," he continued—meaning the Germans—"cannot simply be exterminated to the last man, woman, and child." Surely, the "Soviets cannot actually turn on the workers and farmers," the agent ventured: "they are needed in every state." Perhaps some took comfort in such rationalizations as these. Others turned to alcohol, taking advantage of even the most "meaningless occasion to drink the last bottle, the one being saved for the victory party . . . or the return home of husband or son." People talked openly on public buses and trains "among complete strangers" about things that "only weeks before no one considered deliberating about," and turned their attention, in the war's final days, to practical tasks, laying by emergency funds, looking for places to hide, or securing poison, pistols, and other tools for suicide.[26]

Standing before an abyss of unknown dimensions, filled with dread, some asked themselves what it *meant* that Germany was losing the war, and what sense one should take from monumental defeat and destruction of life. Or worse: they realized there was no sense to be drawn from it. "The perception that there was no meaning in it all has led hundreds of thousands of Germans to experience virtually physical pain," the SD agent wrote. He heard people say things like, "We don't deserve this, that things have gone this way," or "We don't deserve to have been led into this catastrophe." After all, hadn't they done their duty? Done as they were told? Even in the midst of the bombing war's terror, the countless sleepless nights, their burned-down homes and lost family members and friends, hadn't the German people "toiled to the limits of their physical abilities in this war, and showed loyalty, patience, and a willingness to sacrifice to an extent unknown to any other nation"?[27]

Statements that begin by recounting one's virtue and end asking why one has failed are related to theodicy: a search for the meaning *behind* events, for ultimate causes when proximate ones do not satisfy. When mere facts have no power to illuminate, deeper moral and existential questions remain. "I experienced the destruction of Hamburg as a spectator. I was spared the fate of playing a role in it," Hans Erich Nossack recalled. "I don't know why. I can't even decide whether that was a privilege." When the bombs fell, Nossack was on vacation in the countryside, near enough to witness his city being destroyed but far enough away to be safe. Later he would recall that he usually had a "morbid disinclination" to leave home and "squander precious time" on holidays when he could be working. He could not fathom why it was that on this occasion, when his wife, Misi, asked him to leave town, he had said yes. There was "no explanation for the fact that I didn't say no this time as well," he wrote.[28]

. . .

And then, suddenly, after all the chaos and death, it was over. In what remained of German towns and cities, mountains of brick and stone, twisted and charred metal, broken glass, and ragged slabs of concrete loomed where apartment blocks once stood.

Strips of white bedsheets flapped here and there from the windows of surviving buildings or shells of buildings, impromptu flags of surrender. There was little fuel, little to eat, and nothing to buy. Currency was worthless. Diseases raged: tuberculosis, syphilis, diphtheria. Infrastructure had collapsed or been blown up. Millions of refugees were in the country or making their way there. Some were survivors of the concentration camps, force-marched into the Reich by Nazi camp overlords; others were former forced laborers. Still others had fled the Red Army's ferocious assault or been displaced by the bombing war. Soon this "society of the uprooted" would be joined by millions of ethnic Germans who fled or were violently ejected from their homelands in Eastern Europe.[29]

At first, the Allied occupation forces would exercise control over most every aspect of daily life, large and small. The material task was immense. There was rubble to be cleared; streets to be made passable again; railroads, bridges, drains, sewers, schools, hospitals, and apartment buildings to be repaired or rebuilt wholesale. The Allied armies had to disburse resources: fuel, medical supplies, housing, motor vehicles. They had to feed an enormous and diverse population.

As pressing as these concerns were, the moral task was easily as great. Soviet soldiers had begun liberating Nazi camps already in 1944. They had seen things there that most outside the camp empire had never witnessed, things almost beyond human imagination. They found mounds of bone and ash, crematoria and mass graves; rooms of hair and shoes, suitcases and toys. When, a few months later, French, American, and British soldiers began liberating camps in the western parts of Germany, they discovered thousands of sick and starving and dying people. They found the dead, sometimes stacked in piles, sometimes scattered.[30] J. Glenn Gray, an American soldier who would later become a philosopher, helped liberate a camp. "I was conscious," he wrote, "of having stumbled onto an hour of truth that would hardly be repeated."[31]

The Allies had discussed postwar justice and how to structure Germany's rehabilitation even before the war ended. At the Yalta Conference in February 1945, Joseph Stalin, Winston Churchill, and Franklin D. Roosevelt had agreed that upon prevailing in the war, they would "wipe out the Nazi Party, Nazi laws, organizations and institutions, remove all Nazi and militarist influences from public office and from the cultural and economic life of the German people."[32] The victors aimed to see to it that "Nazi organizations were dissolved, Nazi institutions destroyed, Nazi laws abrogated, and Nazis themselves eliminated from positions of power or influence."[33]

What came to be known as denazification would have several aspects. Best known are the Nuremberg Trials, during which the Third Reich's remaining leaders, as well as high-ranking military and government officials, industrialists, and physicians, were tried for crimes against humanity beginning in 1945. Other measures encompassed far wider swaths of the population. The Allies undertook a massive public purge of everything that symbolized the former order. They tore down or blew up Nazi monuments, ripped out street signs bearing Nazi heroes' names, banned Nazi holidays, and chipped offensive insignia and slogans off building facades. Through questionnaires and civilian tribunals, they aimed to determine the extent to which individuals had aligned themselves with the Hitler regime and its organizations, and to sort the population into five categories of relative complicity, from "exonerated" to "major offender." Those considered dangerous were often placed in internment camps. Others, those deemed less culpable, were conscripted to clear rubble, and sometimes relieved of their positions if they held public office. Food rationing was based on the category to which one belonged, with the goal of ensuring, the historian Alice Weinreb writes, "that the better off one had been in Germany during the Third Reich, the worse one fared after its collapse."[34]

And from the beginning, questions of guilt and responsibility, of blame and taint, became practically synonymous with the occupation itself. The Allies "viewed the German people as morally unclean," something they demonstrated by hanging pictures of the murdered on trees and in city squares, captioned by versions of the accusation, as the poster below shows: "THIS IS YOUR FAULT."[35]

They rounded up townsfolk living near concentration camps and forced them to bury or rebury the dead. They produced films as they liberated the camps, recording the sites of torture; the sick, starving, and dying survivors; the ovens and barracks; and bulldozers pushing the broken and emaciated bodies of the dead into enormous trenches. Germans were paraded into theaters to see these films as rituals of mortification and moral retribution. Sometimes Allied soldiers filmed Germans entering or sitting in darkened cinemas, watching the films

(or turning away from watching), in an attempt to evaluate their relative levels of contrition, guilt, or incorrigibility.[36] The images and film footage the Allies used to document what had happened in the camps constituted the "primal scene" of denazification, the first time most Germans were forced into a face-to-face confrontation with mass murder on an industrial scale.[37]

Among Germans, there was some initial support for these measures. But as early as 1945, public opinion began to shift. Denazification began to provoke "private expressions of unease and half-loud demands for fundamental changes."[38] Deciding which category of guilt to place an individual in was an ambiguous process. People who had been convinced Nazi supporters were not necessarily guilty of any specific crime, and practically speaking, it quickly became clear that to remove everyone who had been a member of this or that Nazi organization from public life would form a serious impediment to the reconstruction of the country, to getting the machinery of daily life and the economy up and running again. Sometimes the best person for a given job was a knowledgeable and capable local party member.[39]

Already in 1946, denazification procedures were turned over to local, German-staffed tribunals. The process became increasingly corrupt, functioning on "deceit, back-room dealing, mutual back-scratching, and even outright bribery."[40] Former Nazis (or those sympathetic to them) could influence the proceedings. Investigators could be intimidated. Sometimes witnesses could not be found. Cases wound up being downgraded from a category of greater to one of lesser offense.[41] Germans came to perceive the process as too slow or too harsh or too lenient or too inconsistently applied.[42] They derided the tribunals as "factories" for producing harmless "fellow travelers" whose pasts had been scrubbed clean. Everyone knew of a big shot who had gotten away unscathed, smaller fry who had not. Whatever popular support initially obtained for the process dried up. By 1949, only 17 percent of Germans in the US zone supported denazification.[43]

But corruption was only one reason that Germans resented the initiative. Jewish survivors and the occupiers alike were often struck by a powerful German defensiveness on the subject of guilt. Most Germans appeared fundamentally incapable of admitting any wrongdoing, any antisemitism, any allegiance to the Nazi state and its policies.[44] Some denied the reality of National Socialist crimes, or insisted that all countries had done bad things in the war, or assigned blame to party higher-ups and the SS. Impulses toward knowing the truth varied. What Germans saw, let alone chose to understand, when they looked at posters depicting desperately ill and skeletal survivors and piles of corpses that members of the occupation forces nailed up all over their towns, or when they viewed the atrocity films the Allies made or heard the Nuremberg testimony on the radio, was often quite different from what the occupiers intended. Heaps of bodies from various camps were rendered virtually indistinguishable from one another. Propaganda in the Third Reich had often made use of similar images of violence committed against Germans, raising the question, for some, of just what the concentration camp images actually depicted.[45] Some Germans complained that the images in films had been doctored or fabricated, or insisted that they actually depicted German victims.[46] As a result, Allied pedagogical efforts may have deepened some Germans' sense of alienation.

Many Germans took particular umbrage at being, as they saw it, "indiscriminately and inappropriately charged" with what came to be known as "collective guilt." They feared, in other words, a blanket accusation, of being found guilty without respect to their own actions, what they had done or not done, known or not known, as individuals. The idea of collective guilt produced anxiety so profound that scholars have likened it to a traumatic memory.[47] That memory's powerful effects and cultural resonance may have been rooted in an important linguistic distinction. In German, "guilt" (*Schuld*) carries greater psychic weight than in English, argued the sociologist Ralf Dahrendorf. It "always has an undertone of the irredeemable," of something "incapable of being canceled out by metaphysical torment." This guilt was not the same as being found in court to have committed a crime, in other words. It conjured up a more transcendent sense of disquiet, of a stain that might make one incapable of renewal or salvation.[48]

Scholars debate whether the occupiers actually used the language of collective guilt in official documents. What's more important, though, is what Germans *felt*, and the overwrought defense they mounted against the perceived accusation, an accusation that "no one levied."[49] In this sense, even denials of collective guilt can be perceived as an important piece of historical evidence, an "indirect" or "paradoxical admission" of culpability or shame.[50] The speed with which people came to repudiate a system and ideology to which so many had offered themselves, body and soul, and for which they had sacrificed nearly everything, offers some indication of just how powerful the psychological reflex behind this defense was. Fears of a lasting, even generational, taint produced powerful taboos.[51]

It is true, on the one hand, that liberal humanists, like the philosopher Karl Jaspers, and former exiles from Nazism, like Thomas Mann, dominated the public sphere after the war and made statements not only admitting German guilt, but even connecting the possibility of democratic renewal and transformation to such admission. But on the other hand it is also true that an "obstinate culture of silence" allowed Germans to preserve their sense of honor. To keep quiet was to remain loyal, true to one's authentic self.[52] The historian Thomas Kühne argues that the Holocaust and war crimes were so toxic that they bound all those implicated in them together in a "community of crime."[53]

And yet, however much the shock of catastrophic defeat, the humiliations of occupation, and fears of guilt's ineluctable stain bound some Germans together, these things also came between them. Denunciations continued after the war, with locals writing to report neighbors to Allied officials, whether out of a genuine sense of justice or to insinuate themselves into the occupiers' good graces.[54] German expellees and refugees from Eastern Europe were made to feel their status as outsiders acutely. Arriving in enormous numbers in a country torn apart by war and scarcity, they were generally unwanted and sometimes treated with great unkindness, and labeled by fellow Germans as parasites, thieves, and "foreigners."[55] The refugees, who had often lost even more than other Germans, asked unnerving questions. Why did *we* lose everything—not just our homes, or our families, but even our homelands? "Why did we"—but, by implication, not you—"pay the bill for Hitler?"[56] Alienation also marked family life. Marauding soldiers raped hundreds of thousands of German women and girls of nearly all ages. Since male relatives were often missing or dead or in POW camps, women had little time to recover from such experiences, because they had to shoulder family responsibilities alone.[57] Even those families lucky enough to be reunited fairly quickly found that life did not get easier. Husbands' homecomings may or may not have been welcome. Some came back and beat their wives, or found their children did not recognize them. Some came back without arms or legs, or blind or deaf. Some were unable to work. Some had nightmares, recalling things they had done and seen.[58]

Betrayal and confusion were accompanied by implicit questions of blame. "Am I imagining it all?" a former soldier muttered to his psychiatrist after the war. "Why all the sacrifices and losses? All for nothing."[59]

. . .

Opposition in the western zones of Germany to denazification only grew over time. Those subjected to the process grumbled about arbitrary periods of internment, unequal rations, and the sense that some people, despite being more implicated than others, were often no more likely to be punished. By 1949, many were demanding a final repudiation of denazification while other voices increasingly began calling for something more: they wanted a general amnesty, a slate-clearing for Nazi-era crimes. Under such an amnesty, many hoped, the records of those convicted under denazification would be expunged.[60]

In May 1949, a constitution for the new Federal Republic—the Basic Law—was adopted, and a new West German parliament, the Bundestag, founded. For the first time since the occupation began,

Germans in the western zones would assume a certain control over their own legislative and other affairs. The country would not be fully sovereign until 1955; until then, the Occupation Statute of September 1949 reserved ultimate authority to the Western powers in matters related to West German economic life, foreign policy, trade, and military security, and a large foreign military presence would remain in the country for decades thereafter. But as much day-to-day legal and political authority was taken back into German hands, support for amnesty grew into a significant political force. Various German states considered their own amnesty plans while simultaneously hoping for a sweeping, federal-level pardon.[61]

During parliamentary debates about the matter that December, legislators lamented the "massive confusion" to which the country had lately been subjected. They spoke of the "apocalyptic years" they had endured, and the "evil period" the country had lived through. The confusion, apocalypse, and evils to which they referred were not the iniquities of the Hitler years. They referred, rather, to the trials of the time *since*: the years of occupation and denazification. When a general amnesty was ultimately enacted into law on the last day of 1949, it covered kidnapping and causing bodily harm, "deeds directed against life," as well as theft and property damage committed against Jews, for example on Kristallnacht.[62]

West Germans across the political spectrum supported amnesty— even those political parties that had opposed the Nazis, some of whose members had paid for that opposition with their lives. Why? Why did politicians, regardless of political point of view, regardless of their own experiences during the Third Reich, share the same sense of "need," as one parliamentarian ventured during the debates on amnesty, "to cover the past with forgetting"? There were certain political considerations, to be sure, but more important, as the historian Norbert Frei has shown, amnesty offered all West Germans a clean break with the past and past crimes, not merely in a legal but also in a psychological sense.[63]

By early 1950, the Protestant weekly *Christ and World* would call on the Federal Republic to extend even broader amnesty protections than those guaranteed late in December 1949. Only an even more comprehensive slate-clearing would end what the journal called "the civil war" brewing in West Germany. This civil war manifested itself, the editors explained, in the ever-present possibility of being "tripped up" by some acquaintance—a neighbor, maybe, or a coworker or former associate—who might decide to tip off authorities about one's "former political life," about what one had done in the "most recent past." "As long as this unpleasantness has not been cleared away by a true and extensive amnesty, we will never have peace in society," *Christ and World* warned.[64]

. . .

During the early postwar years, clergy had sometimes described what they called a "fantastic apocalypticism" flowing through popular culture, and urged their congregations to remain faithful to "the true biblical eschatology."[65] Not a few visions were laced with fears of vengeance and punishment, or demands for atonement. In Catholic Bavaria, a dowser and well-digger named Alois Irlmaier gained local notoriety during the war for successfully predicting where bombs would land and how to survive them. After the war, he was sought out for his ability to describe the fates of missing people in the afterlife: when the dead churchgoers in his visions had their backs turned to the altar, he knew they were in purgatory or damned.[66] In 1947, Léon Hardt, an astrologer and telepathist, appeared before a sold-out crowd at Munich's Regina Palast Hotel, warning that the political and economic situation would be "very grave" if a "spiritual rebirth of humanity" were not realized. "We have in our hands the power to actualize heaven or hell," Hardt said.[67] Meanwhile, editors of the cultural-critical literary journal *Der Ruf* bewailed the heaps of letters and articles they received from "faith healers of every kind" claiming to "solve practically every postwar problem from collective guilt to the potato beetle." One, who called himself a "special consultant for cultural rebuilding, religious and political amity, and all related topical life and moral issues," attributed a spate of "extraordinarily dry weather and related forest fires" in 1947 to the German people's "ever-increasing psychic exhaustion."[68]

But in early 1949, a wave of urgent, new rumors of cosmic violence and earthly calamity suddenly began to surge through western occupied Germany. Carried along by newspapers and word of mouth, they warned that evil was flourishing, and predicted retribution and chaos. Sinister speculations multiplied: soon, it was said, the world would be consumed by floods, or split in two. Planet Earth would be obliterated by atomic warfare or airplanes with death rays. Stars would collide, and parts of their bodies fall to earth, setting off a chain reaction to destroy the world. Most harrowing of all, some prophesied, a snow would fall so dense and impenetrable as to smother everything that lived.

Rumors had been a crucial form of communication for Germans trying to sort out and interpret what was happening during the war's cataclysmic end. People had also recruited clairvoyants, palm readers, and numerologists to help them understand what was happening, to avoid falling bombs, to learn what had become of their missing loved ones, and to determine the spiritual fates of those who had died. But the new and powerful wave of end-of-days rumors came amidst tangible signs of reconstruction. By 1949, rubble piles had mostly been pushed into enormous mounds on the outskirts of cities or heaped up beside neatly cleared streets. Rebuilt or newly founded schools and universities were opening. New, democratic political parties had formed. Transportation had resumed. And in 1948, a new currency, the Deutsche Mark, had been introduced within the western zones of occupation with the intention of putting a stop to illicit trading and stimulating the economy. With a trustworthy currency in circulation, goods had quickly appeared again in shops, and magazines and newspapers on newsstands. Life had already begun to take a certain shape.

So what caused whispers of imminent catastrophe and death to resurge again so dramatically almost four years after the war, and after the "big bang" of currency reform, which many histories of the early Federal Republic have seen as the foundational moment of transformation from a postwar setting to one of reconstruction and democratic renewal?[69]

Tracing the origins of anything as ephemeral as rumor is probably beyond a mere historian's ability. But the content of 1949's end-of-days prophesying suggests that, regardless of gradually improving living conditions, clarity on many of the moment's most pressing questions had not been achieved. The future looked not only bleak but laden with spiritual danger.

That we know anything at all about these rumors is because someone took the time to study and publish about them. Alfred Dieck was a scholar of prehistory, ethnology, and folklore. At his desk in the university town of Göttingen, he recorded hearsay, took note of how it circulated, and jotted down the odd permutations that developed in the process of its being told and retold. Dieck considered the rumors' sociology—who had passed along what kind of story, and to whom? Had a woman told a man, a shopkeeper an academic, or an urbanite a farmer? Stories surfaced in many different kinds of places, he noted: industrial cities and trade centers and university towns, Catholic burgs and Protestant villages. But Dieck took special notice of those emerging near Göttingen and in the region around Hannover. He heard the most incredible things on the streets and read even wilder things in the newspapers: that his panicked fellow citizens were apparently spending their last money on alcohol, for instance, or had undertaken religious conversion and baptism en masse. Others, it was whispered, were fleeing to the mountains in terror or committing suicide.[70]

. . .

Getting to the bottom of 1949's doomsday mood was in some ways a project tailor-made for Alfred Dieck. He had a nose for the uncanny and the out-of-this-world. While still in his teens, he had translated into German and published Edgar Rice Burroughs's *A Princess of Mars*. In the 1930s, he had written a dissertation on bog bodies, the remains of mostly Iron Age people preserved in the airless swamps of northern Europe. Many died violently, and may have been human sacrifices. Early in the war, Dieck had been sent to the front, was wounded, and later detained in a POW camp. He understood ruin. Though he would go on to publish widely on many topics, his academic career never recovered after 1945. By his own estimation, he "emerged from the war an eighty percent damaged man."[71]

Dieck concerned himself relatively little with the actual substance of the rumors he recorded, or with analyzing their emotional or religious resonances. He preferred merely to catalogue their appearance and transformations. But he did offer his opinions about what had set off the panic gripping many of his fellow citizens. Four years into the occupation, he acknowledged, the country's mood remained bleak, ruinous, and troubled. For that, he blamed the occupiers. His complaints were numerous and specific. He chided the Allies for failing to offer a credible replacement for the tremendous faith Germans had placed in Hitler—as though that were in their job description. He denounced various occupation policies, like *Demontage*: after abolishing the country's military, the Allies had set about containing industries that could support munitions production, dismantling industrial plants and taking extracted resources as a form of reparations. Dieck condemned the occupiers, too, for prohibiting trade with countries with surplus foodstuffs while Germans, he said, went hungry. He also looked to escalating tensions between the Americans and Soviets with apprehension. And he was convinced that various "tasteless" and "perverse" products of American popular culture, like radio plays, which now filled the airwaves, were replacing Germans' "reverence for the majesty of life and death," as he put it, "with dread."[72]

Dieck also blamed German newspapers. The occupiers had strictly controlled the press after the Third Reich's collapse, and publishing required applying for and obtaining a license. With the 1948 currency reform, however, paper was no longer rationed. "New papers shot up like mushrooms," a *Foreign Affairs* article from 1954 recalled, with numbers rising from 160 to 1,000 between early 1949 and the middle of 1950.[73] This explosion of postwar news outlets produced a highly competitive environment, and, according to Dieck, one that craved sensation. Some papers printed what amounted to divination alongside news, he noted, or even divination-as-news. He cited stories about an imminent shift in the earth's axis, and others hinting that activity at the South Pole was to blame for an approaching "new Flood."

In fact, the prophecies of coming doom ushered in with the year 1949 had originated in word of mouth and then been amplified and augmented by newspapers. While some papers may indeed have hankered for sensation, others were just as willing to poke fun at a population they helped agitate. APOCALYPSE! shrieked one headline. Others warned, ON MARCH 17 THE WORLD WILL END! or observed, shrewdly enough, FAMILIES WANT TO BE TOGETHER FOR THE END OF THE WORLD.[74] In Munich, the *Süddeutsche Zeitung* reported preparations being made in anticipation of the imminent end of time. Butchers were supposedly giving meat away, panhandlers were suddenly raking it in, and lots of "old Nazis" could be seen donning their party insignia once more.[75] Fears of a gathering storm were a big joke, it seems, something to be lampooned as far as the press was concerned. Meanwhile, Dieck heard people talking up any prophetic fragments they heard, trading on the tiniest of auguries. Once published in newspaper accounts, these snatches of information would wend their way back into hearsay, only to appear yet again in the newspapers in new forms, completing a circuit of doom-laden prognostication.

Dieck's explanations for the ominous scenarios coursing through his country don't really help us understand why, four years after the *conclusion* of annihilationist war, Germans living in the western zones of occupation now awaited the end of the world. Of course, emerging conflict with the USSR might have played a role. The Soviets perceived a threat in the 1948 introduction of the new Deutsche Mark. They responded in June that year by blocking land and water access to Berlin, the former capital of the German Reich, which the four powers occupied jointly. This blockade in turn led to the Berlin Airlift, when the Allies flew thousands of sorties to supply the city by air. It was a watershed moment in the early Cold War.

But by the time Dieck took up his study, the airlift had been going on for months, and in any case, he scarcely considered it as a factor. For him, all the telling and retelling and foretelling were evidence of a more generalized "crisis of nerves," as he put it, among the overly credulous and easily spooked, a textbook example of "mass psychosis." Wild rumors had accompanied the 1940 German invasion of France, he recalled. And just recently, in Ecuador in February 1949, a mass panic had turned into riots when a Spanish-language version of *War of the Worlds* was broadcast on Radio Quito.[76]

What Dieck's boilerplate account of "mass psychosis" did not—or could not—acknowledge is that postwar Germany's "crisis of nerves" was not readily generalizable and had more than one source. The rumors, after all, spoke about fears of being damned or punished—preoccupations since the last years of the war. In this, the apocalyptic reports of 1949 become an important piece of historical evidence.

An against-the-grain reading of that evidence—a reading that looks not only for what a source tells us explicitly, but for what it hints at implicitly—would immediately zero in on Dieck's rote insistence that his countrymen and women "felt largely blameless" and "only minimally responsible" for the war's consequences. The Third Reich's "crimes, about which almost no one knew anything," he wrote, falsely, were not much "a matter of debate." Most people, he observed, continued to believe as they had for years that World War II was more or less an outgrowth of World War I, a war that had been foisted upon Germany by what he called "known American financial circles"—code for Jews. What Dieck was saying was this: that "no one knew anything" about Nazi crimes, but also that many of his fellow citizens continued to believe that Jews had been responsible for the war, Germany's defeat, and its postwar predicament. There is a great deal to unpack in that series of fictions and elisions, not least that Dieck's way of explaining a sudden explosion of apocalyptic fear went immediately to an insistence that no one felt responsible for the war or its "consequences."[77]

Even as he asserted that his fellow citizens felt blameless, Dieck ignored some of the implications of his own discoveries. Some of the rumors he recorded, for example, intimated that only the sinful would go under in the coming deluge. Others predicted that only children under the age of two—the truly innocent—would survive. Angels, it was said, would care for the children left behind after the destruction of the world.[78] These auguries, like those that had sometimes circulated during the war, centered more directly on judgment and punishment, blame and guilt—terrors that Dieck was convinced no one felt much bothered by. Not everyone, it seems, was quite so sanguine.

The apocalypticism of 1949 suggests how guilt—and even the sharp rejection of it—found its way into many dimensions of postwar life in sublimated forms. Some perceived the possibility of cosmic wrath, or felt existential trepidation. A sense of unease lingered, one that could not be easily discharged. That day in Lemgo, someone had piped up to say that Germany should expect God's wrath for sending the town's last elderly Jews away to their deaths. Someone remembered that later. But people could also feel guilty for losing the war and seeing everything they had sacrificed for come to naught. Was defeat not itself a sign?

• • •

Apocalyptic thinking is often associated with crisis, but to think apocalyptically is not just to think in terms of disaster. Apocalypse means unveiling—as in unmasking, a view behind the curtain, a glimpse at transcendent truth. "Here is wisdom," it says in the book of Revelation. Apocalypse is about signs, but it's also about interpretation, the *exegesis* of signs. In both the Jewish and Christian prophetic traditions, apocalypse promises a final reckoning, a new era of purity for the elect. Asked by a seeker "what will become of us?"—meaning the

Germans—the Bavarian clairvoyant mentioned earlier, Alois Irlmaier, predicted the burning of churches and the murder of many clergy. But thereafter, his visions told him, the pope would crown three kings, there would be enough food for all, and people would cultivate as much land as they wished. The climate would warm up. Bavarians would grow wine and tropical fruits.[79] Exegesis of signs is required to know who will be chosen to inhabit the redeemed and happy paradise of tropical-fruit cultivation, and who will be damned, and what kind of cosmic battle will ensue in the meantime.[80] The rumors of coming Armageddon in 1949 amounted to just such a search: for visibility, insight, and clarity in a skittish and volatile moment.

Was the world ending? Would anyone survive? These questions may not have been on every mind that year, but many people lay awake at night, thinking gloomy thoughts, pondering unfathomable things. "The world situation worries me, everything looks black," a man told a public opinion pollster. Other respondents to the same survey said that, as they lay down to sleep, they thought about their lost homeland, dead relatives, or those still missing from the war. They worried about money, jobs, health, and lost savings. They worried about strangers, "Gypsies"—meaning, in this instance, almost all "foreigners"—and crime. "I am afraid all the time," one woman said. "But I don't know what of."[81] How should anyone know whom to trust? "We in Germany find ourselves living in a time in which most people no longer know what is true and what is a lie," claimed a mysterious group in Kassel calling itself the Militant League Against Nihilism, whose letterhead featured an image of Hercules slaying the hydra.[82] When asked in 1949 by pollsters whether more people had good or evil intentions, only one-third chose the former.[83] No wonder people still scanned the heavens for signs.

Or, at least, the headlines. Alfred Dieck stayed on the case, marking a new pitch of anxiety in the end-times rumors toward the end of February 1949. Humanity's last day on earth was widely predicted to occur on March 17. Hoping to capitalize on the moment in a dramatic fashion, perhaps, Northwest German Radio broadcast a play, in which an enormous meteor shower threatened the world.[84] If that moment in any way resembled what happened in 1938, when Orson Welles broadcast *The War of the Worlds* to the US public via radio, more than a few listeners held their breath.

2

A STRANGER IN TOWN

Nineteen-forty-nine saw its share of extraordinary events. In August, the Soviet Union would test its first A-bomb. UFOs were witnessed from Japan to New Mexico and beyond. Early in the year, in Los Angeles, a freak snowfall—the biggest in the city's recorded history—blanketed the beaches for three days.[1]

And in western Germany, insistent end-of-days prophecies continued to swirl. But then amidst them, a very different kind of news suddenly took wing. In March 1949—the same month, and indeed on practically the very day that popular rumor had slated for the end of time—in the small Westphalian city of Herford, a young boy who was unable to stand on his own received a visit from a curious stranger. Though no one, not even the boy's parents, quite understood just what had happened, after meeting this man their boy got up out of bed for the first time in months and, slowly and hesitantly, began to walk.

The impact of this single occurrence would be explosive, like a bolt out of the blue. Soon, tens of thousands would stand in the rain for days at a time just to catch a glimpse of the apparent author of the boy's recovery: an obscure, long-haired healer dressed in inky shades of blue and black. Cure-seekers would prostrate themselves in supplication before him, or try to buy his bathwater. Some believed he could raise the dead.[2] He would become the first German celebrity of the postwar era, his image splashed across newspapers and tabloids from one end of the country to the other. Paparazzi, police, and eventually a documentary film crew would trail him everywhere he went. Some called him miracle doctor (*Wunderdoktor*), miracle healer (*Wunderheiler*), wonder worker (*Wundertäter*), cure bringer (*Heilspender*), even savior (*Heiland*). Others called him a charlatan, a demon, a sexual deviant, a dangerous lunatic, an inciter of mass hysteria. To yet others, he was "the Good Son of God." His friends called him Gustav. His name was Bruno Bernhard Gröning.[3]

The headline of one of the first national news stories about him gives us some idea of the stakes as people perceived them in that moment: GOD SENT ME: THE TRUTH ABOUT THE "MESSIAH OF HERFORD."[4] Over the following months, Gröning was interviewed on the radio and featured on newsreels. Mere rumors that he might show up somewhere jammed city traffic for hours. High-ranking government officials extolled his talents before enormous crowds. Aristocrats and sports and movie stars befriended him.

Who was this Wunderdoktor Gröning, and what did he have to say? What made hundreds of thousands, if not millions of people read about him, listen to him, pilgrimage long distances in the hopes of meeting him? In part, the answer is that he was seen as the instrument of something powerfully providential. Herford lay within the geographic scope of Alfred Dieck's study of apocalyptic rumors, which had chronicled dire predictions of the imminent end of the world and terrifying prophecies of planet-smothering snows. Now, the chaos had yielded to something unexpected: healing. For those inclined to look for signs, one had arrived.

Still, exactly what that sign meant wasn't easy to say. Like millions of his countrymen, Bruno Gröning was a former soldier and POW. He had also been a Nazi Party member. He didn't have much in the way of what you might call a philosophy, at least not initially. He didn't preach. He didn't write books or found a church. When he spoke, it was mostly in hazy, elliptical aphorisms, which sometimes touched on vaguely spiritual themes but more often than not circled back to the topic of good versus evil. He also did not really have a defined technique for curing the sick, at least not one that could be plainly articulated in words. It was not even clear to anyone exactly *what* he was healing, or how. His method, such as it was, mostly consisted of being near people who were ill and sometimes training his gaze on them. And that didn't always work: the young boy whose cure became the origin story of this whole affair was back in bed again only a few weeks later. But often enough, the healing seemed to hold.

Many sources convey Gröning's powerful impact on people, and many people testified to his cures. But from history's standpoint, the real story is not him at all. It's *them*: the huge crowds that surged up around him everywhere he went; the hopes, fears, and fantasies they projected onto him; and the vast drama of emotions—usually kept in tight check—that played out in those crowds. The interaction between postwar German society and Bruno Gröning matters because in some very real sense, that society invented him to cure what ailed it—not just disease and injury, but forms of disquiet and damage that were much harder to see. This is a story about sickness and healing, and about the search for redemption. But first, it's a story about a family and a stranger in town.

• • •

Dieter Hülsmann, the only child of Helmut and Anneliese, had been born just three days after the start of World War II. He had been a little slow to start walking. When he did, a little past the age of two, his steps were hesitant, and his feet gradually turned inward as he grew. At four, doctors put painful casts on his legs and feet to straighten them out. They went up to his knees.[5]

Helmut was away at the war then, serving as an engineer in the Panzerwaffe, the Wehrmacht's armored division. Later, he spent some time in a POW camp, returning home to Herford in June 1945.[6] On the way home—whether by train or on foot—he would have seen mile after mile of ruins, the broken remains of a former life: mangled bridges, burned-out buildings, gutted machinery, and roadside graves with homemade crosses. He probably had few illusions that the destruction had been contained at the front, especially since the front had come home to Germany. Letters from home, too, might have mentioned the bombs and the fighting and the endless refugee caravans. But hearing about and seeing are not the same.

Back home in Herford, Helmut found his boy in a miserable state. He had the casts cut off immediately. Still, Dieter's condition worsened. Helmut took his son to the university clinic in Münster, seventy miles away. The diagnosis was vague but grim: progressive muscular atrophy. This assessment was confirmed in a pediatric clinic and by ten other "doctors and professors," but none had any treatment to offer. There is nothing we can do, the doctors reportedly told the family. Over the winter of 1948–49, when he was nine, Dieter took to his bed and did not get up for ten weeks. Nothing warmed his ice-cold legs—not blankets, not hot water bottles, not massages. When

he tried to stand, Helmut later said, he "snapped forward at the waist like a pocket knife."[7]

Anneliese's father said he knew someone who knew a healer. The man had just helped a woman paralyzed for more than five years walk again. Maybe he could help the boy?[8]

One day, an acquaintance brought Bruno Gröning to Herford by car. The relationship between him and the Hülsmanns got a fair amount of legal scrutiny later on, and the historical record betrays some confusion about the date, but it seems to have been March 14 or 15.[9] The calendar promised imminent springtime, but Herford was gloomy, wet, and windy, and the coming days would be colder. Here, in the Ravensburg basin, between the Teutoburg Forest to the west and the low-slung hill country of the Weser River to the northeast, the late-winter sky can turn pitiless and leaden against a landscape of alternating woods and meadows, with towns and farms and villages unfurling into the distance as far as the eye can see. In rainy weather, mist can veil the black-brown earth, merging landscape and sunless sky into a single, inscrutable shade the color of wet wool.

The Hülsmanns made their home in a handsome, whitewashed villa on Wilhelmsplatz. Once, the square had boasted a statue—though not, as one might expect from its name, an homage to Emperor Wilhelm. The subject was a much older hero: the eighth-century rebel Saxon leader Widukind. After fighting the armies of the Frankish king Charlemagne for more than a decade, Widukind was defeated in 785 CE and converted to Christianity. Legend has it that the Saxon, whose name meant "child of the forest," rode to his baptism on a black horse. Whether this was an act of defiance in the face of a forced conversion or Widukind's announcement of the spiritual death of his former pagan self, no one really knows. In lore, certainly, it is a redemption story: a "child of the forest"—meaning not only a pagan, in the thinking of his times, but a child of the Devil—became a Christian, a child of God. Many Nazis, though, saw Widukind not only as a folk hero but as an ideological exemplar, a native Germanic resister against the militant Christianity of Charlemagne, whose Frankish

Empire had destroyed local, pre-Christian gods and usurped the Germanic peoples' historic freedoms. In the Westphalian countryside of the 1940s and '50s, horse heads still decorated houses. Traditionally, it was said that Widukind's spirit lived on in them, protecting homes and promoting health.[10]

From 1899 until 1942, Widukind's statue stood just steps away from the Hülsmanns' front door. But during the war it was toppled and, like thousands of church bells and other treasures, melted down to make guns.[11] If on reaching the Hülsmanns' doorstep on that late-winter day Gröning had turned slightly westward, he would have seen not Widukind forged in triumphal bronze, astride a stallion and wearing a winged helmet, but a naked granite stump.

No documents allow us to reconstruct Gröning's arrival in Herford in any detail. But photographs from the time let us imagine him against a gray afternoon's backdrop, standing before the Hülsmanns' tasteful home, maybe turned to take in that violated monument. He was not tall. His frame, though athletic, could tend toward gauntness. In pictures, his pushed-up shirtsleeves reveal strong, ropy arms.

His hair—wiry, dark, and quite long for the time and place—would often be a subject of interest (and humor) in the press. People commented again and again on his intensely blue eyes, which bulged slightly. His face was weathered, even haggard. He had hands accustomed to work, the fingers stained with nicotine.[12] He dressed simply, seemingly always in dark clothing. He spoke simply, too, many would say. In his pockets, he sometimes carried little tinfoil balls with bits of his hair and fingernails in them. And he had an unmistakable goiter that, he would claim, allowed him to absorb his patients' sick-making energies.

Anneliese Hülsmann was a slim woman who dressed in a plain fashion, her hair tied back modestly. Helmut, for his part, was regarded by some as a bit crass—the sort to chew a fat cigar while talking too loudly at the same time.[13] Still, given Helmut's occupation as an engineer, the Hülsmanns would have belonged to prosperous Herford's

professional middle class. Gröning's origins, on the other hand, were working class. He was not especially comfortable speaking textbook German and by some accounts preferred the dialect of his home region.[14] He chain-smoked American cigarettes—Chesterfields—and drank cup after cup of strong, black coffee. We don't know exactly what happened after he arrived at the Hülsmann home, whether the group first sat together to drink coffee and smoke, to exchange pleasantries or misgivings. At some point, though, Gröning went in to see Dieter.

Scores of people would later attest to the extraordinary abilities of this long-haired, raw-boned refugee. How he seemed to possess the power to know what was going wrong in a sick person's body, and how to talk to those who were ill. How, as soon as he appeared, everything changed. You could hear a pin drop, it was said. Gröning's gaze would travel slowly from one person to the next. He would stand perfectly still and perfectly silent with his hands in his pockets and tell the afflicted not to think too much about being ill. Their fingers would begin to tremble, and they felt things happening in other parts of their bodies as well. He would take the foil out of a pack of cigarettes and work it into a little ball, and then give these foil balls to the sick and tell them to hold the ball in their hands and focus on it until they felt better. He had a habit, too, of repeating strange rhyming formulas, like: "it could also go down the other way around" (*Umgekehrt ist auch was wert*). Patients said they felt a warm current flowing through their bodies or an unaccustomed prickling sensation under his gaze.[15] His brother Georg said Bruno could stop toothaches, just by concentrating on the hurting tooth.[16]

What happened when Gröning first met Dieter Hülsmann would be told and retold for a long time after: initially in rumors, gossip, jokes, letters, and casual conversation; then via newspapers, maga-zines, sermons, speeches, films, pamphlets, and books; then in accusa-tions, denunciations, exposés, police and psychiatric reports, witness statements, court briefs, legislative inquiries, and academic journals and eventually—much, much later—on websites in dozens of lan-guages. Within an hour of encountering the healer, the boy sud-denly had feeling back in his legs, which Anneliese said "almost never happened anymore." There was a burning sensation in his legs and back. His cold limbs had suddenly warmed. The next morning, however unsteadily or hesitantly, Dieter, who had spent much of that bleak postwar winter in bed, got up and walked.[17]

Over the coming days, his condition improved further. At first, Helmut said, he "did not quite believe" what was happening. Yet soon he was convinced that his son was cured.[18] After two weeks, Anneliese recalled, "my boy could move freely and walk without any help . . .

around the house and outside." He still could not climb stairs without help, and he stood on tiptoe rather than with his feet fully on the ground.[19] But his father told the press that he was sure that this too would pass.[20] By then, the Hülsmann family had invited Gröning to come and live with them. And he had accepted.

It was not long before the villa at number 7 Wilhelmsplatz would be inundated with pilgrims, as news of Dieter's cure spread far beyond Herford, and then even beyond western Germany. Thousands would flood this small city, coming just in the hopes of seeing the black-clad Gröning or speaking with him for a moment, seeking relief for maladies of every imaginable kind. He would meet them in the Hülsmanns' parlor or on their front lawn. From time to time, especially late at night, he would appear on the villa's upper balcony to dispense cures to the crowds gathering below. No one quite knew how they worked, but what they heard was wondrous: that people who had been paralyzed, or sick in bed for years, would suddenly stand up and walk. That adults and children with trouble speaking could talk without hesitation or constraint. That stiff and damaged limbs and fingers became supple, and lifelong pain vanished. That the deaf could hear and the blind see.

What brought clarity to the surging chaos of 1949, in short, was not the end of time, as rumor had predicted for months. Instead, it was a tale of miracles, one that almost anyone could recognize. As cure-seekers began trickling into Herford that spring, Wilhelmsplatz became a spiritual destination. The world had not drowned in iniquity; there had been no apocalyptic fire, no death rays to split the earth in two. Instead, there was healing. There was redemption. Soon, what was already coming to be known as "the miracle of Herford" would grip the nation.

• • •

As extraordinary as Dieter's apparent cure was, the man who helped him walk again was in many important respects a postwar German everyman. Born in 1906 to a Catholic family, he was the fourth of seven children and grew up in the Danzig suburb of Oliva. Situated on Danzig Bay, surrounded by forested valleys to the west and north, Oliva was a *Luftkurort*, a place known for having particularly salubrious air. The Grönings lived in a large urban housing block of a type referred to, without affection, as a *Mietskaserne*, or "rental barracks." Like millions of children their age, the Gröning siblings grew up in the shadow of World War I and the British blockade, which brought great hardship to the civilian population: starvation, disease, and death.[21]

Gröning was like millions of others, too, in having been a soldier in World War II and then a POW. He was called up to serve in March 1943, reporting for duty at a *Panzerjäger*—tank hunter—school in Kolberg, a couple of hundred kilometers from Danzig. *Panzerjäger* traveled in vehicles or even on foot, armed with rocket launchers, and looked for Soviet tanks to blow up. It was not a task for the faint of heart. His Wehrmacht records show that Gröning was captured by the Soviets in Köslin, not far from where he had done his training. He spent March to late October 1945 in a POW camp in Frankfurt on the Oder.[22]

Gröning and his wife, Gertrud, had married in 1928 and had two sons. Both boys died in childhood; the elder in 1939 from a faulty heart valve, the younger in 1949 from pleurisy. (It's not clear whether Gröning's younger son died before or after the Herford events.) These deaths strained an already unhappy marriage, and the pair would later divorce.[23] Gröning's work life had been peripatetic. He'd trained for a time as a carpenter, worked as a messenger for an export company, been a waiter, an electrician, and a furniture maker. He'd repaired watches, sewing machines, and bicycles. He'd sold paint.[24] In 1945, when the Allies conferenced in Potsdam and agreed to redraw the map of Europe, Gröning's hometown of Danzig became Gdansk, Poland—and he became a refugee.

In Danzig, Gröning had been a member of the Nazi Party. This, too, was not unusual. After World War I, ethnic tensions ran high in the city. The Versailles settlement placed Danzig under League of

Nations protection, making it a Free City—a quasi-independent city-state. Germans and Poles shared the Free City under extremely trying conditions in an era of hubristic nationalism. When the Nazi Party emerged on the political scene in the early 1920s, it made a great deal of noise about the "fate" of Danzig, and frictions only escalated over time. The Nazis gained traction in Danzig faster than in many places in Germany itself. By 1933, they had an absolute majority in city parliamentary elections.[25]

Still, it is notable that several of the men in the Gröning family, including not only Bruno but also his father, August, and brother Georg, joined the party. While it is not clear from extant sources exactly when they joined, they did so in 1936 at the latest, years before Germany invaded Poland and reclaimed Danzig for the Reich. The family also changed its name: to Gröning from Grönkowski, or perhaps Grenkowski, or even Grzenkowski—Nazi Party record keepers never seemed to get that straight.[26]

What motivated that name change? It's possible that Grönkowski simply sounded too Polish in ethnically charged Danzig. Those who wanted to be recognized as full members of the German national community—not necessarily to join a Nazi organization or serve in the army but even just to get married—had to "establish their racial bona fides" by engaging in "racial grooming."[27] But the name change may also have been motivated by a keenness to showcase the Grönings' German heritage and Aryan identity. Again, the timing is notable: they made the change in 1936, long before Germany invaded Poland and seized Danzig for the Reich in 1939.[28]

Gröning himself never became more than a small-time party member. But as we'll see, as a celebrity he consistently surrounded himself not just with other rank-and-file former Nazis but with more prominent ones.

Soon, hundreds of thousands of Germans would travel to out-of-the-way places like Herford, hoping to see Gröning for themselves and be healed of any number of illnesses. An unlikely person had arrived in an unlikely place and performed uncommon deeds: it was a classic millenarian scenario, a symbol portending transformation.[29] And it so happened that the man at the center of the story was a former Nazi who talked a lot about an earthly struggle between "evil people" and everyone else. Bruno Gröning was plainly a complicated character, but his relationship with his fellow citizens would be no less complex.

3

THE MIRACLE OF HERFORD

That the Gröning story began amidst the low Westphalian hills, in such a conventional, bourgeois-mercantile town as Herford seems as surprising today as it did then. Tidy and industrious, Herford was known for its "healthy entrepreneurial spirit," as one newspaper put it in 1949, as well as for the manufacture of textiles, kitchen furniture, chocolate, and cigars.[1]

To be sure, the thousands of Wunderdoktor-seeking pilgrims who soon began pouring into the town complicated Herford's already considerable postwar tribulations, and probably gave the town manager, Fritz Meister, quite a headache. Meister formed part of his region's new, post-1945 elite. A Social Democrat removed from a prior office by the Nazis in 1933, he was, in classically euphemistic postwar parlance, politically "unburdened."[2] This would not necessarily have made him a hero to all, though Westphalia had been somewhat less enthusiastic in its early support of Adolf Hitler than other places, and Herford itself even less keen than parts of the region surrounding it.[3] While Meister's name suggests a certain suitability for running things, the challenges posed by intimations of miracles and the sudden flow of masses of cure-seekers into his town were considerable, maybe the greatest of his postwar career to that point.

The variety of complaints that people brought to Bruno Gröning, hoping to be healed, was enormous: headaches, asthma, and sciatica; calcification of the spine, various cancers, and neurofibromatosis (which causes tumors to grow on nerves); thyroid, circulation, intestinal, liver, heart, and middle-ear trouble; sinusitis and arthritis. Some had sustained injuries to their larynxes, dislocated their hips, and endured tremors and various forms of paralysis. Others had cerebral palsy, scoliosis, angina, epilepsy, sleeplessness, tuberculosis, and ulcers.

Germans' health had been damaged by years of war, followed by shortages of medical care and adequate housing. What's more, the British occupiers, in whose zone Herford was located, had been committed to the idea that, for justice's sake, the German standard of living should remain very limited. Rations were kept low, something German medical officials perceived to have contributed to an "alarming decline" of people's health.[4]

The health of women, in Herford as in other parts of the country, had been especially imperiled after the war. The consequences of rape, sometimes on multiple occasions, were several, among them unwanted pregnancy and rampant venereal disease. Women carried these burdens alongside many others. Since so many men were dead or remained in captivity, or came home unable to work, they were the ones who began the process of clearing away the rubble left behind in their towns and cities. They took care of the children, procured shelter, and "hamstered" in the countryside, trading objects of value for food to supplement meager rations. At the same time, and as we might expect given their wartime service, the overwhelming majority of people with disabilities after the war were men. Those eligible for war pensions in 1950 included more than 1.5 million disabled veterans; among them were more than 200,000 amputees, 56,000 who had sustained brain injuries, 34,000 with glass eyes, and 6,600 who were blind.[5]

Children's health was also a matter of concern. Infant mortality remained a third higher than at prewar levels until at least 1948. In urban areas, children were susceptible to worms and rickets. Those who had a dead or ill parent or came from large families were more likely to be undernourished, a clinical study published in the *Lancet* in 1948 concluded, but "nutritional health" was a "minor issue" compared with "the dangerous social and psychological environment of the bombed cities."[6] Children were also often born smaller after the war, and were more susceptible to diabetes and circulation problems as well as forms of mental illness.[7]

The city of Herford itself, on the whole, had been relatively fortunate, sustaining less war damage than many places. Still, it had been bombed several times to significant effect. As a result, in 1949 the town's foremost concern was a serious housing shortage. During the air war, thousands of German civilians had been evacuated to the relative safety of Herford, and after the war, they were joined by nearly seven thousand refugees who resettled there—some expelled from the formerly German regions to the east, others migrating west from the Soviet Zone.[8] Because Herford was also one of the bases of operations for the British military government (known as the Control Commission for Germany), British occupation forces had seized more than 600 homes for their use, evicting some 6,500 residents.[9]

The multitude of cure-seekers converging on Herford in the spring of 1949 would only add to this housing problem. At the same time, the thousands of pilgrims annoyed British military authorities living near Wilhelmsplatz, and they soon came calling. If the disturbances did not end, they said, they would have no choice but to requisition additional homes for their personnel, perhaps in quieter areas of town.[10] The pressure on town authorities mounted.

In late April, the chief health officer, a Dr. Siebert, called Gröning into his office for a chat. Gröning responded by organizing a press conference at the Hülsmanns' home, which Meister and other local administrators attended.[11] A few days later, Meister returned to announce, before an audience of some 120 witnesses in their living room, a ban:

Gröning had to desist from "practicing healing" from "that moment forward."[12] But the Wunderdoktor would not be easily dissuaded. Faced with the ban, he (or someone acting on his behalf) upped the ante, hanging leaflets around town instructing cure-seekers that if they wanted to see him, they would have to get permission from a doctor or from Meister.[13]

Pleading letters soon began making their way to Meister's desk, begging him to bend the rules and allow them an audience with the healer. A man named Fritz T., who suffered from tendonitis, kidney trouble, arthritis, and rheumatism, and had used a wheelchair since 1935, wrote to tell Meister that though he had only been "able to speak to Herr Gröning through the window," he "felt lighter, better, more mobile." Upbraiding the beleaguered town manager, Fritz T. said he wished "that those who have forbidden Herr Gröning to practice had to spend just four weeks sick like I am, sitting in a wheelchair as I have to."[14]

Once a hometown drama, news of the Miracle of Herford spread rapidly. And it played out simultaneously with a signal political development: the founding of the Federal Republic on May 23, 1949.

Locals immediately connected the historic establishment of Germany's second republic, with its ideals of democracy, fairness, and egalitarianism, to the Herford situation. "They shouldn't only listen to the doctors," a reporter overheard someone say amidst a group of Gröning supporters gathered at city hall to protest the recent ban. They should also listen to "the people, as is the democratic way."[15] Some citizens lodged pointed complaints in a populist spirit. According to the resident of a small nearby community, the ban contained "not the least trace of democracy, because it was issued against the will of the masses." It was "a punch in the face of the ailing," averred this citizen, who likened the ban to "measures . . . usual in the Third Reich."[16]

The passionate embrace that Gröning received from the public seems likely to have been in part a backlash against the Nazi Party's crackdown on lay healers. Germany had a long history of lay and magical medicine: from the founding of the German nation-state, almost anyone who wanted to practice healing could do so under a de facto principle known as *Kurierfreiheit*, or the "freedom to cure."[17] No less a spokesman than Otto von Bismarck had once declared before the Reichstag that the state had no right to ban the ministrations of those with the "talent given by God and nature to heal."[18] Though the *Kurierfreiheit* principle was never absolute, from the German Empire's origins in 1871 to the eve of World War II a wide array of medical arts flourished. Millions of people visited mesmerists and hypnotherapists, naturopaths and homeopaths, radiation therapists and hydrotherapists, sidereal pendulum practitioners, herbalists and iridologists, layers of hands and prayer healers and purveyors of anthroposophical medicine, to name a few. By 1933, when the Nazi Party came to power, there were around three lay healers for every ten doctors.[19] One prominent physician estimated that unlicensed healers treated more than half of all illnesses. In a single month in 1934, more than a quarter million people paid their own money—since healers, unlike doctors, were not covered by insurance—to be seen by lay healers.[20]

The National Socialists had been initially ambivalent about lay medicine. Lay healers were backed by certain highly influential Nazis and members of the Third Reich's upper leadership, such as Hitler's lieutenant Rudolf Hess and SS chieftain Heinrich Himmler. *Der Stürmer* publisher Julius Streicher headed the Association for German Folk Healing.[21] Hospitals for homeopathy and natural medicine were established in Berlin, Cologne, Stuttgart, and Munich, among other cities.[22] But a state organizing a vast eugenic enterprise and preparing for total war could hardly afford to cede much ground to herbalists.[23] In 1939, the Nazi state moved to end the principle of *Kurierfreiheit*, enacting a new law that banned lay healers from treating the sick unless they first obtained a state license.[24] The law attempted to regulate "the practice of the healing arts . . . in a professional or commercial sense" and to govern the "professional determination, healing, or amelioration of disease, suffering, or injury." A 1941 amendment went further, cracking down on medical practices authorities deemed occult.[25]

As Bruno Gröning rose to fame, many people voiced the opinion that the lay healer ban was a "Nazi" law and should now be purged along with other laws of that era. But the dispute over Gröning began to gain explicitly political dimensions not merely because the healer continued to flout both the lay-healer ban and the Herford edict against him. The controversy also provided citizens with an opportunity to tell their stories, to give voice to their suffering. In scores of letters addressed to Meister, correspondents recounted desperate details of pain and illness, of their travails in the war and since. A man from Lüdenscheid, Walter S., for instance, attributed his "chronic muscular rheumatism" to "terrible mistreatment" in a French POW camp. This experience had left his "psychological equilibrium shattered." Walter S. could walk now only with difficulty and could hardly talk anymore. "I have lost my belief in the world and in medical science," he wrote.[26]

Many of the letters Meister received came from the parents of children who were ill or disabled. A man named Gustav B., who read about the Herford events in the newspaper, wanted an audience with Gröning for his five-year-old daughter, who could neither speak nor walk.[27] Another parent, Hilde R., wrote with "a great request." Her six-year-old daughter was too small for her age and unable to speak "or understand properly what is said to her." Hilde R. had taken her daughter to see some famous doctors, she said, including "Professor Ibrahim from Jena."[28] Dr. Jussuf Ibrahim was a renowned German-Egyptian doctor. Only much later would it become more widely known that he had participated in "euthanizing" children with disabilities during the Third Reich. The daughters of Gustav B. and Hilde R.—and perhaps Dieter Hülsmann, too—may have been spared such a fate only because they had been too small for doctors to have recommended it yet.

Eventually, a commission of doctors from Herford and nearby Bielefeld softened a bit in the face of public pressure and offered Gröning the chance to put his "healing arts to the test" in any university clinic in the British zone or nearby hospitals. Gröning declined, however. He did not see himself as a "lay healer," he would later make clear.[29]

What kind of healer was he, then? And what was he healing?

. . .

That's what the Protestant church superintendent of Herford, Pastor Hermann Kunst, tried to learn during a series of interviews he conducted with Gröning in May 1949, and from talking to "many very different people" about the healer. The clergyman was a significant local personage who oversaw a number of parishes after the war, at a time when the Christian churches were virtually the only intact institutions. He would go on to have an illustrious career in church and conservative national politics, and ultimately become the kind of figure to whom Federal presidents extend public birthday greetings.[30]

In a report he wrote subsequently, Kunst recounted some basic biographical facts. The Wunderdoktor was Catholic. He had not completed his education or learned a trade. He had no "foreknowledge as a lay healer," and had never studied medicine. Gröning did not take his knowledge from people, he explained. He did not read books or newspapers. He sharply condemned hypnosis, which he associated negatively with magic. His gifts, he said, came from God. Kunst also recorded a few hints of eccentricity he'd heard about secondhand: the Hülsmann family "testified that he ate very little and hardly needed to sleep."

Gröning, Kunst explained, would sometimes spend hours with a single patient. Afterward, he might simply tell them, "you are healthy," or "you will be healthy at this or that time." He could heal people from a distance, Gröning told Kunst. All he needed was a scrap of paper from the sick person bearing the message: "I ask to be healed."[31] Local opinion swung between proclaiming Gröning a "new messiah and a swindler," Kunst noted. But "the truth is," the pastor wrote, "that people I know are free of old aches and pains since meeting Gröning and have a new lease on life. With others, their old pains came back after weeks or months." Kunst saw "no reason to believe that Herr Gröning seeks to use his gifts to gain wealth." If anything, Gröning said, he wanted "to stay a poor man." He described turning down large sums to cure rich people, saying he wanted to serve the community and for those he healed to commit themselves to a life of sacrifice. While Kunst found these virtues consistent with a Christian outlook, he also expressed theological concern. Gröning addressed crowds in the name of Jesus, Kunst said, but "aimed only at bodily healing," and not forgiveness.[32]

Kunst understandably assumed that Gröning was some kind of religious healer, and in a certain way, he was. He talked a lot about God, said that his power to heal came from God, claimed to cure in God's name. But whereas Pastor Kunst, steeped in Christian theology, talked about sin and forgiveness, Gröning spoke of evil spirits. In early June, a local Herford paper, the *Freie Presse*, quoted a "reliable source" about a visit Gröning had recently made to a farm nearby, where several people had fallen sick. Gröning recommended that a hole be dug, a foot and a half deep, near the property boundary. The farmer would find a root there from an old dead tree. Cutting it out, Gröning said, would chase away their neighbor's evil spirit and lift a curse plaguing the farmer and causing his family's illness.[33]

That was curious, but so was Gröning's saying repeatedly that he would only help "good" people. "Were he to let himself be moved by the tears of an evil person," Kunst reported, Gröning said he "would get a high fever for two or three days after." Good and evil were states Gröning would often claim the ability to sense, something he perceived inside a person that marked them as a bearer of beneficent or ill will. One contemporary account recorded an instance in which he told an associate to make sure a certain woman left his vicinity: "she is possessed by Satan," he said.[34] Those bearing ill will could make other people sick. But Gröning was also always alert to the ways that even good intentions might be turned to the bad. The healer explained to Pastor Kunst that he had been able to help people since childhood, and had tested his gifts many times to make sure they were God-given and not "from below," that is, from the Devil. Gröning claimed that those he healed who took up wrongdoing afterward would be punished, losing the health they had gained.[35] To be ill, on some level, was to have transgressed, to have done wrong. Illness was a punishment for misbehavior. But there were degrees. Some transgressions and illnesses could be cured, but some could not, because not everyone deserved healing. Gröning was quoted in the press saying he would only help those who were "worthy."[36]

Gröning was indeed a religious healer, but not one who whispered pious prayers at the bedsides of the suffering. The spirituality of his medicine had more than one aspect. On the one hand, he spoke of God and divine energy; on the other, about "evil people" who infected tree roots with demonic spirits and made their neighbors ill. "Evil people" was a longstanding folk synonym for witches.[37] To understand *that* part of Gröning's healing, we have to understand a bit more about the practices of German folk medicine. We have to understand something about witchcraft.

. . .

The era of large-scale witch hunting in Europe ended long ago. The last legal execution of a witch in German-speaking Europe took place in Glarus, Switzerland, in 1782.[38] But that did not end fears of witches. It did not end the dread that among the members of one's community might be those who worked mischief in stealth to harm others.

The early modern witch hunt has powerfully shaped what we assume witchcraft to be about, and it has also limited what we think it is, and when we think it was. But in the most basic sense, to accuse someone of being a witch is to accuse that person of conspiring to do covert evil: to inflict harm, misfortune, and sickness.[39] Witchcraft, in this regard, is a cultural idiom, a way of understanding and explaining the bad things that befall us.

In his 1937 ethnography, *Witchcraft, Oracles, and Magic Among the Azande*, the British anthropologist E. E. Evans-Pritchard famously argued that witchcraft should be understood principally as an explanation for misfortune. Conducting fieldwork among the Azande of east-central Africa in the 1920s, he learned that witchcraft was "ubiquitous," and that it played a part "in every activity of Zande life."

> If blight seizes the groundnut crop it is witchcraft; if the bush is vainly scoured for game it is witchcraft; if women laboriously bale water out of a pool and are rewarded by but a few small fish it is witchcraft; . . . if a prince is cold and distant with his subject it is witchcraft; . . . if, in fact, any failure or misfortune falls upon anyone at any time and in relation to any of the manifold activities of his life it may be due to witchcraft.

The Azande ascribed to the same causality that he did, Evans-Pritchard said, the same set of facts about how the world works. But they also perceived, in any given instance, that there may be different *kinds* of causes and facts in play. And, as Evans-Pritchard said, "the facts do not explain themselves."

The anthropologist offered this famous example: from time to time, he recounted, "in Zandeland an old granary collapses." Sometimes when this happened someone would be killed, since people often sat under the granaries in the heat of the day. The Azande knew perfectly well that granaries collapsed because termites gnawed on the structures. But the event of a granary collapsing and harming those underneath it on a particular hot day could not be fully explained simply by recounting that causality. Knowing that gnawing termites cause granaries to collapse does not explain why they collapse just when they do, or why specific people are sitting under them at the very moment they collapse, and not, say, an hour before. Termites, Evans-Pritchard learned from the Azande, are merely a *proximate* cause. Collapsing granaries also have an *ultimate* cause, and that cause was what Zande people called witchcraft.[40]

For the Azande as Evans-Pritchard described them, witchcraft was foremost a way of making what happened in people's lives intelligible in the fullest sense, of explaining what lay behind such misfortunes as poor harvests and sickness. Narratives proliferate in the spaces between what is known and what isn't, especially in the spaces where life and knowledge are the most fragile. Illness is mysterious. It comes without warning, and its sources are often hidden. By explaining death or illness or bad luck, witchcraft acts as a form of theodicy, a way of understanding why bad things—like granaries collapsing— happen when they do, and to whom.[41]

Witchcraft played a similar, explanatory role in German folk medicine. The first comprehensive textbook dedicated to the topic, Gustav Jungbauer's 1934 *German Folk Medicine*, described a variety of popular ways of understanding illness, what caused it, and how to cure it.[42] A professor of folklore at Charles University in Prague, Jungbauer documented a spectrum of prevention and treatments for maladies of all kinds. Folk medical wisdom, he explained, had its own names for illnesses, and recognized a wider spectrum of health problems than university-educated doctors were trained to do. For example, it acknowledged many varieties of fever with distinctive names, such as "lazy fever" (*Faulfieber*)—an affliction suffered by those whose blood had "gone bad." Folk medicine had its own unique geographies, Jungbauer said, because diagnosis and medical efficacy sometimes depended on climate, and because herbalists could rely on different varieties of plant life depending on location. Folk doctors also had a range of practices they might prescribe (washing in flowing water before daylight on Easter morning) or proscribe (certain activities for pregnant women, for example). Jungbauer's book inventoried a spectrum of therapies: speaking the name of God, offering benedictions, prayers, and incantations; using amulets; holding pictures of saints; transmitting illness (to another person, or a plant, or animal) or burying it in the ground.[43]

What really defined the difference between folk medical conceptions and those of physicians pivoted around how each group *explained* illness's sources. Physicians and folk doctors both began by looking for natural causes. But if folk doctors failed to find such a cause, they might turn to supernatural ones: the alignment of the moon and stars, for example, or the ghosts of the dead, or demons, or sin.[44] From this perspective, illness could be rich in *meaning*. It might betray the machinations of evildoers, such as witches; or, like a scarlet letter, it could reveal personal shame, or religious or social transgression. Illness was shot through with moral concern, and the potential for moral judgment.

Körle, a Hessian village in the Fulda River valley chronicled by anthropologist Gerhard Wilke, offers a rich illustration of how some people might interpret illness, and the ways in which moral values could be conflated with physical well-being. Körle residents mostly worked in agriculture, though some traveled by train to work in the nearby city of Kassel. Villagers largely attended to their own medical needs, visiting a doctor only in case of a serious injury or disease. They relied on signs in nature—a barn owl's appearance at the wrong time of year, an especially large molehill—to anticipate or interpret the onset of sickness. But illness was itself a sign, one that villagers tended to associate with dirt, pollution, and disorder. Illness was often perceived as a form of cosmic judgment, as punishment for improper or irresponsible behavior. It reflected the order of society and the cosmos writ large, and could reveal sins of various orders of magnitude. As such, it structured the community's moral economy: those who suffered from heart disease, or had circulatory problems, villagers believed, had lived wrong. Perhaps they had not worked hard enough, or had behaved irresponsibly, creating a social burden for the community. Cancer and ulcers were perceived as punishments, perhaps for youthful sexual indiscretion. Maintaining health was a sign of one's self-discipline and accountability within a community where people depended on one another to get the work done that allowed the community to continue and to thrive.[45]

To be sure, Körle's inhabitants did not perceive all illnesses as moral judgments or as the result of cosmic sanction. Tuberculosis and pneumonia, they felt, could befall anyone; those were simply two of humanity's burdens.[46] But for many people in communities like Körle, of which there were many hundreds in Germany, sickness and healing were often perceived to have spiritual and social significance, arousing a search for causes *behind* causes. Illness could be a portent, a sign, ripe for speculation and interpretation. In this sense, folk healers performed a service that university-trained physicians, with their natural-scientific explanations, could not, by helping to interpret illnesses' spiritual and moral meanings.

Folk doctoring entailed a certain dualism, or moral ambiguity, another folklorist, Gerhard Staack, argued. Healers "justified ... their craft" by invoking God, he explained, but rituals to banish evil involved arts open to interpretation. "He who avails himself of magic can do so for good or ill," Staack wrote. "He is bound only by moral law; if he behaves arbitrarily, or tries to harm others through his abilities, then he has succumbed to demonic temptation and become a witch." Being a successful healer, in other words, could also entail a reputation for being a powerful *Hexenbanner*—literally, a witch banisher, capable of doing battle with evil or putting it to use.[47]

The moral dualism Staack identified meant that healers known to have the ability to identify witches and break their hexes were by turns feared and revered. Again, the one who could make bad magic harmless, block evil's malignant effects, root out demonic influence, and cure devil-induced sickness, was also perceived as capable of doing bad magic, bringing on misfortune, and calling forth illness and harm. Gröning's estranged brother Karl would later claim that Bruno had been fascinated in childhood by a neighborhood healer, Frau Bialke, whom Karl called the "miracle maker [*Wunderfrau*] of our part of town." People apparently stood in line to take her cures, some of which involved exorcisms. A story went around, Karl claimed, that she had been possessed by a demon and could only give this demon over to a child. When she died, according to Karl, the neighbors became convinced that her spirit had been transferred to "the Gröning boy."[48] That story contains two intertwining elements: one, that an awesome power had been transferred from one generation of healers to the next; and two, that that power—to cure, to benefit, to do good—could cohabit with devilry.

These beliefs and practices were more widespread, evidence suggests, than one might assume in a country with such a powerful and renowned medical and scientific culture. The Atlas of German Folklore, a vast ethnographic study undertaken in the 1930s, gathered information about all kinds of everyday customs and practices, material culture, and forms of language and belief, including folk medical knowledge. Among the practices the Atlas documented was *Besprechen*, which involved the ritual vocalization of prayers and verbal charms to effect healing, and which could include evil-averting magic.[49] Within a rough triangle formed by Hamburg, Dresden, and Danzig—an area centered on Berlin—four out of five people reported the use of *Besprechen* in their communities. In parts of Bavaria, Lower Saxony, Hesse, and Württemberg, between 40 and 80 percent of respondents reported its use.[50] Gröning, as we have seen, came from Danzig, and Bavaria is the region where he would have his greatest success.

German folklorists in the 1930s, '40s, and '50s, including Gustav Jungbauer and Gerhard Staack, were inclined to revere practices they presumed to embody ancient Germanic, pre-Christian forms of knowledge, preserved in the supposedly inert amber of rural places. But where folk medicine was concerned, the distinction between the rural and urban worlds was much less firm than those scholars imagined. Statistics from the Atlas project indicate that while *Besprechen* was somewhat less common in Munich than in its hinterlands, in other large urban centers, like Hamburg or Berlin, there was no significant difference in the frequency of its use between the cities and the countryside.[51] In some parts of what would become West Germany, as many as 90 percent of inhabitants believed that some people possessed the power to hex.[52]

• • •

The fabled dualism of healers—their moral ambiguity—led people to interpret Gröning and his mission to cure the sick in starkly divergent terms. Alongside the many pleading missives that cure seekers sent to town manager Meister hoping to gain an audience with the Wunderdoktor, there are other letters today housed in the Herford county archives, written by people who accused Gröning of being the Devil's own. A graphologist called Ludewitz wrote in May 1949 claiming to have performed an analysis of the healer's handwriting, and denounced him on that basis for moral turpitude and sexual deviancy.[53] A group called the European Mission Society accused Gröning of using the "arts of the Devil" and of being in league with "demonic forces" with which he supposedly intended "to perplex humanity."[54] "We are truly living in a time in which the Devil drives his regiment forward," wrote a representative of the Militant League Against Nihilism. "As a sincere German and Christian," the League's representative declared, "I am duty-bound to help fight evil"—meaning Gröning. This citizen saw in his sudden materialization and fellow citizens' response an explicit reversion to Nazism. "For those like me, who found themselves in the grip of satanic forces in the Third Reich and then were saved," the man wrote, "we see things with different eyes."[55]

The letter writer may have had a point: someone wrote Meister from the nearby town of Gronau, mysteriously referring to Gröning as "the Third Messiah."[56] Did this citizen imagine him as part three of a divine triumvirate, of which Jesus and Hitler formed parts one and two? Perhaps. The postwar moral through-line was never clear, and certainly not around Gröning: a citizen from Werries, another town not far from Herford, asked the town manager in June if he understood the full implications of the ban he'd imposed. Was Meister truly prepared to stand in the way of "the Angel of the Lord, Gröning"? After all, the correspondent from Werries contended, the country's spiritual destiny was at stake: people must "turn themselves earnestly to Jesus" in order to avert "the *Unheil* that still hangs over us." *Unheil* can mean calamity, or catastrophe, or misfortune, but it can also mean evil, and it suggests both the "unholy" and the "unwhole." What was the nature of this calamity? According to the correspondent from Werries, instead of drawing spiritual lessons from the war and the bombing, his fellow citizens had allowed things to degenerate even further. "Whores are back at it," he wrote, "just like the Gypsies, vagabonds, murderers, adulterers, and thieves." Even the youth was "totally corrupted."[57]

A few weeks later, in July, someone from Miesbach wrote to Meister expressing the hope that Gröning would find someone to help support his work, because things had gotten so bad. "We are living through the Jews' fate," the Miesbacher wrote. His analysis of the national condition? That his fellow Germans had "attended too little to the New Testament and dragged along with us too many errors from the Jews' Old Testament about a wrathful God."[58] Obsessed with punishment and divine vengeance, his fellow citizens had not yet learned the spiritual importance of Christian forgiveness.

Germans had been accustomed for at least a generation to see the world in extreme, black-or-white ways, in terms of allies and enemies, good and evil, "Aryans" and others. The letters to Meister bear witness to this, even as they suggest a concerted, ongoing effort among people to interpret fate and seek out the means to salvation. At the same time, they reveal a powerful desire to blame someone for their suffering, and most seem to have been concerned with the "evils" of the *present*, not the past. In that sense, the *Unheil*, the calamity hanging overhead, was not Nazism but defeat, and the occupation: it was these that had driven Germans to prostitute themselves ("whores are back at it"). It was the Allies who failed to "deal with" "Gypsies," murderers, and thieves. It was the occupiers who allowed youth to be "corrupted." The implicit comparison here was with the Third Reich, seen as a positive force: one that had indeed dealt decisively, often murderously, with any perceived social problem.

The press, for its part, paid detailed, practically phrenological attention to Gröning's physical characteristics, as though clues about his origins and class, motivations and talents and habits might provide a window into his soul. Reporters never failed to describe the color and look of his eyes (feverish and bright blue, or were they gray-green?); the color and length of his hair; his gait and frame; his prodigious smoking and coffee consumption. Newspaper and magazine writers sometimes suggested that Gröning might be related to "Indian yogis," or that he was a "Gypsy."[59] The last description—in the aftermath of the Nazi campaign of persecution and mass murder against Sinti and Roma people—had complicated overtones, to say the least. "Gypsies" were considered dangerous and untrustworthy outsiders, but were also perceived to possess magical abilities. To say that Gröning was "related to Gypsies" hinted at desirable qualities—clairvoyance, supernatural abilities—but also dealings with the Devil.

. . .

By mid-June 1949, Herford's town manager expressed concern that, due to their "insufficient insight concerning the necessity of the ban for public protection," several thousand cure-seekers had been waiting outside for days and nights in the rain, "contrary to reason" and "to the detriment of their health."[60] Hoping to disperse them once and for all, Meister announced that he would permit Gröning to perform a "one-time mass healing." But afterwards, the crowds stayed put.[61] By the last weeks of June, automobiles and even buses lined the Hülsmanns' street.[62] With nowhere else to stay—every hotel, inn, and guesthouse was full—weary and ailing travelers camped on benches in the train station, or slept in their cars, or under the stars, on the Hülsmanns' lawn.[63] The *Freie Presse* described crowds in the streets, plazas, and parks of the city forming "a wide and ever-expanding bivouac." Protestors mounted an obstreperous, even threatening resistance to the ban on Gröning's cures.[64] Those who could not come themselves sent letters, "from Dortmund, Koblenz, Mannheim, Munich," one newspaper reported, and even "England, France, Holland, Belgium, and Australia."[65]

Some reporters and editors appear to have been as swept along by the Miracle of Herford as any of their fellow citizens. Even after Gröning's treatments were banned, national magazines like *Stern* continued to repeat the story of his first meeting with little Dieter, and published other wondrous stories besides: that town manager Meister had personally witnessed Gröning, who said he was God's envoy, enable "completely lame adults to walk without crutches within hours"; that "ulcers healed under his very hand."[66]

The Herford press remained circumspect. In early June, the *Freie Presse* had reported that Dieter was "back in bed" again.[67] But his story, whatever the truth of it, had taken on a life of its own. The very same day, an illustrated weekly, *Der Hausfreund*, enticed potential cure-seekers with the news that police posted in front of the Hülsmanns' home were letting people through "if some poor devil had come from a long way off." "Police capitulate under the weight of the facts," the paper editorialized.[68] Meister had to inform the district governor that the situation in his city had become "intolerable."[69] Out-of-town journalists described an "agitated crowd" gathering to protest at city hall, shouting "hang the town manager." Police had to intervene "to stop eruptions of violence." Some demonstrators were arrested. "It was a small uprising," the Munich *Mercury* reported.[70]

As the weeks went by, people continued to stream toward Herford.

"They come from all over West Germany," a correspondent wrote in late June. People thronged the Hülsmanns' home "at all hours. Fifty to a hundred in the morning. Two hundred in the evening. Five hundred at midnight." Only then, very late at night, would a window on the second-floor balcony open. Gröning would "speak to the crowds and hand out photos of himself." Some had "waited already three, four, five days . . . in the rain, almost without anything to eat, camping out at night in waiting rooms."[71] Magazines published photos of happy people returning to work, their nerve paralysis cured, or doing deep knee bends after Gröning relieved them of asthma.[72] The *Freie Presse* warned of Gröning's "almost uncanny influence on people," and suggested that he was mentally ill, observing that a "psychiatrist would doubtless find pathological characteristics in Gröning's peculiar behavior."[73]

A young diabetic stopped taking his insulin when he heard Gröning say that anyone "who had the proper belief in God was healed." He soon became weak and fell into a deep coma. He survived, but would continue to require a lot of care.[74] In response, North Rhine–Westphalia's minister for social welfare asked the district governor to initiate immediate criminal proceedings against Gröning for violating the ban on lay healers, for fraud, and for negligent bodily harm.[75] Gröning obtained legal counsel. His lawyers responded to the criminal complaint by arguing that because their client did not accept money for his work, he could not be said to have violated the ban. Gröning was merely answering the needs of "countless suffering people." He offered help to the ailing out of religious conviction, a sense of charity, and love. Gröning "worked on people spiritually, without medicines," they wrote, and healed without actually laying his hands on anyone.[76]

Soon, the entire state of North Rhine–Westphalia (to which Herford belonged), as well as the great maritime city of Hamburg, would ban the healer outright from treating the sick.[77] Other states, like northerly Schleswig-Holstein, however, declared that they would not obstruct his mission. "Everywhere you go, from Flensburg to the

Rhine, people are talking about the Wunderdoktor," Hamburg's *Die Welt* newspaper reported breathlessly. As "topic number one in the British zone," he had "suddenly overshadowed current events, letting people forget their worries, large and small."[78] At a press conference in Hamburg at the end of June, Gröning was asked whether he was religious. "Yes. I believe in God," Gröning replied. "I live with God."[79]

4

SOUL MEDICINE

People sought out Bruno Gröning to cure them of a wide variety of illnesses, but a striking number of the letters written to Herford town manager Fritz Meister in spring and summer 1949 came specifically from people suffering some form of paralysis. "I've heard that Herr Gröning is supposed to have his greatest successes in dealing with paralysis [*Lähmung*]," a man wrote to Meister in June 1949.[1] A standard image of the day's photojournalism featured people arriving to meet the Wunderdoktor using wheelchairs, crutches, and canes. Journalists describing the scene on Wilhelmsplatz remarked on this trend, and not always kindly. One described the crowds as "dominated by those unable to walk and cripples" alongside "quaverers and tremblers and war wounded."[2] Paralysis of various limbs had been a symptom associated with wartime experiences and the effects of shell-shock since World War I, but according to one account, up to three times as many German veterans were disabled after World War II.[3]

A Dr. Jens Bergfeld, who published an account called *Herford's*

Wunderdoktor in 1949, also described several cure-seekers whose ability to speak had been affected by war injuries.[4] Another publication related the story of a woman who could no longer speak or hear "after losing her only son, and from the circumstances of the Russian invasion" (the hazy reference to "circumstances" was likely a euphemism for rape).[5] Some supplicants were described as suffering from war blindness (*Kriegsblindheit*), a condition also familiar from World War I.[6] While many other ailments continued to be part of the parade of affliction, illness vaguely attributed to war damage and impairments to sufferers' limbs and sensory organs were especially prominent themes.

The historian of medicine Anne Harrington describes various instances of "bodies behaving badly"—when ailments' origins, rather than being related to individual physiological, biological, or psychological factors may be located instead in *social* experience.[7] Thomas Mann, who spent the Nazi years in exile from Germany in the United States, once remarked that members of the exile community "seemed to be particularly susceptible" to "heart attack, in the form of coronary thrombosis or angina pectoris." Considering the pain and terror of their experiences, Mann remarked, this was "scarcely to be wondered at."[8] He once referred to the "heart-asthma of exile."[9]

Harrington asks whether experiences of "betrayal, interpersonal alienation, and power politics" might help explain some manifestations of illness or sudden disability. One of the striking examples she gives, which will be familiar to US readers of a certain age, concerns the air-traffic-controller crisis of the early 1980s. In 1981, air traffic controllers went on strike to protest their working conditions and the intolerable stress associated with their jobs. But though researchers readily conceded that the controllers were under stress, they could find no physical evidence of it, like heightened levels of cortisol or elevated blood pressure. Ultimately, Robert Rose, a prominent psychiatrist on a Federal Aviation Administration team researching the problem, concluded that the cause of the controllers' suffering was not so much stress as a lack of social support. They felt that no one cared about how hard their work was, or how they fared in their jobs. The stress they experienced, Rose became convinced, wasn't just biological or physiological, and it "wasn't just inside the individual."[10] Their illness was a product of social experience.

Applying these ideas to postwar Germany, we might ask how pervasive unease, a sense of collective failure, persistent questions of blame, and fears of betrayal might have influenced the ways people experienced the fragility of their bodies after Nazism. Did people become suddenly blind or deaf because they could not bear to see or hear what was happening around them—could not bear defeat and its consequences? Did some suddenly lose the ability to walk as a form of unconscious protest against volition, against agency, against responsibility for genocide and war crimes? Did they lose the ability to speak because there were so many things that could not be discussed out loud—the persecution and mass murder of the Jews above all, but also the anxieties denazification provoked, and shame over losing the war? Defeat, an anonymous Nazi intelligence agent wrote in the closing days of World War II, had caused *bodily* suffering. Under social conditions that some contemporaries described as a simmering "civil war," the philosopher Maurice Merleau-Ponty's idea, that a loss of speech can stand for a "refusal of co-existence," seems like a potent possibility.[11]

Bruno Gröning and the phenomenon that mushroomed around him in 1949 offer us a chance to think through these striking questions. That many people were ailing after the war is clear. But what sent them, in huge numbers, to seek cures from an obscure little man in rumpled pants, and a former Nazi at that? What led them to spend nights sleeping outside in the rain in the hopes of meeting him? Why did they call him "messiah"? Clearly, many Germans invested Gröning with qualities far exceeding those of ordinary doctors. It's not clear how, but the Wunderdoktor was able to touch pains those doctors simply could not reach.

. . .

Following the Hamburg press conference where he said he lived with God, Gröning suddenly slipped out of public view. After the tumult he'd created in Herford, this disappearance only added to his mystique, and he continued to dominate headlines even in absentia: in early July, his image appeared on the cover of West Germany's newsmagazine of record, *Der Spiegel*, seemingly unmoored from the earth and floating above a sea of transfixed women. The accompanying article was far less than insightful about what had brought people into his orbit, being itself largely transfixed by various lurid details about him—"the messiah" who sat "together with his disciples" in the evenings, in "an atmosphere straight out of Edgar Allan Poe."[12]

It would soon emerge that Gröning was ensconced in a rented villa in Heidelberg called Rutenberg House (chosen in part for its high garden hedge, to help keep the public at bay), where he had embarked on what would be described as a novel set of experiments. The enterprise was the brainchild of a popular illustrated newsmagazine called *Revue*—in form not unlike the *Saturday Evening Post* but with celebrities and pinups.[13] Two enterprising reporters, Helmut Laux and Heinz Bongartz, had been given the task of recruiting him along with some doctors willing to observe his work and "test it clinically."[14] The results were to be published in weekly installments between August and October 1949. The series was a blockbuster, with each issue selling between 100,000 and 400,000 copies.[15] The first cover story suggests why. It featured a full-page closeup of a soulful Gröning above the arresting, bold-type headline: REVOLUTION IN MEDICINE? The series' initial issues were dedicated to the proposition that an "intolerant" medical establishment was standing between the people and the restoration of their health. "I cure the incurable," Gröning told *Revue*.[16]

Laux and Bongartz's assignment required considerable legwork. They enlisted the aid and expertise of a Marburg physician and psychologist, Professor G. H. Fischer. In Heidelberg, the journalists hoped, Gröning would work with test subjects they had identified, while Fischer and other doctors observed.[17] Driving north from their Frankfurt

7. JULI 1949

DER SPIEGEL

PREIS 1 DM

HANNOVER · 3. JAHRGANG · NR 28
ERSCHEINT JEDEN DONNERSTAG

„ICH HABE VERBOT", RIEF GRÖNING

„Aber ich will es noch einmal mit Deutschland versuchen" (siehe „Deutschland")

offices to Herford, they turned up people Gröning had already helped, who were willing to talk about their experiences, as well as some who had not yet met him. Among the former were the director of a health insurance plan named Lanzenrath who suffered from kidney trouble but had been pain free since Gröning treated him two months earlier; a man named Klüglich from Bielefeld who had been shot through a kidney during the war, but had experienced "growing relief from his suffering" since communicating with Gröning; and a Herr Kargesmeyer, forty-seven, from the spa town of Bad Oeynhausen, who suffered severe headaches that developed into a trigeminal neuralgia, but whose terrible pain had been ameliorated after meeting with Gröning. Among the new patients were a widow from Bielefeld who owned a bicycle shop and suffered from rheumatism; a Frau Joest, of Hemsbach near Heidelberg, afflicted with stomach trouble and digestive complaints; and a Herr Strobel of Mannheim, who had been wounded three times in the war and was living with Bechterew's disease, an inflammation of the spinal column.

Finding such people was easy; the healer himself proved more elusive. After failing initially to locate him, Laux and Bongartz left word with Lanzenrath, the health insurance official, asking him to relay a message. A telegram from Gröning soon arrived, and the Wunderdoktor himself materialized in Frankfurt shortly after in a borrowed Volkswagen. The Rutenberg House in Heidelberg was secured, and the stage was set.[18]

Though Gröning resided in the villa (where, despite the hedge and the efforts of *Revue*, big crowds gathered, parked their cars, and clustered around the gate), the experiments would take place at the Ludolf-Krehl Clinic at Heidelberg University, which Fischer had recommended.[19] The clinic was known for a special focus on psychosomatic medicine. Laux and Bongartz seem to have assumed from the start that the illnesses Gröning had been so successful in treating were, as they described it, *seelisch*.[20] This word literally means "of the soul," but depending on context, can also mean spiritual, psychological, emotional, or mental.[21] Laux and Bongartz also frequently used a somewhat outmoded term for a psychologist, *Seelenarzt*—literally, "doctor of the soul"—to describe Gröning. His medicine, the *Revue* series repeatedly suggested, was soul medicine. According to Fischer, too few physicians knew how to treat *seelische* illnesses, and so patients "wandered without a cure from doctor to doctor and medications do nothing for them." That, he said, explained their "fanatical hope for a miracle"—and for an audience with Gröning.[22]

At least initially, Fischer was convinced that Gröning had the potential to redeem medicine, to breathe new life into it, to offer new understandings of the interactions between mind and body. In a manner characteristic of the time, he never said explicitly why this redemption was needed. He did not talk, for example, about how in the Third Reich medicine had been instrumentalized, and placed in the service of the state's eugenic program, with no corner of it remaining untouched by a racial-technocratic impulse. He did not discuss the invidious categories of racially based wellness and illness the state contrived, categories that had radically redefined and narrowed human value, producing a stark, exclusionary social hierarchy of "fit" and "unfit." Those deemed "fit" in the Third Reich—those, that is, with an "Aryan" racial identity, freedom from hereditary disease, and an ability to work vigorously and produce—had received lavish benefits from the state, including the privilege (though sometimes, since abortion was criminalized, the obligation) to reproduce. The "unfit," by contrast, were deprived of the most basic care and sustenance. Regarded as biologically dangerous, they were excluded for such perceived inadequacies as race (as Jews, Sinti, or Roma), disability, and a range of illnesses or conditions that were inherited (or believed at the time to be). German physicians had underwritten a system that led to at least 400,000 involuntary sterilizations and the medical murders of some 260,000 individuals whose lives were, in the state's parlance, "not worth living."[23] Fischer did not mention that either.

Nor was Heidelberg University's recent history a topic on which Dr. Fischer or the *Revue* series commented. Situated on the verdant banks of the Neckar River, the university is one of Germany's most ancient. Faculty and students had nazified it shortly after 1933. Jewish, pacifist, and socialist professors were purged. The remaining faculty and students adapted themselves to the prevailing winds, their attitudes toward the new regime generally ranging from enthusiastic to accommodating. The American occupiers, who led Heidelberg's denazification after the war, screened the faculty. The procedure, intended to be just but thorough, would remain distinctly incomplete. In the case of the medical faculty, the desire to reopen the university's doors quickly meant that though "most doctors" had "formal Nazi affiliation," almost half were deemed eligible for reinstatement.[24]

Heading the clinic where Gröning's experiments were to take place was neurologist Viktor von Weizsäcker. He had only returned to Heidelberg in 1945, having served as director of the Neurological Clinic and Research Institute at the University of Breslau (today Wrocław, Poland) beginning in 1941. Von Weizsäcker was the scion of an aristocratic family (his nephew, Richard von Weizsäcker, would later serve as president of the Federal Republic). Viktor's brother, Ernst, former state secretary in the Foreign Office and ambassador to the Holy See under the Nazis, had just been sentenced at the US military tribunal at Nuremberg in April 1949 for his role in the deportations of French Jews to Auschwitz and for war crimes.

In Breslau, Viktor von Weizsäcker had been involved in obtaining the brains of "euthanized" children for scientific research. He defended euthanasia and human experimentation even after the Nuremberg Trials, professing his opinion that "violence and human sacrifice" were "a necessary part of the tragedy of human history."[25] Von Weizsäcker had long held these views, having reflected since at least 1933 on how "constructive" a "policy of extermination thought out to its logical conclusions and implemented nationally" would be.[26]

Yet von Weizsäcker is still perhaps best known as a key figure in the history of psychosomatic medicine. The field, which had its origins in early nineteenth-century European romanticism, had been institutionalized in the German-speaking countries by the 1920s. It focused on afflictions, often chronic, that were physical but influenced by pathological interactions between mind and body. Psychosomatic practitioners tended to be critical of more mainstream medicine, finding fault with what they perceived as an overly reductionist attitude among fellow physicians, one that failed to treat patients as whole beings, body and soul.[27] Psychosomatic doctors rejected narrowly natural-scientific ideas about illness and disability and sought, alongside science, to engage questions of meaning. They placed patients' biographies and social environment at the center of their treatment and philosophy. Von Weizsäcker's teacher and mentor Ludolf von Krehl believed that healing required knowing a patient's "entire nature." Von Krehl declared himself to be no "mystic," and "also no occultist or such. But what is spirit is spirit," he said, "and a human being is a totality, spirit and body."[28]

Von Weizsäcker was much influenced by these ideas, believing that one had to contemplate seriously not just the appearance of disease or organ dysfunction but also its symbolic aspects. He listened to the stories his patients told for clues about the meanings of their troubles. From their life stories, he wrote "pathosophies"—narratives that analyzed aspects of his patients' lives to unlock hidden significance about their ailments. Rather than asking his patients "What seems to be the trouble?" von Weizsäcker asked, in the way a psychoanalyst might, "Why this symptom? Why now?"[29]

A major argument laid out in the *Revue* series did feint, if ever so tacitly, toward the past: medicine had failed patients, the magazine maintained, by treating their bodies like failing machines while neglecting their souls. Gröning would prompt medicine's psychosomatic transformation toward a more holistic approach to treatment that would take people's inner lives and life experiences into account. He would, *Revue* repeatedly argued, restore "trust." Why trust had to be restored—the recent history of forced sterilizations and "mercy killings" of those with disabilities—was once again left out. As was true in so many instances in postwar West Germany, the elision itself becomes a piece of evidence, the elephant in the room. Yet given that the Gröning experiments took place at a barely rehabilitated

Heidelberg University, and in the clinic of a doctor who had defended euthanasia, the avoidance of any mention of Nazi-era medical depredations is hardly surprising.

Much of the attention the Wunderdoktor received in Herford had been religious in nature. Pastor Hermann Kunst, while finding certain of Gröning's ideas troubling, also judged him to be a pious figure. The healer's lawyer had rebuffed charges that his client violated the ban on lay healers by explaining that Gröning healed *spiritually*. And if the first conceit of the *Revue* series was that medicine had failed to treat patients by neglecting their souls, the second was that what Gröning did could be explained through the methods of science—through experimentation and observation—in an environment primed to receive favorably the idea that a damaged soul could make the body ill.

Yet most of what was captured in the series involved little more than Gröning's talking to patients and asking how they perceived their bodily sensations. He would read these less as clues that might indicate a specific kind of distress than as indicators of an internal state constantly in flux, over which he—or some unseen, external force—might achieve influence. Frau Joest, for example, a patient of von Weizsäcker's, suffered from digestive trouble, constipation, headaches, and a benign uterine tumor. In a transcript of their treatment session published in the magazine, Gröning asked her not to dwell on her suffering. Rather, he told her, she should "concentrate fully and completely" on her body. "Do you notice anything happening in your body?" he asked at one point, "Is a wave going through?" He assured her that he did not want to tell her what to feel, insisting only that she "make sure to tell the truth . . . just always tell the truth." As in other instances, Gröning spoke elliptically, never articulating anything as specific as a method, but quietly bantering with patients while seeming to intuit their shifting physical states. "We will get there," he told Frau Joest, but "you must not think so much about your suffering—it disturbs me—I can't get to it. That does not need to be." The details of what Frau Joest felt, unfortunately, we can't know much about.

Revue recorded only her most basic responses: a feeling of warmth in her kidneys, pain in her lower back.

In a sidebar, Laux and Bongartz explained other things to their readers about Frau Joest, things that sounded like one of von Weizsäcker's pathosophies. She had suffered without relief for more than ten years. At the age of twenty-two and against her family's wishes, she had married a fifty-five-year-old widower whose wife Frau Joest had taken care of before she died. The wife had suffered from an unspecified abdominal or gynecological complaint. For a time, Frau Joest worried that she had been somehow "infected" by this complaint. She and her husband had one child of their own, a son, and three daughters from his previous marriage. She wanted more children, he did not. Von Weizsäcker had attributed Frau Joest's "agonizing stomach trouble" to guilt about her husband's first wife and her tumor to "unfulfilled wishes for more children."[30]

There is no evidence that any of this had anything to do with the way Gröning treated Frau Joest or anyone else. As in Herford, so too in Heidelberg observers projected onto him what they believed they saw—and in this case, what they saw was a kind of psychotherapist. Whatever else he did for the many thousands who appealed to him for help, the *Revue* series made plain, Gröning seemed willing to listen. He inspired trust. As Pastor Kunst had observed in Herford, he would sit for hours, listening to suffering people talk about their troubles. He spoke to them "quietly," Laux and Bongartz wrote, "and full of confidence."[31] Gröning's significance for those who sought his cures lay in his "wild, unrestrained natural talent, one that inclined sometimes toward error but had a powerful ability to treat souls."[32] The term they used, *Seelenbehandlung*, could also be translated as "psychological treatment," but they clearly imputed Gröning's success less to technique than to some inborn facility with hearts and minds.

The religious ideas Gröning had often expressed in Herford were little in evidence in *Revue*'s pages. God was barely mentioned. Instead, the series presented him as an earthy, lay therapist, an intuitive rustic with mysterious abilities. He was clairvoyant, it said, and

Anneliese Hülsmann, Dieter's mother, sometimes worked with him as a medium. At Gröning's request, she would intuit the ailments of supplicants and describe them back to Gröning, who could work cures even at a distance.[33] Readers learned, too, about the tinfoil Gröning took from his packs of cigarettes and rolled into little balls. These served, he said, to conduct the therapeutic energy he possessed, which he called the *Heilstrom*, the healing current.[34] Laux and Bongartz described an instance in which Dr. Fischer had unsuspectingly sat in a chair Gröning often used when treating patients. Suddenly, Fischer's face had turned "deathly pale." He "struggled for breath" but then quickly collected himself. It was as if "he had been touched by a mysterious power whose origins he could not explain."

Convinced that some of Gröning's energy had collected in the chair, Fischer summoned twenty-one-year-old Anni Schwedler, visiting from Darmstadt. During the war, Anni had been buried alive with twenty others in an air raid shelter beneath a brewery as the building began to burn. She managed to escape, but over the next days her bearing became less certain; she began stumbling and gradually lost the ability to walk. Now, as she sat in the mysterious chair, Fischer began telling her how Gröning had already helped many paralyzed people in that very room. Then he showed her a picture of the healer. When Fischer next "commanded her . . . quite suddenly to stand," Anni "raised herself up almost energetically," the article recounted, "and was so astonished by being able to stand that at first she did not wager a step." With a faltering gait, after a couple of attempts, Anni was ultimately able "to cover the entire distance across the room, out of the house and across the yard to an adjacent street."[35]

. . .

Anni Schwedler's miraculous steps told two stories at the same time. One was about Gröning's mystique; the other was a war story, about how paralysis gradually came over a young girl after she narrowly escaped death. "The Second World War, with its many convulsions, left behind a flood of illnesses," Laux and Bongartz noted, including "immense numbers of stomach complaints and rheumatic illnesses as well as instances of neurosis and paralysis."[36] Many such illnesses, the journalists suggested, had their roots in "conscious or unconscious *seelische* shocks."[37]

As summer turned to fall, new installments of *Revue* hit newsstands, including the results of a survey Dr. Fischer undertook of some eighty thousand letters that cure-seekers had sent to Gröning to date, explaining their troubles and asking for his help. From a sample of some two thousand, Fischer found that a little more than half (57 percent) came from women. He surmised that most of the letter writers tended to be between twenty and sixty years old and most came from the middle and lower classes. Fischer deduced this from their writing styles, which he sometimes found "awkward," with "the clumsy expressions" used by "those unaccustomed to writing."[38] If Fischer was right, some of the letters' authors could have been among those most harmed by Nazi eugenic policies. A common mechanism for determining who should be sterilized in the Third Reich was "intelligence" testing, biased toward the kind of knowledge presumed in a middle-class subject with a middle-class education. This placed working-class people with practical educations at a distinct disadvantage.[39] In Herford, for example, most of the people sterilized came from the lower classes—workers in the city's cigar factories, farmhands, and young people in the welfare system.[40] Much the same was true elsewhere.

Stylishly written or not, the letters to Gröning related more than the details of illness and infirmity. Cure-seekers told him of their lost homes and lost loves; of grief, guilt, and disappointment; of family conflict, fear, and shame—most connected, in one way or another, to the war. "My son, six years old, has been in the hospital for six weeks," a mother wrote. "His kidneys have stopped working. His condition is very serious." The mother was convinced that her son's illness had to be attributed to "*seelische* causes": her husband died in the war, and she and her son had been forced to go and live with her unsympathetic parents. Another mother wrote to say how much worse her rheumatism was since she was bombed out in 1944. It had "become ever-more difficult" to walk. "I have to be carried everywhere, am always dependent on others."[41] *Revue* trained particular focus on a man named Herr Weiland, who had been mustered out of the Wehrmacht in 1943 as "fully unfit to serve" because his eyesight had gradually vanished. But after meeting Gröning in Herford, a portion of his vision had returned.[42]

According to Fischer, some 25 percent of correspondents said they had been diagnosed by their doctors as incurable. Many others suffered from "chronic ailments that . . . had their origins in *seelische* causes." Fischer characterized many of those who wrote to Gröning as "spiritually disoriented." They saw "no way out," felt terribly lonely, thought of suicide, and had "no one in whom they could confide." One correspondent described his wife as *herzkrank*—heartsick—after losing their daughter. Another woman described how her daughter had been raped eight times, had been sick ever since, and no longer wanted to eat.

For most doctors in 1949, unless there was an "organic basis" for illness, that illness did not exist. When patients complained of pain for which no manifestly physical cause could be located, doctors sought other explanations. Not unlike the problem of chronic pain in our own day, these explanations could cast a shadow on the sufferer's moral constitution, suggest a family taint, or hint at a lack of personal integrity.[43] Perhaps the patient was a malingerer, angling for a disability check, or lacked the fortitude or individual strength of character to overcome hard times. Perhaps the patient was too sensitive or weak-willed, or there had already been something wrong with him or her before the war.[44]

The letters to Gröning, Fischer was convinced, provided ample evidence that conventional medical opinion about the narrow applicability of psychosomatic medicine would have to be revised. The illnesses described were not phantom ailments: they were manifestly physical maladies with origins in the soul. Individual stories of distress revealed what Fischer called the effects of "mass fate": "nights under falling bombs, . . . flight and hunger, fallen fathers, fallen sons, assaults and rape."

Gröning, Fischer claimed, had shown psychosomatic illness to be "the epidemic of our time." The letters certainly documented stories of individual suffering, but they also revealed, as he put it, "the history of German suffering." People whose limbs suddenly refused to move, or who had stomach ailments, or whose children's kidneys were failing—these were the products not so much of individual experience, the physician suggested, but of the nation's collective fate. They were "reactions to the extraordinary burdens" that had been the "yield of the events of the last years."[45]

Fischer's language here is worth examining. First, when he wrote about fate-driven mass illnesses, he was not speaking about psychological trauma. Though in our own time trauma has become a nearly universal explanation for how terrible events can affect individuals' lives long into the future, the idea had little if any currency in Germany when Gröning arrived on the scene in 1949.[46] (When the term did get used, it referred to a physical shock or damage, not the effects of an emotionally disturbing experience.) Rather, Fisher was talking about maladies that resulted, as he saw it, from *collective* fate—maladies specific to Germans' experience "of the last years," as he put it. He noted that quite a few "foreign countries . . . especially Sweden, Switzerland, and the U.S.A." had recently seen "a not-quite-explicable growth of [psychosomatic] illnesses." But these countries' "*seelische* shocks," Fischer said, had been "few relative to ours."[47] He was talking about illnesses linked to German experiences in particular.

And when Fischer spoke of the "yield of the events of the last years," he was not talking about the Nazi era, or even about World War II—at least, not as a whole. He was talking only about those last, fatal years in which the war came home. German readers would have known this, when they saw references in *Revue*'s pages to bombing and especially to rapes. That, they knew, meant defeat and occupation—and occupation, of course, was the first product of defeat, the collective failure from which all other humiliations had flowed. According to Fischer, it was defeat and occupation that had destroyed the health of so many Germans.

Focusing only on a very restricted sense of what had happened "in the war" and talking only of their own losses, sacrifices, and struggles allowed the nation as a whole to exonerate itself. In the emerging postwar narrative, West Germans came to think of themselves as the true victims "of a war that Hitler had started but everyone lost."[48] When Hannah Arendt visited western Germany in this period, late 1949, one thing that struck her particularly was what she called Germans' "pervasive self-pity." When she revealed to fellow Germans during that visit that she herself was a Jew who had been forced into exile to save her life, they responded again and again by talking about "poor Germany."[49] The vast criminality of the Third Reich, which required millions to take part and millions more to turn away—all of this was now ascribed to a few "fanatics," namely Hitler and the SS, who had supposedly seduced the nation and led it fatally astray. Collective memory of victimization was of a piece with the sharp rejection of denazification and the movement toward a slate-clearing amnesty for Nazi-era crimes. All were born of the desire to "cover the past with forgetting," or at least to preserve only a highly restricted form of remembrance.

Emphasizing German losses was, above all, a means of evading charges of collective guilt. After the war, the historian Atina Grossmann writes, Jews in Germany—whether German Jews who had returned to the country, members of the various occupying forces, or those en route to permanent new homes in Israel, the United States, Canada, or elsewhere—sensed an "inchoate shame" among Germans "that led to a deep resentment." The nature of this shame was not exactly what we might expect from our vantage point today. Jews, Grossmann writes, "were a constant affront" to Germans, a "reminder of German crimes and losses." In other words, they were a deeply unwelcome reminder of defeat.[50] We might note, too, that Fischer spoke of *mass fate*: something that had *befallen* everyone. The language neatly obfuscates: the term "collective guilt" would have implied agency; mass fate permits none.

At the same time, in this era of curious elisions and roaring silences, it's interesting how much West Germans wanted to *talk* to Bruno Gröning. "They all long for discussion," Dr. Fischer wrote in *Revue*.[51] Expressing such a desire was unusual for this time and place. A culture of fierce stoicism had developed in the Third Reich. For the Nazis, existence itself was a life-or-death contest that only some people had a moral right to win. Honor dictated that suffering be borne in silence. The Nazis prized discipline and emotional restraint in the face of pain, praising the unsentimental acceptance of death and loss as a specific virtue: "noble resignation" (*stolzer Trauer*). Party leaders even occasionally chastised the public for sadness, which appeared to them to be a particularly malignant and "unheroic" feeling.[52] Prominent doctors argued that suffering and ill people should not be coddled, but learn to tolerate pain with equanimity.[53]

During the war, the remedy prescribed for terrible experiences was not talk, but hard and uncomplaining work.[54] Hard work, that is, and silence. A psychological study conducted in 1944 with people who related their symptoms of illness to experiences in the wartime air raids cautioned that talking about feelings could lead to depression.[55] A culture of silence, in other words, was not only a generalized social imperative born of taboos surrounding Nazism and the war, it was an authoritative medical recommendation.

And yet, people wanted Gröning to hear their troubles. The authors of the thousands of letters addressed to him had chosen not to dwell in silence as directed, but instead revealed to him their feelings of shame, sadness, guilt, pain, and inadequacy—feelings otherwise kept under tight wraps. As much as Fischer sought to expose a stratum of morally complex and unresolved human suffering in postwar Germany, the *Revue* series was itself a cri de coeur. Whatever else Gröning did with mysterious energy and tinfoil balls, to many thousands who appealed to him for help, he seemed willing to listen. He inspired trust.

Maybe best of all: he wasn't a doctor.

5

MESSIAH IN MUNICH

The first installment of Helmut Laux and Heinz Bongartz's series for *Revue*—with its jaw-dropping stories of sudden cures and chairs laden with magical energies—hit newsstands in early August 1949. Gröning had been out of the public eye for weeks. Now he suddenly resurfaced: "Since lunchtime the day before yesterday," the *Süddeutsche Zeitung* announced, "the Herford 'Miracle Doctor' has been in Munich."[1] Some weeks beforehand, a Hamburg newspaper had reported that Gröning had been invited to Bavaria by a "circle of interested Munich scientists," who wanted to offer him a country house where he would practice his treatments, pending "support from state and church sources."[2] Whatever the truth of that story, the healer was indeed now in the Bavarian capital as a guest in a private home, "with a small staff, including two doctors." He had come, it was said, to try to restore the sight of a blind woman, and had "reportedly . . . already healed" another, "older woman, who had suffered for years from full paralysis in both legs." For the time being at least, Gröning did not wish his whereabouts known.[3] Nonetheless, as local press began to print key details from the *Revue* series about spontaneous healing, officials girded themselves, given what had happened in Herford, and prepared for a flood of supplicants.[4] State interior ministry officials warned the government of Upper Bavaria that Gröning had no license to treat the sick, and that practicing without one—because of the ban on unregistered lay healers—remained illegal.[5]

The *Revue* series highlighted specific forms of illness that seemed to afflict so many people in postwar Germany—chronic maladies and forms of distress doctors deemed incurable. Nowhere would this idea find such resonance as in Munich and nearby Rosenheim in the summer and fall of 1949. The magazine had presented Bruno Gröning as a soulful antidote to the sterility and detachment of modern medicine. He listened to human troubles; he could cure problems no one else seemed able to touch, heal wounds no one else could see. The crowds that greeted the healer in Bavaria positively dwarfed those witnessed in Herford. An unseen world of pain and illness, previously confined to the privacy of home and family, was increasingly revealed. Even Gröning was surprised. "Every house in Germany is a hospital!" he told reporters.[6]

Witnesses to the scenes the healer provoked in Bavaria often saw them not through the lens of science, as had been true in Heidelberg, but religion. They called them biblical, and claimed they heralded a mass spiritual renewal. And as we'll see, there was good reason to interpret what was happening that way. Religious emotion seemed to overflow in the scenes around Gröning during this period. That is striking for many reasons, not least because historians have noted only a modest and short-lived "return to the churches" in postwar Germany (both in Catholic regions like Bavaria and in Protestant ones).[7] The spiritual thirst on display in Munich and Rosenheim—expressed not at Sunday mass but in a muddy field full of thousands of fellow sufferers—may not have been conventional, but it was undeniable. Ultimately, this religious sentiment would again, as in Herford, take on the character of a popular, if inchoate, revolt "for" democracy and "against" Nazi medicine.

As the story of Bruno Gröning and the Federal Republic continued to develop, and the crowds continued to swell, the nature of the
Gröning story changed. By the time he reached Munich in August
1949, the Wunderdoktor had developed an expanding and colorful
circle of followers and associates. This shifting retinue would eventually include publishers, photographers, lawyers, even a trailing sculptor working on a bust of Gröning, as well as Helmut and Anneliese
Hülsmann from Herford and a pair of documentary filmmakers
named Rolf and Erika Engler.[8]

There was also one Egon Arthur Schmidt, who had formerly toiled
in the radio division of the Third Reich's propaganda ministry and
became Gröning's first manager.[9] He dealt with the press, scheduled
appearances, and handled correspondence. Schmidt also published, in
1949, a book about the events in Herford, *The Miracle Healings of
Bruno Gröning*. In it, he made the now-familiar argument that a medicine that failed to account for the life of the soul was a failed medicine. "Belief," he wrote, "is a miracle's most beloved child."[10] Beliefs
were something the former propaganda ministry employee was no
doubt familiar with. Notably, his NSDAP membership file includes
an X-ray, which reveals that he had severe arthritis of the hip joint,
making it difficult for him to walk.[11] Maybe this trouble was what
initially drew him to Herford, where he first met Gröning. Or maybe,
like some ex-Nazis, he simply had a hard time (for a while at least)
landing a job.

What began in a middle-class living room in Herford had by
this point expanded outward to touch thousands of cure-seekers
in many parts of the country—first Hamburg, then Heidelberg, and
now Bavaria. With the assistance of an ever-eager press, Gröning had
become a nationwide phenomenon. As his entourage changed and his
celebrity grew, the figure he struck in public shifted, too. If what precisely Gröning was healing at the time was unclear, it is no more
obvious to us now, observing him from the distance of many decades.

· · ·

When Gröning arrived in Munich, the signs of defeat were still everywhere. A total of 66 air raids between June 1940 and April 1945 had completely destroyed some 13,000 of the city's 60,098 buildings. Another 8,000 were heavily damaged. In central parts of town, like the area around the main train station, up to 74 percent of structures had been demolished.[12] Within a short time, much of the rubble had been neatly organized at the foot of ruined buildings and the streets swept clean. But four years after the war, as the photo on the next page shows, signs the American occupiers had posted on buildings still warned with macabre irony about the permanence of death.

Munich was electrified by Gröning's sudden arrival. Newspaper editorial offices found themselves besieged by people looking for him or seeking information about him—their phones rang off the hook.[13]

STADTARCHIV MÜNCHEN

DEATH IS SO PERMANENT
DRIVE CAREFULLY

STADTARCHIV MÜNCHEN

Doctors' practices were overrun with patients asking how they might get a chance to see him.[14] On one occasion, police had to be called to the home of a deaf couple named Metzger, where some six hundred to eight hundred people had collected just because of rumors that Gröning planned to appear there.[15]

This response outstripped anything seen in Herford by a wide margin. Granted, Munich was a much larger city. Even with its population sharply reduced by the effects of the war, it still had fifteen times Herford's inhabitants. The cities were different in other ways, too. While Herford was heavily Protestant, Munich was overwhelmingly Catholic. And though Munich voters had been relatively reluctant Nazi voters—more reluctant than the citizens of Herford—their city was nevertheless the birthplace of the NSDAP, a fact the party commemorated by christening it the *Hauptstadt der Bewegung*, the "capital of the [Nazi] movement." It had been in Munich that the Austrian Adolf Hitler enlisted in the Bavarian army to fight in World War I. It was there that he lived after the war, working in military intelligence to ferret out political subversives. The 1923 coup he helped launch in the city—the Beer Hall Putsch—brought him to national attention for the first time.

But Munich had worn other hats. During the 1918–19 German revolution, it served at the front lines of socialist insurgency, and as capital of the short-lived Bavarian Soviet Republic. As "Athens on the Isar," the city had embodied a certain ease and broad-mindedness, and historically played host to a large and variegated community of artists, writers, performers, and scholars, not to mention esotericists and fabulists and avant-gardists of various stripes. Before World War I, these included the Cosmic Circle, a group that combined spiritualism, sexual liberation, paganism, and poetry readings, and, after the Great War, the ultra-rightist, occultist Thule Society—named for an Atlantis-like lost Nordic city. (Many Thule Society members would become major players in the Nazi Party.)[16] In the Weimar years, Munich emerged as a center for paranormal research.[17] The diarist Victor Klemperer might have summed things up best when he observed, reporting on the 1918 revolution, that in Munich, art, politics, and performance were hard to separate.[18]

It's fitting for all these reasons that Gröning's Bavarian idyll began in Munich, though the crowds surrounding him would reach their greatest dimensions in nearby Rosenheim, at a former horse farm repurposed as a country resort and casino called the Trotter Farm (Traberhof). It was an unlikely venue for scenes of mass spiritual revival. Situated on a generous expanse of meadow in the alpine foothills some forty miles southeast of the Bavarian capital, with racetracks and clear views all around, the Trotter Farm was a pleasant place to enjoy coffee and cake, play tennis, dance, take a stroll, or have a drink. According to at least one journalist, when full of "elegant ladies and gentlemen," the resort's restaurant "smelled like money."[19]

The Trotter Farm's central building, a two-story, whitewashed structure painted with kitschy horse shoes and racing carriages, had a second-floor balcony. A gravel parking lot formed the structure's apron in front.

The resort's owner, businessman Leo Hawart, reportedly had a relative suffering from paralysis whom he hoped Gröning could help, which is why he had extended an invitation to the healer. But as a "money-maker with great instincts," he may have had more than one motivation.[20] Within a week of the first press reports announcing Gröning's arrival in Munich, hundreds of cure-seekers were massing on Hawart's property.

Officials took notice. When an officer of the county police, Detective Käsberger, went out on a Saturday evening to have a look, he found a crowd of around five hundred people gathered in the Trotter Farm parking lot, waiting. The central building's balcony offered an elevated place from which to gaze out over the grounds (and the crowds) below. Around 8:15, Gröning briefly materialized there, Käsberger noted; he stood for just a minute or so without saying anything and then disappeared back inside. Leo Hawart came out for a moment with a message: that Gröning would be back, but he needed time to concentrate. In the meantime, a third man appeared with some directions for the people waiting: they should make a little space between themselves. This was a common instruction Gröning would issue; by making some space, supplicants would not "short-circuit" the flow of healing energy and thus the possibility of a cure. Around 8:30, Gröning reemerged, now with a statement of his own. He "had not asked anyone to come," he said, "on the contrary." It seemed to Käsberger that maybe Gröning was a bit overwhelmed by the crowds. Gröning said that "people should wait until he had permission." He "wanted to help everyone," the detective scribbled, "but he wanted things to be orderly, and not so mixed up." Gröning also said that he could "only help those who believed in him, and who had a firm belief

STADTARCHIV ROSENHEIM

in the Lord God, who had given him, Gröning, the power to heal." Gröning said he "was only doing his duty and his job like they all did their jobs." "All the sick people who came to him could leave their money at home; he did not need it. They had to bring their illness and their time. Those he would take from them."[21]

Detective Käsberger wasn't the only observer in Rosenheim that Saturday; a journalist and editor named Alfred Heueck was present too. Heueck had been on a bike tour in the Alps when he heard that Gröning was in the region. His reporter's instincts piqued, he decided to make a detour to see what was going on. Armed with a "determined sense of skepticism," he pedaled onto the property just before lunchtime and began mingling with the crowds. For five hours he listened as cure-seekers talked about their many ailments—both "visible and hidden."[22]

Detective Käsberger's report had a "just the facts, ma'am" tone, dry and relatively dispassionate. Heueck, by contrast, described a rousing scene, a "spiritual revolt." Gröning's effect on the crowds was palpable and extraordinary, he wrote: as soon as he appeared, a "deadly stillness" enveloped the assembly. According to Heueck, it was like "being at the movies when the film suddenly jams." Faces in the crowd "furrowed with worry and suffering" were "magnetized" by "this unimposing little man" wearing wrinkled, threadbare trousers and a dark-blue shirt buttoned all the way up. At one point, "Gröning paused for a long time, motionless," Heueck narrated, with his "piercing blue eyes . . . fixed somewhere in the distance, rather than on the masses below. His ascetic face was exceedingly tense." When Gröning did begin to speak, he did so very quietly, and seemingly without moving a muscle. His hands were still. He did not gesture. For Heueck, Gröning appeared to be a man of "innocence and genuineness," who "must be truly pious."[23]

At one point, both witnesses recalled, Gröning asked the crowd who among them was in pain. According to Heueck, "At least 200 people demonstratively raised their hands." After a few minutes, he asked again.[24] He told those still in pain to put their hand on the place that hurt and close their eyes. After ten seconds, he told them they could open their eyes, and asked what they felt. The answers varied, but all said that they felt a strange prickling sensation.[25] Gröning then withdrew to a corner of the balcony where there was some shade, to smoke a cigarette. He was "clearly exhausted," Heueck noted.[26]

Detective Käsberger went back to the Trotter Farm a week later, this time with a colleague in tow. By then, the crowds had multiplied to several thousands. They "greeted Gröning jubilantly."

Addressing the crowd, one of the healer's associates rejected glorifying the healer, but at the same time, in Käsberger's view, "skillfully promoted" him as a "miracle doctor and cure bringer for the poor and the sick." While he mingled, Käsberger talked to people in the audience. A woman he called Frau L., seventy years old, told him and his colleague that she "had been paralyzed in both feet since April and could no longer walk." But now, as Käsberger watched, she was able to walk "sometimes alone, sometimes lightly guided" some thirty to fifty meters. The parents of a nine-year-old child who "had never been able to move his head freely" and had been "paralyzed since birth" said that he suddenly "could move his head." Though he was still not able to stand or walk, his father could bend and move the child's legs (the detective reasoned that the child "naturally had no strength in his legs"). People told Käsberger "that they now felt quite different from before." It was the detective's view that "we are dealing with inner illnesses here."[27]

. . .

Bruno Gröning cured people. There are endless attestations to this fact in the archives, the contemporary press, and other sources. The question though, is what was he curing them *of*? If he was a savior, what kind of redemption did he offer?

In 1951, as we'll see in some detail later on, Gröning would be hauled into court to answer for violating the lay healer ban. On that occasion, the court recruited psychiatrist Alexander Mitscherlich—who had

STADTARCHIV MÜNCHEN

once been a student of none other than Viktor von Weizsäcker—to give his expert opinion on the case. Though a generally conservative figure in the 1950s, the anti-Nazi Mitscherlich had not been afraid to let his social conscience speak after the war. The damning report he and colleague Fred Mielke wrote on the Nuremberg Doctors Trial— translated into English as *Doctors of Infamy*—offered undiluted evidence of medical crimes under Nazism. The book was loathed by his fellow physicians and almost cost him his career.[28]

What Mitscherlich argued to the court in 1951 seems fitting for a psychoanalyst: he described Gröning as the projection and product of other people's wishes and needs. It was the crowds around Gröning, Mitscherlich argued, that *made* him. They elevated him to an emissary of the divine.[29] Their enthusiasm and hopes and dreams, and their powerful desire for a cure, had willed a savior into being.

Mitscherlich offered an astringent assessment of Gröning's personality. The Wunderdoktor had no capacity for self-criticism, the psychiatrist said. He lacked self-control, was incapable of honesty, lived in a magical world. He was "to a considerable degree" "pathological in the sense of a neurotic disruption of his personality development." His healing mission was merely a "symptom" of this "problematic nature."[30] The Gröning Mitscherlich described was inconstant: easily led, capricious, moody. The healer had no fundamental core, and while he was no charlatan, he was also no miracle worker.

Mitscherlich was especially troubled by Gröning's supplicants' inability, as he put it, to think for themselves, to be self-critical, to be honest—though he declined to say exactly what they were supposed to be critical and honest about. The relationship between the healer and his followers was a dangerous two-way street, Mitscherlich held: the masses needed Gröning as a haven in a world in which they could find no other succor. He in turn needed them to bolster his deranged craving for attention.[31]

For all his frankness, though, even Mitscherlich—an outspoken critic of the Nazis after the war—was tentative about making overt

connections between that past and the present Gröning phenomenon. His report for the court was abstract and replete with indirect language. This kind of distancing was common among intellectuals after the war and took various forms. Rather than speaking directly to recent events and their implications for the course of German history, for example, historians would insist that German history had always been rooted in what they perceived as universal and timeless values—like "civilization" or Christianity or "the West."[32] In this way, they skirted specific questions about what had gone wrong in Germany to produce National Socialism.

Mitscherlich's evaluation of Gröning fit this pattern of elision and displacement, but in this case, couched in the language of psychoanalysis. For example, the psychiatrist described the healer's "psychic-labile, security-seeking" (*haltsuchende*) personality as a sort that would be familiar to those who "know the history . . . of the founding of sects and political parties." Yet Mitscherlich failed to name even one of those sects or parties. Of course, he didn't have to be specific: anyone reading his report knew what he meant. He continued in this vein, writing that those familiar with such history would have noted the "pathological sense of mission among some individuals"—by which he seems to have meant the founders in question—"and the equally pathological search among others" (their followers) "for some form of refuge." The combination of mission-driven leaders and deeply needy followers constituted for Mitscherlich a "psychopathic phenomenon," one that, while "potentially resurgent in any moment," was "especially threatening" in the present.[33]

Though the psychiatrist declined to put too sharp a point on it, the former Nazi and Wunderdoktor gave Mitscherlich a way of talking about Hitler without actually mentioning his name. In Mitscherlich's estimation, Gröning and his supplicants were separated by only a hairsbreadth from Nazism. What made them "especially threatening," the psychiatrist was convinced, was their need for stability, for some kind of "refuge." That's what Gröning's cure-seekers were missing, and that's what he gave them, Mitscherlich argued—someone to trust, a place, if one will, to call home. They, in turn, gave him their desire.

Alfred Dieck, the collector and analyst of apocalyptic rumors mentioned earlier, claimed that the occupation had failed because it had been unable to offer a credible replacement for Hitler—a substitute for the Führer, in whom Germans had reposed such tremendous faith, even love. It's interesting, too, that Mitscherlich and his wife, fellow psychoanalyst Margarete Nielsen Mitscherlich, would later write an enormously successful diagnosis of West German society, *The Inability to Mourn*. In the book, the pair would argue that Germans had identified so thoroughly and positively with Hitler that, after the war and defeat, they had to break "all affective bridges" to him and to the past he represented to remain psychically intact. This, the Mitscherlichs said, had stunted Germans' ability to confront the crimes of the Third Reich, to experience shame or guilt, and to come to grips with their own complicity in what had happened. Instead, they fled into a kind of perennial busyness: constant work, constant rebuilding, constant improvement and tinkering.[34]

In 1949, Mitscherlich's analysis of Gröning and the trip to court that occasioned it still lay in the future. But the elements of that analysis were already on display that summer at the Trotter Farm. Rolf and Erika Engler's film crew had begun shooting footage for their documentary about Gröning.[35] Now, when the Wunderdoktor came out to speak to the crowds, klieg lights illuminated him in the night. The scene must have felt reminiscent of earlier times, when another wild-eyed charismatic mounted a stage in the darkness and fed crowds words like manna. Rosenheim in 1949 was hardly Nuremberg in 1934, but as Gröning stood on that balcony—gazing out over the masses in his own kind of uniform—he may have telegraphed, at least for some, a specific and undeniable memory: that of Hitler addressing the Volk.

That memory, those aesthetic elements: they charged the air with emotional fervor, at least, for those inclined to be so enchanted. This is not to discount the religious significance so many attached to Gröning's presence and ability to cure the sick. There is no reason in fact to separate those two things at all. For some of the people standing in that field in Rosenheim on an Alpine summer's night, seeing Gröning must have been a little like seeing a friendly ghost. That encounter had enormous, even curative, power.

. . .

Reporters described many people getting suddenly healed at the Trotter Farm, especially of paralysis, and trouble with their ears or eyes. Maria Würstel told the journalist Heueck how she had suffered since 1938 from near-paralysis of the spine. The slightest movements caused her terrible pain. Her doctor had recommended she see Gröning. Heueck saw her run like a child, "partly laughing, partly crying from happiness." Another woman—she'd had polio and had used a wheelchair since the age of three—got up and walked too. A man who said he had suffered brain damage in the war rejoiced, "The buzzing in my ears is gone, my head is free again!"[36]

Amidst these scenes were accounts of "hawkers of Gröning photos, sausages, cigarettes, cake, and tin foil balls" plying their trade.[37] Siegfried Sommer, a Munich journalist (and later, novelist) known for his depictions of local color, saw "limousines, taxis, a Red Cross van, countless vehicles . . . some carts, some wheelchairs" standing in the Trotter Farm's parking lot, which had been "freshly strewn with gravel." He saw crutches leaning up against chestnut trees, kids hollering, and beer barrels stationed under tables to keep cool. Sometimes, Sommer wrote, people brought photos of their sick relatives—perhaps those too ill to travel—and held them up before the resort's windows in the hopes of receiving Gröning's energies.[38]

As news of these gatherings and cures multiplied, the crowds grew larger. It worried police. "These people cannot understand why anyone would hinder him practicing," one reported, and said he feared a riot if anyone tried.[39]

In truth, banning Gröning's healing work, as Herford officials had done, was not much discussed in local papers. Rather, something like the opposite was generally true. A number of local politicians and officials spoke up for him publicly. Munich's police commissioner, Social Democrat Franz Xaver Pitzer, thanked Gröning personally in front of the Trotter Farm crowds for helping him over an illness.[40] A state parliamentary representative, Hans Hagn of Bavaria's conservative party, the Christian Social Union, exhorted the crowds to "believe in the healing power of Gröning and to trust him." Even the highest officeholder in the Bavarian government, Minister President Hans Ehard, openly expressed support for Gröning. The healer should not be subject to a lot of "red tape" (*Paragraphenschwierigkeiten*), Ehard said.[41]

Members of the press were as smitten as politicians. One local paper described the public's trust in Gröning—"a simple, uneducated man . . . the son of a Danzig bricklayer"—as "limitless."[42] The very air in Rosenheim, correspondent Hans Bentzinger rhapsodized, was "filled with a special excitement" that "grows from hour to hour, as it becomes known that Herr Gröning will speak to the waiting crowds."

Bentzinger described an "unbearable" tension, the atmosphere "so laden with the energy of expectation that one can hear his own heart beating and that of his neighbor at the same time."[43] Journalist Viktoria Rehn was transported, writing of how she was "reminded, instinctively, of the great events of the New Testament and Rembrandt's Sermon on the Mount picture." "Everyone and everything in Germany," she wrote, "is waiting for some kind of miracle."[44] Another journalist, Kurt Trampler, had been amongst the Trotter Farm crowds almost from the first. In early September, he published an account of his own healing. He had walked with a cane since being injured during a bombing raid. At a meeting where he was to interview Gröning, Trampler said the healer "turned to me and asked me to tell what I sensed." Trampler told him that he was a reporter, not a patient. Gröning responded that he would no longer need his cane. After that, Trampler said, he walked without one.[45]

Within two weeks of Gröning's arrival in Bavaria, some twelve to eighteen thousand people were massing at the resort on any given day.[46] The atmosphere became even more overtly religious. People began spontaneously to sing hymns, like "Great God We Praise You," and prayed out loud.[47] Some had ecstatic experiences.[48] Newsreels captured the enthusiasm for national audiences. In one, women can be seen prostrating themselves on the ground, while men carry children on stretchers and others implore heaven.[49] Trampler described members of the crowds shouting, "Thy kingdom come!"[50] The scene, he said, was "of such shattering poignancy, that no one who saw it would ever forget."[51] "Here and there, someone throws his crutches [away] . . . or a mother calls out: 'my child is cured!'"[52]

Mail for Gröning began to mount up in Rosenheim as it had in Herford. It came not just from all over West and East Germany but also from Austria, The Hague, even locales as far away as Croton-on-Hudson in New York.[53] Newspapers began hinting that Gröning might leave Germany if he were not given express permission to carry on with his work. The *New York Times* reported that James A. Clark, chief of the US military government's political affairs division, who suffered from gastritis, had met with Gröning. "I can't say that I felt better immediately but on the next day I was able to eat heartily for the first time in weeks and soon I will be well again," Clark said.[54] Gröning now had to take detours to elude the crowds and journalists, "jumping over garden railings and slipping through the stables to get to his lodging."[55]

A fantastic, increasingly fervent spectacle was developing, generated by newspaper headlines and wild hopes, among crowds of expectant people transported by spiritual rapture and buoyed by the glamour of klieg lights and Gospel-like tales about the lame taking up their beds and walking. In Munich, crowds formed spontaneously, sometimes in the thousands, on any rumor that Gröning might appear. People desperate to see him stopped traffic, forced streetcars to be rerouted, and sometimes became unruly.[56]

Around noon one day in early September, three hundred people clustered in a park in Solln, in Munich's south, waiting for the healer. Word went out that he had been delayed at the Trotter Farm: "thousands of people had lain themselves in front of his car," police reported, and said "he should heal them or run them over." Murmurs went through the Solln crowd—"we won't let him leave until he cures us either." By eight o'clock, police reported, there were two thousand people waiting in Solln and more arriving. Two hours later, someone announced that "thousands of people" had held Gröning up near the city center.[57] Elsewhere in town the same day, yet another crowd awaited Gröning's arrival. At four o'clock a van with a loudspeaker drove by, announcing that he could not come. Though most people departed, a few lingered. The "greater part of the public," a police officer on the scene concluded, "is visibly and obviously in favor of Gröning's continued work and will not accept police restrictions without active resistance."[58] The following day, these scenes and sentiments repeated themselves. A crowd of eight hundred, having heard that Gröning would appear in the Ganghoferstraße, gathered there. When they were told that he would instead turn up in the Lindwurmstraße, they all decamped for an address that, it later turned out, did

not exist. Despite another round of announcements by police that there must have been some mistake, and that waiting was probably pointless, some two hundred people stayed put—a few until 1:30 a.m.[59]

As 1949 rolled on, stray rumors of a coming apocalypse continued to course through the country. To prevent the end of days, the Hannover *Presse* reported in September, a woman in the Palatinate had recently offered to sacrifice her child.[60] But Gröning inspired hopeful counterpredictions. A publisher in Munich reprinted an old popular prophecy that seemed to point to the larger meaning of his appearance: "The great preachers will arise and holy men will work wonders. The people will have their belief back and there will be a long, peaceful time."[61] Gröning became the sign confirming other signs: of redemption, renewed faith, and the possibility of miracles. A visiting Benedictine from Italy preached to the Trotter Farm crowds. "To me it seems that we are living at the end of time," he said, and referenced prophecies foretelling a period of great healing.[62] A headline quoted Gröning: "My Power Is Not a Human Power."[63] As the fourth installment of Laux and Bongartz's *Revue* series appeared in early September, two competing narratives about the source of Gröning's power—God or nature—continued to develop. Was he "the carrier of an electrical field or wave?" the journalists asked. The healer himself, they explained, was "certain in his conviction that he could absorb and act as a 'transformer' of the energies of human suffering" and "send out healing powers" in return. This, the *Revue* suggested, even influenced the size of Gröning's goiter, which absorbed his patients' "morbid energies."[64]

Gröning was now a portent registering the meaning and fate of the universe, and tracing out the cosmic horizon.[65] His powers appeared heroic, even limitless; they might defeat the greatest dangers of the age. The local Rosenheim *Alpenbote* compared the Trotter Farm with Lourdes and asked, "Can Gröning's powers secure world peace, stop tanks, and defeat atomic weapons?"[66]

Not everyone was so sure. Some mingling at the Trotter Farm had come merely out of curiosity and "spoke snidely about the Wunderdoktor." They were silenced with a "threatening gaze."[67] Few dared to break the spell with skepticism.

• • •

Other kinds of people found themselves pulled toward these astonishing scenes—not just journalists, not just those who beseeched Gröning to heal them, not just clerics who hoped he would lead the people back to God, but also some health officials and elected leaders. Many doctors (though certainly not all) were quite skeptical; several local political figures remained conflicted. On the one hand, newspapers reported, authorities intended to treat the healer's work as an act of "voluntary charity." As he was not acting in a professional capacity—say, by taking money to treat the sick—Gröning would not need a license.[68] Still, not all officials agreed, and the pressure exerted against them by the crowds, in Rosenheim and on the

Munich streets, began to gain more overtly political dimensions—
just as it had in Herford.

A representative to the Bavarian State Parliament requested, in
an emergency motion, the immediate abolition of the lay healer law
"to allow Gröning to work."[69] Meanwhile, among members of the
Munich city council, considerable acrimony prevailed in discussions
of what to do. A council member named Bößl declared that prevent-
ing Gröning from working on behalf of the people was the "height
of injustice."[70] When a colleague disagreed with him, Bößl suggested
that his opponent needed to visit Gröning himself: it was well known,
he said, that Gröning could help the mentally ill.[71] State Secretary in
the Interior Ministry Josef Schwalber reported to the Bavarian Council of Ministers that "a warning should be dispensed concerning the
health-hazardous circumstances in Rosenheim."[72] To the press the
following day, he declared himself ready to sit down with Gröning
to determine how he might be permitted to carry on, if his practice
were purely charitable and if he could stop people around him from
"taking advantage."[73] Hans Ehard, the Bavarian minister president,
told the press that the state "should not make difficulties for Bruno
Gröning." Exceptional people "should not be hindered by bureaucratic laws."[74]

On the streets, black marketeers traded tinfoil balls for outrageous
prices. Local entrepreneurs offered to provide "the exact address of
wonderworker Gröning" for fifty marks.[75] The healer was reportedly
the only topic of conversation on Munich's Number 22 streetcar one
day in September. If he were forced to leave Germany because of some
"bureaucratic misunderstanding," one man said, there would be a
"storm of outrage." He was "the most popular man in all of Bavaria,"
piped up a retiree. A young woman called him "a simple, humble
man of the people." Others found the matter laughable. "I'll believe
in Gröning after he liberates me from my chronic lack of cash," joked
one passenger. But at least a few saw something more forbidding at
hand, something reminiscent of another time when their fellow citizens had been lured by a character promising to fix all that ailed

them. As an older woman on the streetcar observed, the "Pied Piper only has to whistle and the children come running."[76]

Summer was coming to an end, and the weather began to turn. The Trotter Farm by now was said to resemble an "army camp."[77] Crowds had swelled to such proportions that the Red Cross had to provide tents to shelter the supplicants.[78] Local officials laid straw in the market halls in Rosenheim to provide emergency shelter for the sickest people.[79] Some had lung ailments and polio.[80] The head of the local health office warned of the possibility of an epidemic. Officials resolved to ask the American military police to provide security.[81]

At a meeting of the Bavarian parliament's Committee for Law and Constitutional Questions, Social-Democratic representative Josef Seifried urged immediate action: "against Gröning's will," "mass hysteria" was developing. Things could not be allowed to go on as they were. Seifried blamed a "swarm of people" around the healer for a difficult situation. Wolfgang Prechtl of the Christian Social Union noted in Gröning's defense how neglected natural healing had been by modern medicine. Seifried responded, shouting damningly, "doctors are mostly agents of IG-Farben!"[82] It was quite an indictment. The chemical giant had manufactured Zyklon-B, used in the gas chambers at Auschwitz. Its directors had been tried only one year earlier at Nuremberg for war crimes.

In the end, though, it was not police, parliamentarians, or city councilors who had enough, but Gröning himself. Around September 10, he announced that he no longer wished to appear under the "unregulated circumstances" of the Trotter Farm. He had a better plan in mind, he announced: to establish cure centers near Rosenheim, where he could treat the sick in regular appointments, under the supervision of doctors. From the Trotter Farm's balcony, Gröning asked the people to go home.[83]

The next day he met with authorities in Miesbach, a short drive from Rosenheim. A Dr. Beck, the district manager, had recently visited the resort and been moved by the religious fervor of the crowds. "For

KOMMUNALARCHIV HERFORD/STADTARCHIV HERFORD

me it was staggering to see thousands of people shouting 'Healing! Healing!' and singing 'Holy God, We Praise Thy Name.' The people are gripped by a deep religious feeling," Beck told the press.[84] He invited Gröning to set up a clinic in Miesbach. In the meantime, he appealed to the American military governor for field beds for the sickest among the cure-seekers.[85] Newspapers reported that "Gröning needed rest."[86] Despite his departure, thousands remained at the Trotter Farm, waiting for his return, in the wind and the rain. Some lay on the ground, ill and wrapped only in blankets.[87] Rosenheim's district manager declared a public emergency.[88]

    Tabloid headlines from that time offer a snapshot of the moment's burning issues: WORLD EVENTS 1950: RETURN OF THE RUSSIANS?, HITLER MURDERED HIS NIECE, GRÖNING'S MIRACLE CURES REVEALED, and the by now ubiquitous IS THE WORLD GOING TO END?[89]

. . .

At the end of September, an illustrated tabloid called *Quick*, like *Revue* published in Munich, printed an article titled "Gröning and the Crisis of Medicine." The masses of desperately sick people the healer had unwittingly brought to public attention symbolized a bleak present, according to *Quick*. They had been "broken spiritually, suffered appalling things, and saw no way out, could find no helping hand." This focus, of course, echoed similar themes in the *Revue* series, especially the comments of Dr. G. H. Fischer about the need for a more holistic medicine, one that treated both body and soul. The people who sought Gröning out certainly knew that "there are educated doctors," *Quick* explained, and "many had already consulted with them"—to no avail. The tabloid bitterly recalled the legacy of wartime doctors popularly referred to as *kriegsverwendungsfähige Maschinen*: physicians who robotically described every man put before them, regardless of his state of health, mental or physical, as "front worthy." Medicine was an "ossified science" that had become "artificial," offering "ever more pills" and operations. For *Quick*, medicine reduced "the sick to mere numbers" and practically denied "the possibility of *seelische* problems."[90] Gröning, by contrast, as Pastor Kunst and Dr. Fischer had observed earlier, spoke to those who sought his cures "very simply, person to person," as Viktoria Rehn put it.[91] People trusted him, and trusting him made them feel better.

Such praise aside, though, a certain drift can be discerned in the documentary record around the end of September 1949. Many in Munich and Rosenheim had been sympathetic to Gröning, from state and city government officials to members of the press to the passengers on the Number 22 streetcar. In a brief time, he had developed a considerable, if ambiguous, reputation—whether as a Wunderdoktor or a natural psychotherapist, a pious man of God or simply a symptom of hard times. But now a power struggle developing around him began to break out into the open. Damning revelations came to light, often flowing from the pens and being pounded out on the typewriters of those who had until then been counted among the healer's inner circle. The shift highlights the instability and unease then so

pronounced, and how treacherous it might have seemed to trust anyone, even a holy man speaking in the name of God.

As noted, Gröning had acquired a fluid and expanding entourage, one many perceived as a bit less than savory. A recent addition
was one Count Michael Soltikow, a journalist. For a time, Soltikow
claimed in the press to be Gröning's legal advisor and to have power
of attorney over his affairs.[92] A fractious figure, Soltikow had been
adopted as an adult by a childless pair of exiled Russian aristocrats
(hence the title). In the early 1930s, he spent time in jail for fraud.
Though he wrote antisemitic tracts during the Nazi era, he would
later claim to have done so under duress and to have been involved in
counterespionage from within the German intelligence service during
World War II.[93]

One could now add publishing to Soltikow's curriculum vitae. In
September, he put out a bombshell pamphlet concerning his erstwhile
legal advisee. Under a bright red masthead and the headline GRÖNING
UNMASKED, Egon Schmidt—Gröning's former manager and toiler in
the Reich propaganda ministry—offered up various sordid details
about the healer. According to Schmidt and Soltikow, Gröning was a
swindler, a con man, a drinker, a misuser of young women, a Hitler:
someone who believed his own press and thought he was a messiah.
Dieter Hülsmann, whose dramatic healing was the origin story of the
Gröning phenomenon, was nothing but a spoiled brat whom Gröning
had not cured but merely taken in hand. And Gröning was having an
affair with Dieter's mother.[94]

There was a degree of truth to many of these allegations. Multiple sources attest that Gröning had a sexual relationship with Dieter's
mother. And as we'll soon see in some detail, Gröning did like a drink,
and he could be given to self-aggrandizement. But other assertions—
like those about Dieter, for example, who was in fact a very ill boy—
were false, and Soltikow's real goal was character assassination. In
the wake of his pamphlet's publication, a flood of articles appeared
alleging financial malfeasance and dissension among the Gröning

circle, greed and general flimflammery, and featuring quotes from angry local officials. *Der Spiegel* reported that Trotter Farm owner Leo Hawart had reached the end of his rope with the Gröning crew: "I can't stand by anymore, watching . . . how Gröning brings new, complete strangers into his circle daily and houses them in my Trotter Farm."[95] Gröning responded to the scandal by initiating legal proceedings against Soltikow and Schmidt both.[96]

The general storyline that had emerged about Gröning now appeared even more complicated. Could Gröning be the man Soltikow and Schmidt described and still conduct divine energies? Would he still be able to restore trust, reach illnesses that medicine had misunderstood or neglected, cure what ailed people? What had begun as a story about a nine-year-old boy who could not get out of bed and then did had become another story about corruption just below the surface, corruption both general and specific.

Reports of iniquity did not stop people seeking Gröning's help, at least not entirely. Though he had left the Trotter Farm, the crowds waiting for him dispersed only slowly and reluctantly. In late September, Dr. Paul Tröger met a man who had been waiting there for five days. He was out of money and did not know whether to stay or go home. Hadn't Gröning promised to help? the man asked.[97] The same day, the editors of *Revue*, which had championed Gröning so vigorously only weeks before, now published an open letter in which they chastised the healer for irresponsibly awakening "hopes that can't be fulfilled."[98]

By October there was a distinctly retrospective quality to the stories people told about Gröning. In the brief spell between March and October 1949, it was as if a comet had shot into view and then disappeared, leaving only faint traces (and many questions) behind. Nothing had "raised as much public dust or unsettled so many minds," as he had, one journalist wrote. None of the most noteworthy events of the previous year—President Harry Truman's reelection, revelations that the diaries of Eva Braun, Hitler's consort, were fakes, Rita

Hayworth's wedding that May to Prince Aly Kahn in Cannes—had riveted the public as much as Gröning's story.[99]

Rolf and Erika Engler's Gröning documentary premiered in October, but not before the Bavarian Health Ministry, Bavarian State Medical Association, and the Lay Healers Association directed a joint telegram to the American High Commissioner, the American State Commissioner for Bavaria, the West German Federal Parliament, and the film censorship board denouncing it. The telegram was read aloud on Bavarian radio. The film, officials hoped to make clear, was a danger to public order and public health.[100] Gröning, it now seemed, had been nothing more than "an apparition" of postwar chaos, according to the *Upper Bavarian People's Paper.*[101]

Strange events continued to unfold around the Trotter Farm. A correspondent got a tip that police were questioning a group of Jehovah's Witnesses in connection with a plan to blow up the place and poison Gröning.[102] Rosenheim police announced, perhaps somewhat improbably, that they needed a Japanese translator, because so many Japanese were looking for the healer. Nonetheless, "one had the sense that the momentum . . . was gone," a local reporter remarked. "The searchlights were missing and so were the huge mobs of reporters."[103]

Official opinion had turned against the Wunderdoktor. In mid-November 1949, 120 cure-seekers petitioned the Bavarian parliament for permission to found cure centers where Gröning could treat the sick. Bavarian interior minister Willi Ankermüller responded to the request by stating that even if Gröning had offered some people relief, health officials had not confirmed any lasting cures. Most of the afflicted people who came to the Trotter Farm, he claimed, had returned home disappointed. On top of that, Ankermüller observed, waiting outside in all kinds of weather had probably hurt people's health, and a responsible state government could hardly overlook the fact that "an improvement in the health of some sick people was purchased at the cost of a considerable damage to the body of society as a whole." Ankermüller also noted that even after Gröning left the farm, other people standing in for him had treated the sick with some success. "This affirmed the supposition," he said, that the "whole affair had been a matter of mass psychosis, for which sensational press reports were more than a little to blame."[104]

But far outside Munich and Rosenheim, the legend lived on. In November, a woman from Hohenfichte, a village in the Ore Mountains in Saxony—in what was by then the German Democratic Republic—wrote to Rosenheim officials about her daughter, suffering the effects of polio. She had "heard the miracle stories from Bavaria," this mother wrote, "that the savior of the twentieth century was making the lame walk and the blind see in Rosenheim."[105] From Husum, a maritime city in the Federal Republic's far north, came these lines: "To Herr Gröning! We sick people of Husum plead from the bottom of our hearts that you will come, we wait with pain every day that you will free us from suffering. Many cannot walk and wait with great yearning. Please come and help the sick! We trust you!!! Please come soon! We are waiting every day!"[106]

Just before Christmas, a Nuremberg paper announced that a Gröning cure center would open in Upper Bavaria the next year. Patients would be treated there in regular appointments within the bounds of a "scientifically manageable healing method," on the basis of their particular illness and "spiritual readiness" and without respect to their financial situation.[107] Several papers ran this story. All returned to a theme: that Gröning was not to blame for the excesses of those around him. "After looking in the available files," a reporter wrote on Christmas Eve, "it is beyond doubt that Gröning knew nothing of certain things that happened around him, things of which public opinion has accused him."[108] Still, the redeemer of Herford and Rosenheim would not return to the Trotter Farm. "Where once thousands of cars parked on the fields here, where hundreds prayed, sang, suffered, and hoped, geese and turkeys walk now in the warm winter sun," reported the *Abendzeitung*.[109]

"Have you heard anything about what's become of Gröning?" a doctor from Ulm wrote to a colleague, Dr. Wüst—an assistant to Viktor von Weizsäcker who had been involved in the experiments conducted with Gröning in Heidelberg. "The myth melted away pretty fast, is anything left?" And with that, the Ulm colleague wished Wüst the best for the New Year.[110]

6

IF EVIL IS THE ILLNESS,
WHAT IS THE CURE?

When Renée Meckelburg and her husband, Otto, went in search of Bruno Gröning in spring 1949, Renée was suffering from myxedema, chronic constipation, and hearing trouble. Like thousands of other people, she hoped for a cure. Traveling in their older model Opel P4, she and Otto followed the healer first to Herford, then Rosenheim.[1] At the Trotter Farm they met members of his inner circle and were even on hand for the first screening of the Gröning documentary.[2] They did not, however, manage to meet the man himself until Ernst Heuner, Gröning's press officer and the former editor of a regional newspaper based in Rosenheim, allowed that the healer might be in the picturesque Black Forest town of Schwärzenbach. By that point, Heuner would later tell police, Otto "already had a solid plan in hand."[3] That plan was to launch what Otto seems sometimes to have conceived of as a veritable empire of hospitals and spas where Gröning would treat the sick under medical supervision.[4]

Such a venture naturally required capital. Otto did not have any. What he did have were "unofficial" invitations from hotels on the tiny East Frisian island of Wangerooge, in the North Sea, where he formerly dealt on the black market and still kept an apartment.[5] If Gröning liked what Otto had to say, maybe the trio would visit Wangerooge; Gröning could treat the sick there and raise money for the cure centers. And that, as Otto liked to say, would put things on an orderly footing.

The Meckelburgs and Gröning soon formed a partnership, whose finances eventually became the subject of a great deal of police interest. Detailed accounts—most given as witness statements by people who had been members of Gröning's ever-changing circle or occupied its fringes—sit today in the Bavarian State archives in Munich. Renée Meckelburg's own statement to police, dated June 1950, took the form of a seventy-two-page, single-spaced typescript she titled a "report of the facts." It reveals her to have been a prim and starchy personality.

She describes, to give only one example, how disturbed she was by the scene she observed in Schwärzenbach when she and Otto arrived there, sometime in October 1949. The Meckelburgs found themselves in an inn, waiting to see Gröning amidst hundreds of other cure-seekers, while a couple of American GIs and their dates took in the sights and danced to jazz records. The inn's proprietress, a "large woman," according to Renée, walked among the patients, cigarette in hand, big diamond cross dangling at her chest. After hearing all the miracle stories, Renée assumed that the Wunderdoktor himself would soon burst in like a wrathful Jesus to expel the moneylenders from the temple. "You don't know Bruno," someone reportedly told her. "He would join in"—an apparent reference to the music and dancing. "He loves good-looking women and goings on—here a woman, there a woman—and he forgets all about the sick folks waiting. Who knows where he is now." This news discomfited Renée, who found being forced to wait "degrading and cruel."[6] What's more, Nazis—and Otto and Renée were certainly Nazis—hated jazz.

The Gröning story had already begun to take on new dimensions in Rosenheim. The enormous crowds waiting in the dark to catch a glimpse of their savior in the spotlight already hinted at a direction not altogether obvious in the first weeks after Gröning turned up in Herford. The details that Count Soltikow revealed to the world, too, suggested that there might be more to the Wunderdoktor and his entourage than met the eye—something more, that is, than a man of the people dispensing soul medicine. But the introduction into the fold of Otto and Renée Meckelburg, a former SS man and his wife, represented something new. These individuals would run Gröning's affairs in a "businesslike" way, cultivating specific audiences for him in various locales and collecting the proceeds. In these more intimate settings, Gröning grew more voluble and developed a disproportionate sense of his mission.

Many of the witness statements used to reconstruct events in this chapter were made by people with angles—book manuscripts they hoped to publish, ideals they sought to defend, spouses they wanted to exculpate. The depositions do not always agree, but they do allow for a detailed account, especially when one can be compared against others or against newspaper accounts or other documents. Taken together, these sources reveal that alongside the spiritual and physical needs that Gröning helped bring to the surface also bloomed forms of corruption characteristic of early West German society. In the Third Reich, the historian Frank Bajohr writes, corruption had been endemic, an "essential characteristic of National Socialist rule. Patronage, nepotism, camaraderie, and systematic protection became the foundation" of Nazism's "political economy."[7] Grift, mutual back-scratching, and systems of procurement lingered on into the postwar era in ways large and small. For that reason among others, it seems inadvisable to take the people involved in this story strictly at their word.

· · ·

Otto Meckelburg was born near Danzig, Gröning's hometown. There is no evidence that the two ever met before 1949, but they were near contemporaries: Gröning was born in 1906, Meckelburg five years later. After Danzig became a Free City in 1920 under a League of Nations mandate, the Meckelburg family chose to leave. They migrated to Essen, in western Germany's industrial heartland. Otto joined the Hitler Youth in 1929 at the age of eighteen. Within months of the Nazi seizure of power, he had joined the SS.

Otto was a true believer. There are pictures of him in uniform in his file today in the Federal Archives in Berlin. He is probably around twenty-five. In some pictures we also see his fiancée, under her maiden name of Renée Brauns, because part of the file deals with their engagement. SS members' potential spouses—particularly important as their official reproductive partners—were stringently vetted, their family trees traced back to the eighteenth century. This genealogical work sometimes required a considerable effort to gather documents: in Renée Brauns's case, from as far away as Switzerland, where some of her family were from. These were minor inconveniences, however, compared to the questions one might be called upon to answer. Heinrich Himmler, head of the massive Nazi police state apparatus, personally granted (or denied) permission to SS members to marry. Before Otto could marry Renée or anyone else, Himmler declared, he would need to produce a full clarification of why there were people in his family tree with names like Recklenburger and Krackau. These names were "used," the documents in Meckelburg's file note, "by Jews." The dangerous insinuation here was that Meckelburg's family tree might include non-"Aryan" branches.

In photos, both Otto and Renée—who called each other "Bobby" and "Stupsy"—look young and proud and cheerful, though he also affects a posture of great seriousness and cocky authority in some of them, his black cap set raffishly to one side. The SS file includes a biographical statement from Renée, in which she indicates that she had trained as a nurse. In one photo, she holds a pair of white gloves in her hands and wears matching white shoes.

Both Meckelburg and Brauns had been Protestants, but in the genealogical questionnaire they filled out to have their wedding plans approved, they described themselves generically as *gottgläubig,* or "believers in God." The Nazis had invented this designation. Calling oneself a "believer in God" was a mechanism for uniting Christian Germans, who, as simple "believers," rather than Protestants or Catholics, would theoretically no longer be divided by confession. The future Meckelburgs also registered specifically on the forms that they would be married by civil authorities alone, and not in a church. At least one other member of their family—one of Otto's relations, named Walter—was also in the SS. Himmler must have been satisfied by whatever clarification Meckelburg made about the names in his family's past, because Renée and Otto indeed got married.

Being a member of the SS in a society like Nazi Germany was a matter of considerable significance. In the Soviet Union, another revolutionary society, people who rose into the elite were called "new people." They were people of the future, liberated from old norms, and distinct from the nobility of the old regime, who had attained their rank and privileges through birth or wealth. The SS were the new people of Nazi Germany. But their distinction was based less on class (as in the USSR) than on the perception that they had especially good blood. This was their entrée into the elite of the new world under construction.[8]

Early in the war, Otto Meckelburg served as an adjutant in the Death's Head regiment, which oversaw the administration of Germany's concentration camps. No "task was ever too much" for Meckelburg, his boss wrote in 1940; he was always "fresh and eager to work." Meckelburg participated in the Germans' early campaigns in Poland and the west, and later at the Eastern Front and in Yugoslavia. He was decorated a number of times during the war and moved up the ranks. In September 1942, he was made company commander in the notorious Prince Eugen Division, whose counterinsurgency operations involved numerous war crimes, many against civilians. Whatever the precise nature of his wartime deeds, Meckelburg would be repeatedly lauded by his superiors for "particularly successful leadership" and promoted. The officer urging his promotion to *Sturmbannführer* in 1943 described him as "open, direct, and straight-as-an-arrow," with an "impeccably SS attitude." He had, another assessor observed in 1944, an "instinct for the possibilities of a given situation."[9]

Otto was a new person, and it was a new world. It is not entirely clear whether he completed his career (in the Waffen-SS) at the rank of *Sturmbannführer*, as his file in the Federal Archives indicates, or the even higher *Obersturmbannführer*, as the contemporary press reported and as Meckelburg himself claimed to police.[10] If the latter, he held the same rank as his much more notorious compatriots: Rudolf Höss, commandant of Auschwitz, and Adolf Eichmann, who had organized the deportations to Auschwitz of many of Höss's victims.

In May 1945, the world changed again. Some of Otto Meckelburg's former compatriots, in despair over the loss of their ideals and their leader, or because they feared reprisal and did not want to know what was coming next, committed suicide. Under Allied denazification policy, every member of the SS fell prima facie into the category of Major Offender, and the SS itself was deemed a criminal organization. Some former new people spent time in internment camps. Others went underground. Barred (at least hypothetically, or for a period of time) from certain lines of work and certain professions, from unions, and even sometimes from having a driver's license, former SS men had to be resourceful, at least in the short term, to get by.[11] Many found their way into business, if they had the contacts.[12] You could say they had to have an instinct for the possibilities of a given situation.

Later, as police became increasingly interested in Otto Meckelburg, and particularly in the money his partnership with Bruno Gröning would generate, they interviewed people who knew him. Witnesses offered various stories. Two men said that both Renée and Otto had been interned after the war because they were experts on the V-2 rocket.[13] A salesman named Prawatke told police that he met Otto Meckelburg in 1948; Meckelburg told Prawatke that he was involved in the development of rockets, and that Hitler had promoted him "ahead of schedule as a special colonel because of his competencies."[14] There were also stories that Otto wound up in an American or perhaps British detention camp, where he spent two years before escaping in April 1947. Whatever the case may have been, at some point after the war, Otto began insisting that people call him not Meckelburg but Land.[15] He went to live with Renée's family in Celle, her picturesque hometown of timber-framed houses in Germany's northern heathland.[16] He had gone underground. In the parlance of the day, he became a *U-Boot* (that is, a submarine) or a *Braun-Schweiger* (a "silent brownshirt"). Living that life, a journalist wrote in 1949, required "a cold-bloodedness in fateful situations." One needed "a large measure of caution and the ability to make cool decisions," as well as "courage, perseverance, enterprise, and that essential flair—for staking it all on just one card."[17]

Ernst Heuner, Gröning's press secretary, who throughout this period seems to have been preparing a book on the healer under the title *That Was Bruno Gröning*, later told police that Otto had personally claimed to possess plans related to the V-2, which, improbably or not, he had been trying to sell to Adolf Galland, a former Luftwaffe general and fighter pilot working in the government of Juan Perón in Argentina.[18] In the meantime, Otto made a living from the black market. He traded in cacao, tea, and coffee, which he claimed had been placed at his disposal by "personnel related to the Berlin Airlift," high-ranking American officers with whom he professed to have a good relationship. He was able to obtain wagonloads of manure for use as fertilizer when, as was true of many other agricultural supplies (seeds, equipment, and the like), no one else could get any. The former SS officer even managed to get through denazification as a mere "fellow traveler," in category IV.[19]

Right around the time that Otto met Bruno Gröning, the government of Federal Chancellor Konrad Adenauer placed an amnesty for Nazi-era crimes on its agenda. "We have such perplexing times behind us," Chancellor Adenauer told his cabinet in September 1949, "that a general tabula rasa is advisable." Only a slate-clearing would allow the country to move forward, the chancellor felt.[20] Perhaps sensing an imminent change in the atmosphere, Otto abandoned his alias. Otto Land went back to being Otto Meckelburg.

Not everyone who went underground resurfaced in the same manner. Also living near Celle around the time Renée and Otto first heard about Gröning—or rather, in the forest nearby—was another Otto, a forester and later chicken farmer named Otto Heninger. At least, that's what he called himself. In a former life, he too had been a new person. His real name was Adolf Eichmann. Heninger sometimes cycled into Celle on Sundays. A group were known to gather at his place in the woods discreetly to enjoy a beer and talk nostalgically about the good old days.[21] Who knows, maybe Otto Meckelburg was one of them.

. . .

Gröning cured Renée Meckelburg even before she met him, she would say. As she and Otto waited uncomfortably, forced to listen to jazz at the inn in Schwärzenbach, the phone rang. Renée began shivering, shaking, and could not breathe. She became very warm, then cold. She began to cry. Then, she said, "something strange happened." Heuner, Gröning's press secretary, reached to hand her one of Gröning's tinfoil balls. She had already "been given two before, at the Trotter Farm," but they'd had no effect. This time was different: Renée "received a blow," she said, like "an electric shock." She screamed. But when Otto actually placed the foil ball in her hand, it suddenly restored her calm. It turned out that Gröning, who had been on the phone with Heuner, had sent a "healing wave"—allowing her to regain her equilibrium. She found this frightening. It was "so inexplicable, unfathomable."[22]

As a result of this experience, the Meckelburgs became even more keen to meet Gröning in person. They finally did so at a Bavarian spa called Alpenpark, in Bad Wiessee. In 1934, Bad Wiessee had been the site of the Night of the Long Knives, when Hitler had key members of the SA—the *Sturmabteilung*, paramilitary stormtroopers of the NSDAP—murdered. The Alpenpark of 1949 betrayed none of that grim history. Handsome and well-appointed, the spa had a staff Renée recalled as "nice and friendly" and well-trained. Nevertheless, she did feel some foreboding about the place, sensed something "uncanny" in the atmosphere.[23] In the breakfast room, hundreds of people were camped out, waiting for Gröning.[24] Renée met the owner, Frau B., an older lady, plump, and "a picture of piety." Grateful to the healer for successfully treating what Frau B. called "water in my legs," the spa owner had offered him a place to stay. As she related wondrous stories about his clairvoyance and other gifts, Renée began to think that Gröning must "be a saint." When she finally got her chance to meet him, she found his eyes were "good, pure," and she knew in that moment that she "would be healthy again." When the two shook hands, Renée recoiled again "as if shocked by a jolt of electricity." The following day, she felt reborn. Her head was light; she felt happy and cheerful and could hear clearly again. Her digestive trouble cleared up. She wanted to cry out with joy and gratitude to "this man, who satisfied my soul." Otto was impressed. "If he can do things like this," he told Renée, "then it is a crying shame if he does not make it available to humanity."[25]

Renée had sought Gröning out hoping for a cure; Otto wanted a new life, a chance to get back to the center of things. So when offered an audience with the healer around the end of October, he spread out a map of the island of Wangerooge on a table and made his pitch for Gröning to conduct some healings there.[26] Shortly after, Otto resigned from a promising job at a newly founded Hannover publishing house to work for Gröning full-time.[27]

A contract was drawn up and signed.[28] Otto would have power of attorney over Gröning's financial affairs and sole control over income related to the healer's treatments.[29] The Meckelburgs and Heuner formed an organization called the Assocation for Research and Promotion of the Gröning Healing Method. The group planned to publish a newsletter to inform members of important developments, and solicit loans and donations. The funds would finance cure centers where Gröning could work with patients and laboratories for studying his methods. Otto even had a location for the cure centers in mind: a Bavarian guesthouse called the Pension Landes, in Mittenwald, which had functioned as a children's home during the war and would later serve as a home for the elderly.[30] Creating the Association for Research amplified a rivalry amongst various Gröning followers. Earlier, in Herford, a group called the Circle of Friends and Patrons of the Works of Gröning had formed. It was not formally registered, but it did have a bank account.[31] Egon Arthur Schmidt and the Hülsmanns (in some unclear combination) had been in charge, but the three had since fallen out, bitterly.[32] According to press secretary Heuner, forming the Association for Research and Promotion of the Gröning Healing Method placed Otto Meckelburg "officially in the running" in the power play developing around Gröning.[33]

As smoothly and impressively as their initial meetings had gone, significant differences soon emerged between the Meckelburgs and Gröning. Renée was often struck by how quickly the atmosphere around the healer could change. She described a cure session where the room "smelled of sweat and sick people," and it seemed as though all the air "was used up." Then Gröning appeared. "The sick people became agitated" by his "magnetic" glance. But just moments later, Renée wrote, "everything had changed" again. The ailing people stopped being agitated. Gröning "stood in the middle of the room," and everyone became still and silent. "Some of the ill began to tremble," Renée wrote. "Calmly, hands in his pockets," the Wunderdoktor let his gaze travel from one patient to the next to the next. "You could have heard a pin drop," Renée recounted. "Everyone was under his spell, he seized all of us with his glance." Then, just as suddenly, "he tore himself away, made an abrupt gesture . . . and went straight toward one of the sick," as though "precisely this person had drawn him." Moments later Gröning changed again, and "chattered away, here and there, freely and easily."[34]

Just as striking to the Meckelburgs as Gröning's influence on people was his relationship to money. Until he met Otto, Gröning did not take money for his treatments, at least not directly.[35] Since the initial days in Herford, when the Hülsmann family had asked him to come and live with them, he had subsisted largely on invitations and gifts. He and his staff were guests everywhere they went.[36] Months after the healer left Rosenheim, nearby communities were still trying to get Leo

Hawart to pay off debts incurred while Gröning was his guest at the Trotter Farm.[37] But the money issue went deeper: Gröning simply— and, to Otto and Renée, inexplicably—related to it differently than they expected people to do. He not only refused to take money for his work, he did not even want to handle it, except perhaps to give it away. This may have had less to do with an ascetic streak than, simply put, with magic. Folk healers in Germany were known to refuse to take money, for fear it would compromise their abilities.[38]

If money was not handled, though, it certainly was spent: Gröning would run up bills in hotels and bars, and expected others to pay. As Renée observed, "he did not know the difference between fifty pfen- nigs and a thousand marks." Gröning reportedly once asked Otto to buy one of his female companions a car, "like a kid" asks for "a cap gun or . . . a model train for Christmas," as Renée put it. He got his teeth fixed, and was so happy with the result that he wanted to pay extra.[39] In Herford, cure-seekers had freely placed donations in a fruit bowl sitting on a table in the Hülsmanns' home. Sometimes, Gröning reportedly reached into this bowl to hand out fistfuls of cash to his neediest patients.[40]

Otto expected this to change.[41] Those seeking treatment would need to pay, or at least make a donation to the Association for Research. Donations would allow the organization's work to go forward: investments could be made, cure centers founded. But the Meckelburgs' desire to "bring order" to Gröning's affairs in this way had additional dimensions. Gröning was mercurial, by many accounts, and often blew in and out with the wind. He liked to take a drink; he caroused. One night, at an inn in Herford, a big party ensued, during which large quantities of Steinhäger gin were consumed. At one point, according to Renée, Gröning reached across the table and asked her husband to "call me Bruno." This struck Otto as embar- rassingly familiar. "Will you help me do my great work?" Gröning reportedly demanded. To which Otto Meckelburg replied: "If you go the way of order, yes. If not, I will break your neck, because you're not worth the trust thousands of people have in you." Blanching, Gröning retorted, "No human being can break my neck!" Savagely drunk, he soon passed out. After half an hour, he awoke, Renée recalled, and, seemingly sober, proposed to go to the Hülsmanns' house with a fresh bottle of Steinhäger.[42]

According to Renée, Gröning could be moody or "childlike."[43] He got in fights and was often late. He got drunk with police and then made them gifts of bottles of schnapps.[44] He handed out tinfoil balls in bars while cabaret stars sang him songs, like the chart hit "My Rosa Comes from Bohemia."[45] His personal habits were also a matter of concern. "I don't need much, I am so modest, I don't eat much, drink only my coffee," Gröning reportedly said. "The only thing I really need is a cigarette." He indeed ate erratically, Renée observed: nothing for two or three days except a great big glass of beaten eggs or cream. He bathed daily, but owned only one set of clothes, which he carefully washed and placed on the heater each night to dry. Renée tried to get Gröning out of such habits. She claimed that he began to shave and care better for his hair, and that she taught him—like a child, she said—"to eat properly," all the while demurely tutoring him about "the internal world" of women's "delicate feelings."[46]

Because women were a bit of a sore point. Gröning seems to have had a lot of relationships with them. Both Meckelburgs suggested in statements to police that Gröning was a womanizer, and they were not the only ones who made such claims. Press secretary Ernst Heuner went so far as to describe Gröning as "lacking in any ethical connection."[47] There was even an accusation of rape, lodged against Gröning by a young woman who had served as Dieter Hülsmann's nurse.[48] (As it happened, the woman later married Gröning's former manager, Egon Schmidt.) These allegations were said to lie behind Schmidt's decision to deliver what he knew about Gröning— including details of the affair between Gröning and Anneliese Hülsmann, Dieter's mother—to Count Soltikow.[49] It was Schmidt's exposé of the Wunderdoktor that made banner headlines just as Gröning's fame crested in Munich.

In time, Schmidt would actually resume his job as the healer's manager, apparently dropping whatever qualms he claimed to have about Gröning's treatment of his wife. Nonetheless, the Meckelburgs described a number of occasions on which they seemed to think that "getting women" for Gröning was important lest he "fall on" unsuspecting women "like an animal."[50] Meckelburg at one point claimed that only his "deft intervention" had hindered Gröning from behaving in an "indecent way" with women among the cure-seekers.[51] There were also those among Gröning's circle who vigorously denied any such unseemliness.[52]

Whatever the case may have been, the Meckelburgs' bourgeois self-righteousness can only be perceived as grotesque against the backdrop of their recent Nazi affiliations. As much as the differences between the couple and Gröning often seemed to center on class, Otto also perceived them—as a former SS officer might—as differences of race. In a statement to police in June 1950, he described Gröning as coming "from Gypsies in Frankfurt." Meckelburg regarded much of Gröning's entourage as "parasites."[53] He saw it as his job to get rid of them.

As the Meckelburgs began the task of organizing Gröning's tour of the Federal Republic's North Sea coast, they assumed new roles: as fee-collectors, couriers, contract negotiators, and figures of stern but yielding parental authority. The couple wanted to bring a middle-class respectability and business sense to Gröning's life and work. Renée's views swung from one extreme to another as she tried to describe her relationship with the temperamental healer. On one page of her typescript, she describes Gröning gently talking to the sick, handing out silver tin-foil balls, caressing the heads of children. On the next, she declares that she has given up on him. "Why was a person with such gifts afflicted with so many negative, and yes, squalid human weaknesses?" she plaintively asks.[54] For Renée, a healer of the spirit had to be selfless and morally pristine.

• • •

In that, Renée was not so different from many others. People had used strong words to talk about Gröning from the very start. He was an angel of the Lord and an agent of the Devil, a messiah and a bringer of calamity, God's emissary and a charlatan. Moral dualism was a noted characteristic of successful healers, but even those who spent the most time with him seem to have changed their minds about him regularly, suggesting that his was a particularly unpredictable, protean character. "He did not lie, not directly, it was simply his way," said Renée. "It was as though he was an actor living in a role." At other times, she saw him as "a child," whose "sensitive soul had to be protected very carefully."[55] Press secretary Heuner, too, wrote of a conflict in Gröning's soul.[56]

But what if, whatever Gröning's personal failings may have been, those around him simply misunderstood what he was healing, or how his healing worked? Over and over, as he rose to fame, he had raised the possibility that only "good people" could be cured. In his book about the Herford events, *The Miracle Healings of Bruno Gröning*, Egon Schmidt wrote that Gröning openly and publicly refused to treat people who he said were evil.[57] Later, at the Trotter Farm, Viktoria Rehn remarked how Gröning told "old and very simple truths. 'You must believe in God.'" But she also heard the healer voice other views. "Things only go well for good people . . . only they find their way to health and to the Almighty. I can't help bad people."[58] Gröning's diagnoses of the mass illness he saw in Herford and Rosenheim could sound broadly ecumenical and "religious" in a rather unspecific sense. "All people were worthy of being healed," he reportedly said once, "no matter their nation, race, or religion. . . . We are all children of God and have only one father and that is God."[59] Yet he also said that God had empowered him to heal only those who were good and deserved healing, and God would not allow those who were bad to be healed.[60] Ninety percent of people, he once claimed, were evil's "prisoners."[61]

In Rosenheim, a Frau H. visited Gröning hoping to be cured of infertility. As her pastor later wrote to the Lutheran state ecumenical council in Bavaria, she returned home in a state of "total spiritual and religious bewilderment," plagued by the most "anxiety-provoking visions and seized by the belief that she was possessed by the Devil." Frau H. had been a healthy woman, her pastor wrote, "but now gave the impression of someone ready for a psychiatric clinic."[62] A very different story was reported by the Munich *Mercury* in Herford in June 1949. A woman had come to ask Gröning for help with what she described as "huge stomach ulcers." "I was getting thinner and thinner and could no longer sleep from the pain," the woman explained to reporters. "The Devil is grinning out of your face," Gröning told her. "I cannot help you. Please go." Yet despite Gröning's rebuke, this woman found the effect of being under his uncanny gaze somehow liberating, as though having her own "evil" identified had freed her of it, like a visit to the confessional. "He looked at me, and it was as if the ulcers dropped away like stones falling to earth. Since then," she told a reporter, "I have had no pain any longer."[63]

How people responded to Gröning's medicine and to his judgments clearly could vary widely, and may have had as much to do with particular individuals' own perceptions and biographies and circumstances as anything else. For example, there was an occasion in Bad Wiessee when Renée Meckelburg heard about a woman who had gone blind after learning of her son's death in the war. Gröning told the woman, who was there with her husband, to dry her tears. When she did so, the woman found that she could see again. But Gröning also announced that her husband's beatings were what had made her blind, not her son's death. The husband, white as chalk, was forced to admit it.[64] Somehow, bringing the woman's abuse to light had helped her, had returned her sight.

But what did Gröning mean when he said that some people were evil, bad, unworthy of cure? Two things are worth noting. First, to secular ears, "spiritual healing" may have the ring of easy benevolence. In Christian tradition, though, it has had more complex theological and moral overtones. As one scholar puts it, illness and disability have been regarded as having "spiritual implications, either as punishments

from God or as manifestations of malevolent powers."[65] Intrinsic to
the logic of redemption is fallenness: you cannot be redeemed unless
you are corrupted. Christian healing is fundamentally concerned with
sin and the forgiveness of sin. God tests the good with suffering and
punishes the wicked with misfortune to bring them to atonement. To
be told that one was beyond cure, incapable of being healed, in other
words, could have dire spiritual implications, and some people interpreted Gröning's invocations of evil in precisely this manner. Dr. Karl
Weiler, president of the Bayerische Landesärztekammer, or Bavarian State Medical Association, took issue with the idea, denouncing
as "infamous" Gröning's claim to be a divine messenger, since that
implied that those who could not be cured had been marked by God.[66]
They were marked, that is, as damned, beyond salvation.

At the same time, in those crowds surrounding Gröning, if you
weren't evil, this might be interpreted as signifying that you were
spiritually "safe"—meaning that you could be not only cured but
also redeemed. In the postwar context, in the wake of defeat and
denazification, when many people felt the weight of guilt and judgment, Gröning might have represented a special kind of salvation.
Styling himself as sent by God, he expressed an authoritative voice
of divine consolation when he told people that they were capable of
being "healed." That had both physical and spiritual connotations,
and it is striking that the afflictions the Wunderdoktor appeared to
cure most often were precisely those described in the Gospels, especially in John, when Jesus of Nazareth commands a man to take up
his bed and walk. He says to the man, "Behold, thou art made whole:
sin no more, lest a worse thing come unto thee." To be cured was not
only to regain physical strength or mobility, but also to be purified
and released from the bonds of sin—with the admonition that one
should commit no further transgression.

Yet Gröning also meant something else, something more, when he
spoke of evil. "Evil people" was another word for witches, after all, as
in: those who infect tree roots, those in cahoots with the Devil, those
who plot in the shadows to undo others and bring them low. When the

Wunderdoktor demanded that evil people be removed from his presence, he was not just talking about sinners who could be redeemed and cured. He was talking about witches, incarnate evil. And he was issuing a warning: one had to be aware of the "evil people" lurking in one's midst, whoever they might be.

If evil is the illness, what is the cure?[67]

• • •

In January 1950, Otto Meckelburg—having by now traded in his old Opel P4 for a "faster, more dependable" Opel Olympia—announced that a small group of cure-seekers, perhaps thirty, would be invited to meet with Gröning at a hotel on Wangerooge.[68] Instead, every hotel and inn on the island filled up.[69] There were so many people coming in with the train, said eyewitness Wilfried Voigt, a pastor, that many had to be turned back. "Only those suffering paralysis, and crippled people, adults and children, and also the blind and those hard of hearing, were allowed to stay."[70] The sources do not say why this may have been the case, but since Gröning's efficacy in such cases was well known, it's likely that Otto wanted some success stories for the newspapers. He also made sure that only people who paid gained admission.[71]

On a Monday night around 9:30, Pastor Voigt took his seat in the seventh row of the movie theater of the Hotel Hanken, which doubled as a ballroom. It was full of island folk and visitors, quite a lot of them children.[72] The large stage was darkened, the curtains closed.[73] When Gröning finally parted them and walked through, it was almost four in the morning.[74] Though people had been waiting for hours, the "effect was enormous," according to Heuner. Experience had shown, he would later write, that creating an atmosphere of "maximum suspense and faith" would prepare cure-seekers "spiritually for the great event and focus their attention completely."[75]

"Good evening, ladies and gentlemen!" Gröning greeted the assembly. "Are you in pain?" Some people raised their hands. "Then you *had* pain," he said. After pausing briefly, he asked, "Who of you still has pain?" Fewer people raised their hands. "Don't tell me anything about your sickness!" Gröning insisted, "The greatest wealth that we have is health. Money is filth! Are you ready to give me your sickness?"

Turning once more to the theme of good and evil, Gröning became expansive. "I want to tell you why and for what reason I am doing all of this. Human beings in the last few years have gotten very, very bad," he said. "They have lost their belief in our Lord God. I want to give humanity back their true godly belief." He did not spell out what he meant by "the last few years," but for reasons that are now familiar, he's apt to have meant the period since defeat. It was in those years that people "lost their true godly belief," as Gröning put it, *then* that they strayed from the path of righteousness.

Now he continued, in a different, more conciliatory vein:

> I could do much more than I'm doing now. I could cast a spell on this little piece of earth, this island, so that whoever steps on to it, would be cured. Don't forget, you are children of God. God is the greatest doctor, not Gröning. . . . I am telling you now as before: love your enemies! Love your neighbor more than yourself. . . . Strife and stress, hate and envy must be buried once and for all.

To which enemies did Gröning refer? That was not made clear, but some among the crowd were plainly enthusiastic about what they had witnessed. "Isn't this just great?" a Dr. Siemens, whose patients were apparently in the ballroom, asked Pastor Voigt, with an ecstatic look on his face.[76] A newspaper reporter saw something quite different: "a phenomenon of the time, sick down to the roots."[77] Press secretary Heuner, meanwhile, felt he had witnessed a biblical tableau: "every person in the room who was lame, and then suddenly could walk, every blind person who sensed a shimmer of light, every child who stopped whimpering, became calm, and fell asleep, was seen by the other sick people as a revelation. An atmosphere developed that cannot be described."[78] Gröning walked over to Pastor Voigt and told him, with a shrug, "Yes, when the people don't want it, I can't help them." He then broke up the gathering by announcing, "The presentation is over. Whoever leaves their sickness behind will be healed." It was 5:40 a.m.[79]

Gröning went on from Wangerooge to make other regional appearances. In the East Frisian city of Oldenburg, about forty miles inland from the North Sea, he appeared in the Hotel Astoria on successive evenings in February.[80] As many as a thousand cure-seekers gathered waiting for one event, despite the rain. For a time, some very ill people lay on stretchers outside. Some were crying. A few became unconscious.[81]

Once inside, however, despite the hard chairs and stale air, not a sound could be heard, except the groans of the very ill and the fussing of little children. Gröning arrived at 2:30 a.m. wearing his uniform of black suit, shirt, and tie. His long, wavy hair had been oiled back, a doctor observing the gathering noted.[82] Trailed "half a step behind" by a young woman in a red dress, Gröning shut his eyes and rocked back and forth on his tiptoes, fingering a gold ring. Police nearby stood holding their hats. A flashbulb popped, though Gröning appeared not to notice. He walked straight to the stage in the front of the room and stood silently. All eyes were on him. "My dear cure-seekers!" he began speaking. "I see this picture everyday, everywhere, the same; everywhere sick people who look for help and healing." At one point he began to go among the crowd, speak to the sick, work with them, talk to them. "Those who are free of your suffering, rouse yourselves!" he said. A man laid his crutches to the side, uncertainly. His wife began to cry. A little girl bent her knees and moved her arms. "Please, no force. Do only what you believe you can do," said Gröning. Another man pulled himself up from his stretcher and began to walk, hesitantly.

When the session ended, it was 4 a.m. Some people could walk again, but according to one reporter, others experienced little more than the feeling of having donated their last money to little effect. Yet despite the hour, people outside still clamored to get in.[83]

On a single evening not long after, Meckelburg took in 34,000 DM in donations.[84] Amounts collected ranged from 300 DM to 1 DM or even 50 pfennigs. (Ten marks was about the price of a sports shirt, or a bottle of brandy.[85]) With this kind of money at stake, tax authorities began to get interested.[86] With a brief from a local prosecutor, the physician Julius Ahlhorn mixed among the crowd at a session on February 9. He found that Gröning struck a "ridiculous pose" on stage that reminded him "uncomfortably of Hitler" (one wonders whether the crowd's worshipful adoration made Ahlhorn equally uncomfortable). According to the doctor's observations, there was not "the least doubt that Gröning is a serious paranoid or a . . . psychopath with paranoid reactions." As "practical examples" supporting this diagnosis, he offered Gröning's claim never to sleep, and his assertion that he could take illness from one person and give it to another. In one especially grandiose moment, Gröning said that if he summoned the German people, there would be "the greatest revolution the world had ever seen." Ahlhorn observed with distaste the effects all this had on the assembly. He witnessed a young girl with a flower in her hand; with it, "she touched Gröning's pants leg and stroked her own forehead and chest."[87]

If such displays were not disturbing enough, Ahlhorn also heard Gröning say that he gauged "quite fast who is worth being healed and who isn't." Revising earlier comments about the spiritual state of 90 percent of humanity, he said, "I can heal 90 percent, 10 percent are trash—it's not my fault."[88] He had made a similar comment once in Herford, of those for whom his medicine had not worked: "they belong to the 10 percent of humanity that I call the marked ones. They don't believe in anything, and they can't be helped."[89]

At the end of his report, Dr. Ahlhorn drew his own conclusions. "All in all, one gets the strong impression that the whole Gröning operation is the ingenious swindle of a small criminal clique that has the mentally ill Gröning fully in its grip." He suggested the group would make of Gröning "what they will and use the panicked mood of our times to relieve desperate and simple people of their money."[90]

. . .

Gröning's tour of the Federal Republic's northwest ended around mid-February 1950. He and his retinue made their way to the Pension Landes, the inn in Mittenwald that was supposed to be the site of the first Gröning clinic. The inn's "glorious view" of nearby mountains was not enough to persuade Gröning to stay, Renée Meckelburg reported; he found the place dirty, its owner too loud.[91] Still, he conducted healing sessions there, for which Otto collected considerable sums—one hundred to three hundred marks apiece.[92] The pair meanwhile kept a watchful eye on their charge and accompanied him when he went out, not least because they feared he might be borne off by another potential manager.[93] Gröning slipped away nonetheless, acquired a quantity of pineapple punch, and was later discovered in a woman's room. A screaming fight ensued, after which Renée claimed Gröning begged for forgiveness and said he'd never touch another drop.[94]

More troubling for the group than these antics were the continual delays their plans faced. In January 1950, regional newspapers reported that a cure center with thirty-five beds would open on February 1. Local authorities contradicted this story, telling the press they'd received no official notice of these intentions.[95] Otto Meckelburg needed a concession from the Bavarian government to open a cure center, but that was not forthcoming.

As the wheels of bureaucracy slowly turned, Gröning continued his adventures. He traveled to Bayreuth. Despite appearing incognito, word got around at the hotel where he stayed, and the owner had people clamoring for the Wunderdoktor's bathwater.[96] Gröning was invited to a performance of the Emmerich Kálmán operetta, *The Gypsy Princess*, by its star, whom he had successfully treated. The next day, the Meckelburgs awoke to find that he had invited not only the star to his hotel but most of the cast.[97]

Yet it wasn't Gröning's cavorting holding up the cure center. It was Otto's own reputation—not as a former SS officer (which never

seemed to come up), but as a grifter. The head medical advisor to the
government of Upper Bavaria, Dr. Fritz Aub, agreed to give his consent to the center only if Meckelburg resigned from the leadership of
the Gröning organization.[98] A meeting was arranged. Otto arrived,
lawyers and a secretary in tow, this time driving not an Opel but a
new Mercedes.[99] The problem, as Aub told the *Süddeutsche Zeitung*,
lay in Otto's heavy-handed and exploitative tactics with cure-seekers.
"I have heard that Herr Meckelburg puts pressure on patients who
are less than willing to pay." Aub continued, "One does not hear much
good about the man. It appears that he wants to have the Gröning
sanatorium in his own pocket." The State of Bavaria had "no interest
in giving a license for a profit-oriented Meckelburg enterprise."[100] It
was around this same time that state police learned of Otto's black
market dealings and alleged V-rocket plans.[101] Various witnesses
also told police about the couple's tendency to issue threats when
they wanted something. Dieter Hülsmann's mother, Anneliese, now
estranged from the group, recounted Otto's threatening to "destroy"
her if she did not do as he wished and leave the Gröning circle.[102]
Prawatke, the salesman who had known Otto earlier, remembered
that when he tried to get in touch with the former SS man about a
business arrangement involving his father-in-law, Renée told him it
was none of his affair, and that he shouldn't get "fresh" with her since
her husband "was really good at boxing." Otto should be "deemed a
con man," Prawatke told police.[103]

   Where Gröning himself was concerned, Bavarian officialdom never
really spoke in a single or consistent voice. Dr. Aub told the press that
he "personally" had nothing against Gröning's practicing, as long as
he did so under a doctor's supervision and the various legal cases
pending against him—presumably meaning a charge of negligent
homicide in North Rhine–Westphalia from the Herford days—were
settled. The president of the Bavarian State Medical Association, Professor Karl Weiler, declared it out of the question.[104] Yet as would later
be reported, several politicians had appealed to Gröning on behalf of
acquaintances who hoped he would treat them.[105] All were Bavarian

Social Democrats: Georg Hagen, lord mayor of Kulmbach and vice-president of the state parliament; Josef Laumer, a representative to the state parliament; and Josef Seifried, a state minister.

Notwithstanding his own travails, and despite red tape and foot-dragging, Otto remained confident: the cure center would open. Taking his case to the court of public opinion, he explained to the press, "We are doing hard work in the service of a great thing." "It's unbelievable, the difficulties being made for us."[106] One of these difficulties was removed when the group learned that an investigation into the rape accusation against Gröning had been abandoned for lack of evidence. The negligent homicide charge was also abandoned; an individual treated by Gröning had indeed died, it had been determined, but the patient had already been given up on by doctors. While a case remained active in North Rhine–Westphalia, alleging that Gröning had violated the lay healer ban, at least one newspaper reported that it too would be abandoned if Gröning's bid to open a cure center in Bavaria were successful.[107] Bavarian officials—including some from the interior ministry—met in May 1950 to discuss the matter, but without result. A local newspaper chided Minister President Ehard, reminding readers that the previous year he'd publicly said that "we cannot let a phenomenon as exceptional as Gröning crash against the rocks of the law."[108]

Under the weight of fruitless negotiations and a growing sense of estrangement, the Meckelburg-Gröning partnership crumbled. Meckelburg was stripped of his power of attorney. The state police investigation of his financial dealings led to his brief arrest.[109] His lawyer admitted that the Association for Research and Promotion of the Gröning Healing Method had taken in huge sums—around 100,000 DM—but insisted that a great deal had also been paid out, for telephone and hotel bills, taxes, office workers, lawyers, and "Gröning's cigarette and coffee requirements, which were extraordinarily costly."[110] In July, preliminary proceedings began in Bavaria to investigate both him and Gröning for fraud and for violating rules governing public assembly and the lay healer ban.[111]

The Meckelburgs misunderstood Gröning in a variety of ways. Differences of class proved hard to overcome: both Renée and Otto found Gröning too rough for their tender sensibilities. The image of a saintly healer never quite squared with Gröning's Rasputin-like reputation for drinking and womanizing. A messiah should not "thirst after the masses," Renée once wrote.[112] Otto, former SS Death's Head adjutant, went so far as to suggest wistfully to police investigators that, with his help, Gröning could have become "ethically and morally clean," upholding the standards befitting "a normal, civilized central European."[113]

The Meckelburgs and Gröning went their separate ways, though they would spend a good deal of time in court together over the coming years, answering charges of fraud, profiteering, and having violated the lay healer regulations, among others. Each time they went free. Charges were dropped for lack of evidence or suspended, even as police and prosecutors probed new lines of inquiry.

Gröning and Meckelburg were not the only suspects who continued to evade the reach of the law. Around the time of Otto's brief arrest, his SS blood brother Adolf Eichmann escaped American detention and set sail for Argentina, where he would live, in reasonable comfort, for years to come. The press, meanwhile, began clamoring around a new Wunderdoktor, a Düsseldorf hair dresser called Pietro Tranti. Buses from as far away as Hamburg and Austria were now besieging *his* house.[114]

7

SICKNESS THAT COMES FROM SIN

By 1950, West Germany was being rebuilt. A British visitor that year took note of an array of positive changes. The "food shortage, once so acute, has been overcome; hospitals are working, industries are working, long-distance trains are working, and so are local train and tram services in the big towns." There was still underemployment, but all in all things were looking up. The "countryside I saw was very well cultivated," even if "probably in any case uneconomic" because the fields were too small. But, in an early sign of returning prosperity, "very many chickens and geese were to be seen," and the cigarette, a once-ubiquitous form of currency on the much-despised black market, had been restored to its rightful place in vending machines.[1]

Like the neatly swept streets of Munich, the surface of things was being smoothed over. And yet, tensions about the past continued to bubble away, and they had a habit of surfacing in spiritual contexts. Many people continued to find themselves in need of spiritual consolation, sustenance, and blessing. They were wary of the machinations of evil, worried about demons, and sought protection from harm.

Catholics in particular had traditionally seen war, like epidemics and hunger, as punishment for disobedience, sinfulness, and a lack of faith.[2] Five years after the end of World War II, many still feared divine judgment, dreading the possibility that God would bring about future wars to induce atonement.

In October 1949, just after Bruno Gröning's abrupt departure from the Trotter Farm, a group of little girls gathering autumn foliage for a school project and telling ghost stories chanced upon a lady dressed all in white, her hands folded in prayer. It was the Mother of God, the girls said. They told their families and the local priest. Within days, pilgrims had descended on Heroldsbach, the Franconian village where these events transpired. Counted in the tens of thousands, they came by bus, train, bicycle, and on foot.[3] The apparitions continued over the next three years, and included not only the Virgin, but also Joseph, angels, various saints, and incarnations of Jesus—some three thousand visions in all. Between 1949 and 1952, an estimated one and a half million people would come to the village to witness them. While Heroldsbach, which lies about twenty miles due north of Nuremberg, became a mass phenomenon, nearly a dozen smaller-scale apparitions were reported in other West German Catholic enclaves—Fehrbach and Rodalben in the Palatinate, the tiny Rhineland locale Niederhabbach, and cities like Würzburg and Munich. Not all of these visions inspired thousands of pilgrims to take to the roads, but many did.[4]

Some people came to Heroldsbach seeking cures for a variety of fairly commonplace ailments: fevers, rheumatism, eczema, and headaches.[5] Others were after less concrete relief, as folklorist Rudolf Kriß learned when he visited Heroldsbach in October 1952. He spotted an elegantly dressed woman scooping up sanctified earth from the apparition site and tucking it into her handbag. It would indemnify, she told Kriß, against future wars. Others took soil, they said, to protect themselves from harm and as insurance against illness and "demonic temptations."[6] This seemed to some like a real and fearsome hazard: a visiting priest warned of mistakenly confusing a divine apparition with a "devilish copy," and the visionaries themselves reported seeing the Devil himself in February 1950.[7] Pilgrims sought proximity with the girls, whom they believed to be invested with Mary's power, and asked the visionaries to lay hands on them.[8] They came seeking blessings, and bearing rosaries, the bark and leaves of trees, earth, wax, water, and other substances and objects for Mary to bless.[9] They daubed the wounds of a crucifix, donated to a Heroldsbach chapel, with cloths that they believed would carry the healing power of Jesus's blood to homebound relatives.[10]

Some pilgrims sought out the services of exorcists. Kriß, who wrote extensively about the apparitions, described a man named Herr Unsinn who would lead groups to a crucifix in the woods, a spot where Mary had previously appeared, and ask everyone to kneel down. In an "energetic and commanding tone," he then prayed aloud for "all evil spirits, cursedness, demons, temptations, and sicknesses" to "relent in the name of the Holy Trinity." Unsinn repeated this prayer three

times, raising his voice and gesturing with his fist toward the earth, each time repeating the word "relent" and calling on all wickedness to abate. He followed with Our Fathers and Hail Marys and a well-known charm used to heal wounds and stop bleeding. Unsinn would also pray what he called the "Hebrew Our Father," better known as the Sator formula—Sator Arepo Tenet Opera Rotas—a Latin palindrome used in folk magic.[11]

Not everyone was willing to accept the apparitions. The episode caused much friction between two opposing groups of Catholics: those who believed in the visions' reality and those who did not. The believers accused their opponents of faithlessness and blasphemy; their antagonists denounced them as disobedient, and as heathens and sectarians.[12] They repeatedly befouled a pool where the faithful went to take the waters, which they believed had been blessed and made curative by the Virgin. In March 1950, opponents of the cult chased off the visionary children with chants of "the Devil, the Devil!"[13] The next month, Mary herself was said to threaten that if her will were not done—if the pilgrims' antagonists did not leave them in peace to commune with her—"the Russians will come and smite you! Much blood will flow!"[14] The Virgin warning of a Russian invasion: this was not just an allusion to the Cold War and to the godless Soviet communism that obsessed Catholics in the 1950s, but a menacing reminder of the death, defeat, and occupation that had been the harvest of 1945.

The tensions only increased when the Holy Office in Rome weighed in. On the apparitions' first anniversary, a representative of the archbishop in Bamberg appeared in Heroldsbach—under heavy police protection—to announce that the visions were not supernatural in origin and to urge the faithful to keep their distance.[15] When pilgrims continued to come to the site in droves despite the decree, the Pope ordered clergy not to give them communion. The local priest was moved out of town. Eventually, many of those involved—the priest and various adherents of the apparitions, including the visionaries themselves—were excommunicated. A supporter of the Heroldsbach visionaries who had spent years in the Sachsenhausen concentration camp for disseminating anti-Nazi leaflets castigated Church leaders for their use of such heavy-handed tactics and compared them to the Gestapo. Finally, on October 31, 1952, Mary made her last appearance in Heroldsbach.[16]

While some of the sources of these intra-Catholic divisions were, in a sense, doctrinal—a good Catholic should be obedient to church hierarchy—the situation forced believers to choose between such obedience and standing with the visionaries. But the dissension was also rooted in people's relationship to the "most recent past." A "disproportionate number of men attracted to Catholic mysticism" in the postwar years, the historian Michael O'Sullivan observes, "had endured concentration camps, POW camps, or expulsion." In both Heroldsbach and Fehrbach, locals indicted Catholic leaders for their decidedly mixed, and often complicit, record during the Third Reich.[17]

Throughout the 1950s, as scattered groups of people joined prayer circles, sought to exorcise their demons, gathered in huge numbers to hear fiery preachers, and witnessed apparitions of the Virgin Mary, the customary silences sometimes stopped being observed. Accusations were met by recriminations, and fears of spiritual infection and spiritual punishment spilled forth. The hordes who came to Heroldsbach were exceptional, but many other, often quite different settings also saw displays of dread—whether of divine judgment or the demonic.

Most of the sources we have available to study these matters are limited in various ways. They are often fragmentary, diffuse, and episodic. There is no archive for fears of spiritual punishment the way there are archives of social movements or political parties or government bureaucracies. But if we place into one frame a variety of instances in which postwar West Germans experienced, talked about, preached about, and diagnosed spiritual illness, we start to develop a picture we would not otherwise be able to see: a strong undercurrent of malaise, one that those involved in scenes of spiritual tumult often connected, directly or indirectly, to the Nazi past—even as the country as a whole turned away from any direct form of confrontation with that past, and collective memory tacitly agreed on a general moratorium against speaking about its most sinister aspects.

. . .

One night in late 1951, Munich police were called to a villa on Leonhard-Eck Straße, on the east bank of the Isar River, not far from the city's famed English Garden. An investigator approaching the house found all the lights on inside. Though this still afforded only a partial view, he could nevertheless make out around fifteen people, praying so loudly that he could hear them in the street. Then the front door suddenly swung open: two men stood inside. The older one, a Lutheran pastor named Henninger, explained that his church had asked him to come and observe the prayer circle meeting there. They were involved, some said, in *Teufelsaustreibungen*—devil expulsions.

The prayer group members were Protestants, not Catholics, so the connotation is important. Protestants have historically avoided the term exorcism, a Catholic rite too close, from their point of view, to magic. What this Munich prayer group called devil expulsion could be accomplished only through fasting and prayer.[18] And indeed, in the elegantly furnished living room, the police investigator found a group "so deep in prayer that they had not even noticed" his arrival. Most were over fifty, though there were also a few younger people. All were dressed "simply," suggesting they were of modest income, but in their Sunday best, and appeared to police to be "really pious believers." The officer found nothing untoward to report.[19]

The police learned about the devil expulsions on Leonhard-Eck Straße by way of a former tenant of Marianne D., the owner of the house and a senior civil servant's widow.[20] They later questioned Frau D., because seeking to "profit or otherwise achieve some benefit through ostensible magic or exorcism" was punishable under Bavarian law with a fine or jail time. Of the spiritual cures being worked in her home, Frau D. told the police that people who wanted to make their peace with God had been coming there for years. Originally, she said, she had been asked by a senior council member of the Protestant Trinity Church to help found prayer circles in church members' homes. On regular occasions, "friends and acquaintances" would "spend time praying and reading the Bible together." Frau D. called her group an "independent circle of Christ-serving people." Recently, two men from outside the group had come. They had a reputation for having a "particular authority, from God," she told police, "to save people from the grip of hell, heal the sick, and lead the people back to Jesus." The men were Möttlinger Brothers—members of a circle of Pietists in Württemberg, connected with the Salvation Ark (*Rettungsarche*), a religious center founded in 1909 by a visionary and healer named Friedrich Stanger. They had been trying to help a Frau Jagemann, who could not find her peace with God. Frau Jagemann's family, Frau D. told police, had suffered under the control of Satan for many generations, and "she wanted keenly to be free." Frau D. explained that the brothers had ultimately succeeded in breaking the Devil's power and sent hundreds of demons fleeing from Frau Jagemann with loud shrieks.[21]

Over that fall of 1951, Munich police heard more reports about Leonhard-Eck Straße. The local deanery of the Lutheran Church had written to urge police to investigate a "Gypsy" named Schröder—a traveling textile salesman performing the demon expulsions, whose name turned out to be Fritz Köhler.[22] Police also took a statement from an Antonius Kirmayer, who had been on the fringe of the Gröning circle at one point.[23] In the fall of 1949, he told a reporter that he experienced Pentecost at the Trotter Farm, and predicted that a great wave of renewed faith would soon surge through the land, with the power to banish darkness and disarm an atom bomb.[24]

Both Kirmayer and Köhler had been in concentration camps—Dachau, Mauthausen, and Buchenwald, in Köhler's case.[25] It was in the camps, Köhler later told police, that he "found his way back to the Savior." Working for the American occupiers after the war, he said, he saw "how depraved the world is," and prayed to God to change him. We cannot know what experience with the Americans had exposed him to such depravity, but together with his time in the camps it had inspired him to begin his work as a spiritual healer.[26] Kirmayer, for his part, explained that he too belonged to a circle of prayer healers. This group, he said, had recently cured the sister-in-law of a bank manager of stomach cancer and another woman of being possessed. Grimacing devils had contorted her face, and the group had to pray for hours to liberate her from them. Casting out devils was a Christian duty described in the Gospel of Mark, Kirmayer explained to police; the Bible enjoined all believers to banish evil spirits.[27] So successful was the woman's treatment that the police investigation was later dropped—the ostensible victim reported to police feeling "a great spiritual harmony and happiness in her soul" since having her demons expelled.[28]

Spiritual illness and salvation from it were also the fare among popular postwar preachers. The circle of prayer healers to which Kirmayer belonged included aviation pioneer Gottlob Espenlaub and Hermann Zaiss, a razor manufacturer from Solingen. Espenlaub had preached and exorcised demons to cure the sick since the end of the war in his native Baden-Württemberg.[29] Zaiss, once a salesman on West Africa's Gold Coast, had become an evangelist even before the First World War, but then turned away from God for twenty years. What brought him back was seeing his house bombed out in 1944, which he seems to have perceived as a warning from God to set his life right.[30] Together, Zaiss and Espenlaub traveled the country evangelizing after the war, performing healings for mass audiences and proclaiming a harsh theology.[31] A witness at one meeting, a Pastor Bickerich of Wuppertal, reported having heard them preach that if a person were not cured of illness, if their demons could not be driven out, it was because their belief was not strong enough.[32]

In 1956, Zaiss gave a series of sermons in a Wuppertal cinema, Odin's Palace, to capacity audiences. These were collected and published after he died in a car crash two years later. Zaiss oriented himself around a few principles: spiritual healing, he said, was not a supernatural event but rather represented the reharmonization of nature. Illness was "against nature," healing "godly and natural." Illness came from being disobedient toward God. "In every sin lies a curse," he said.

Zaiss is a particularly good historical source because he also spoke much less abstractly about specific sins than many of his contemporaries tended to do. All sins, he said, "would punish the sinner, whether now or later." He urged those who came to hear him to "pay attention to what God's word says: I will bring misfortune to this nation. . . . Misfortune, plagues, pestilence, sickness of every kind . . . can come over a whole nation according to the Holy Scripture." Zaiss warned that those who falsely claimed that they had never been a party member and "never had anything to do with Adolf Hitler" had "added to their sins a lie." He continued even more trenchantly: "We knew that . . . the Jewish people among us were despised, mocked, beaten, and robbed—one only has to think of Kristallnacht—everyone knows what happened then." And Zaiss went further, "Six million Jews were killed, and *our people did that*."

The German nation's punishment, according to Zaiss, precisely reflected that sin's magnitude: "Six million Germans died in the war. An eye for an eye, a tooth for a tooth: exactly six million! Exactly as many as the Jews we murdered." Of course, Zaiss continued, not all Germans died, "only 7 or 8 percent." But that did not mean that "the other 92 or 93 percent" could "boast their innocence. . . . Unfortunately, by the laws of the living God, some people . . . have to reckon with what the community as a whole had earned."[33]

Zaiss's message resonated. By the late 1950s, there were some three hundred "Zaiss communities"—independent charismatic churches, mostly in northern and western Germany, but some abroad as well.[34] Precious little scholarship exists on these churches. What is most striking about them is not their numbers, though, but the impassioned and, for that time, almost inconceivably direct manner in which Zaiss preached to fellow Germans about the need to repent their role in the murder of six million Jews. The introduction to Zaiss's published sermons claims that those who flocked to hear him preach came from "every stratum of society—from modest workers to factory owners, single and working women and housewives, poor and rich, sick and well." His preaching about healing the sick, it was said, "evoked particular interest." Sunday after Sunday, the auditorium in Wuppertal would "fill to the rafters, to standing-room-only capacity," including even the walkways and stairs.[35] When he died, Zaiss's funeral attracted some three thousand mourners.[36]

According to a preacher like Zaiss, sickness was not just a physical condition in postwar, post-Nazi Germany. It could also be a metaphysical state, and a spiritual sign: a sign of a curse, of divine disfavor, of sin and the refusal to atone for it. Similarly, visitations from the Virgin Mary could hold out the hope of salvation, of redemption, but also provoke fears of future wars, and future punishment, for sins most people did not care to name.

• • •

Sufferers continued to seek out Bruno Gröning's form of soul medicine during this time, and he continued to dispense it. Having broken with the Meckelburgs, he began working cures in the Munich offices of a lay healer named Eugen Enderlin, treating patients suffering everything from circulatory and nerve problems to palsy and arthritis to mutism connected to wartime air raids. Newspapers reported that Enderlin, a monocle-wearing chain-smoker, had to set up a special office just to manage the volume of correspondence that arrived for his new partner from all over the world.[37] Patients lined up from the early morning hours to see Gröning, gathering in the stairwell of Enderlin's building all the way up to the third floor, so thickly that they prevented those living in the building from getting in and out of their apartments.[38] Gröning also regularly gave lectures, both at Enderlin's and in local pubs, on the subject of "the godly way and the Devil."[39] A police investigator attending such a gathering at the Wagnerbräu, a Munich alehouse where Hitler had once rallied his supporters, puzzled over how Gröning seemed to think of the Devil as "some kind of higher power."[40]

The relationship between evil and sickness remained the Wunderdoktor's chief topic in the fall of 1950, when he appeared with a
healer named Josef Günzl for the benefit of a group of cure-seekers
at a local swimming spot near Munich. Two witnesses, a sergeant of
the state police named Meier and a Dr. Bachmann, representing the
Bavarian State Health Department, later turned in reports about what
they observed there one late October afternoon. Most of the fifty to
sixty guests, they reported, were women between the ages of twenty
and sixty-five "from the middle class and down to the humbler circles," but a good number—some ten to fifteen—Meier described as
"respectable, educated visitors." Many attendees held egg-sized tinfoil balls and read from pamphlets about Gröning, which could be
bought for 20 pfennigs, as they waited.

Günzl, a "small, slight man," addressed the crowd first. He spoke
about many things: miraculous healing, the "mind-body problem,"
the dangers of eating too much meat, and a jumble of Christian, Bud-
dhist, pantheist, and anthroposophical ideas, according to Bachmann.
But the main portion of his presentation had to do with sin: sins
people committed, sins that God punished with illness. All people
had a piece of God in them, Günzl told his audience, a piece of God
that spoke to them through their conscience. God was put out of
sorts by sin, and—as Hermann Zaiss would also tell those whom
he evangelized—sin caused sickness. Sin irritated the God present in
people, Günzl said, creating spiritual disharmony, and making them
ill. To return to health, Günzl advised the gathering, God demanded a
sacrifice, a form of recompense. God demanded atonement.

Gröning seemed never to use the word "sin." He spoke of evil: the
harm that some people did, the bad intentions and ill will they harbored. Standing with his hands in his pockets, his face expressionless,
he paused frequently for effect, or to collect his thoughts (Meier
and Bachmann were not sure which). For an hour, in his rambling and
elusive style, he talked about how people were like radios, and about
some of his recent cures. Then he talked about God and the Devil,
and evil people who stopped good people from being well. He talked

about helping good people. Only they could have the benefit of his treatment. When he could not heal the sick, he said, it was because evil people were blocking waves of healing he sent.[41] "Protect yourself from bad people," he advised the crowd.[42] At the Wagnerbräu a few days before, he said that God was like a power station and human beings were like lightbulbs, whose power could be "interrupted" by those who "have never done anything good, and from whom we can't expect anything good, because they are bad." These people, Gröning said, "I call satanic." They "have become slaves to Satan." He counseled his audience to "stay on the natural, true, and divine path."[43]

On Wangerooge a few months before, Gröning had told his audience that "human beings in the last few years have gotten very, very bad" and urged cure-seekers to bury hate and envy once and for all.[44] He did not ask anyone to reflect further on the nature of this hate and envy, or flesh out exactly what he meant by his injunction. He probably didn't have to: different attendees could fill in the blanks as they chose. But for Gröning, there was no contradiction between urging people in one moment to lay aside hatred and in the next to avoid "evil people." Evil people were covert bearers of malice—witches—to whom no quarter could be given.

• • •

These were, after all, times of spiritual malaise, of mistrust and heightened suspicion. In an atmosphere of determined, willful refusal to acknowledge basic facts, who could be blamed for imagining that evil lurked behind the false screen of apparent events? "God's will is sure," Gröning would say. "God wants the person to be helped who has recognized that evil lowers him. Owning up is the best way to recovery." But, he continued, "don't come to me and tell me that you've never had a *Schweinhund* inside you. . . . There are people . . . who still carry a beast inside them."[45] *Schweinhund*—literally "swine-dog"—is a highly offensive, insulting term in German, carrying roughly the same connotation as "bastard" in English. The term had been generally used by German soldiers in World War II—and Gröning, of course, had been one—to mean the inner reticence one must overcome to get something done, often something distasteful.

What did this theology—a soldier's theology, an ordinary man's theology—sound like in the 1950s? Unpleasant things had to get done, and we did them. We all know what we did. *Don't tell me you've never had a Schweinhund in you.* Former soldiers who spent time as POWs sometimes described the time they spent in camps in Russia and Poland as a "necessary atonement," a form of penance they hoped would wash away their sins. Other ex-soldiers, sure that their postwar psychological troubles were connected to wartime misdeeds, sometimes sought psychiatric care and tried to offer their confessions to their doctors.[46]

In the 1970s, ethnographer Jutta Dornheim interviewed a group of West German World War II veterans. All, she found, independently raised in discussion their ideas about punishment and illness in relation to their wartime experiences. One veteran, Herr Lang, suffered from cancer. He insisted at first to Dornheim that God did not punish people with illness. And yet, he continued hesitantly (the dashes indicate long pauses):

> I always think, I've, I've, I've never harmed anyone in my life, and something—of what should I?—I've, I've never stolen anything from anyone, I have never again gotten up to anything big (*gross was angestellt*).—Although, although I was in the war, right—and———except for—I mean, it's all—it is all really a thing of its own.—When you—when you were a soldier, right—I mean—I really don't know.—I was in Russia four years.———Right, yes—but I mean—that is really another matter.

Dornheim tried for more clarity. Did Herr Lang mean that he would set war aside as a special case when thinking about whether God punished people with illness? "Yes," he said. "I have a good conscience that I———didn't hurt———that is———any defenseless people, or should we say that———I did not do that." No one blamed Herr

Lang for anything. Still, he sought to justify or rationalize the possible ill effects of his earlier acts on his health, whatever those acts may have been.

Another man, Herr Opp, also had cancer in the 1970s, and he too associated it with his wartime experiences. "I was in the heavy infantry, I had a machine gun, and a lot, a lot, happened with us, that is—with the Russians. . . . I never did anything else to anyone since then, just at the front, we had to." A drum- or belt-fed machine gun, such as the MG 34 used by the German army, could fire eight hundred to twelve hundred bullets per minute and had an effective range of two thousand meters. The people Herr Opp shot at as an infantryman might have appeared to him as no more than dots in the landscape. Maybe that's what he meant when he reported telling his wife when he returned home, "I didn't—see a single thing."

Though circumspect about what exactly happened in the war, both Herr Lang and Herr Opp associated their illnesses with their wartime acts without anyone's encouragement. Unbidden, and without being accused of anything, both sought justification. They related the mystery of cancer to whatever they did in the war. Yet neither *wanted* to think their sins were being punished, or that God was punishing them.[47]

At the Trotter Farm in summer 1949, *Süddeutsche Zeitung* reporter Siegfried Sommer had interviewed a man sitting in a dusty Mercedes, waiting for Gröning to show up one hot afternoon. He had not moved from that spot for thirty-six hours. "I am a master butcher from Fulda," the man told Sommer, as if to say that he was a man of substance, a skilled and hardworking man. Since 1946, he said, he had not been able to move his hands anymore and his legs were both paralyzed. "I never did anything to anyone," the butcher said.[48] He had explained, without really explaining, that his paralysis was not warranted, he did not deserve it. He had not done anything to anyone: there was no larger cause for his affliction.

We cannot know what sins people wanted to be free of when they sought healing and got their devils cast out in Munich or Heroldsbach or Wuppertal. Nor do we know exactly what Gröning referred to when when he spoke of an inner *Schweinhund*, or when his partner Günzl said that God punished sin with illness and that people had to atone, offer a sacrifice, to be well again. We have no access to the thoughts of those who sat waiting for Gröning or feared, after the war, that their bodies were inhabited by demons. The preacher Zaiss, from Wuppertal, was quite clear about what the sin was: the persecution and mass murder of six million Jews, the horror of which was compounded by pretending one had known nothing about it. Feeling spiritual unease could also arise from direct participation in war or war crimes, as Herr Opp's and Herr Lang's stories powerfully hint. Yet we cannot assume that our sense of right and wrong maps neatly onto the moral and emotional lives of people in the past. Postwar Germans could feel blamed and guilty and punished and wronged for many things: for a lost war and lost family members; for failure and defeat and whatever judgment they feared might lie behind failure and defeat. And for some, it was perhaps simply the guilt that came of asking, "Why are they dead, and I am still alive?"

· · ·

Talk of guilt and sin and punishment bubbled up in other milieux, where talk of the Devil never would have. By renewing an old debate about who had the right to heal in Germany, Bruno Gröning's rise to fame had called the future of the ban on lay healing into question. In 1950, Dr. Richard Hammer, a parliamentarian and distinguished physician (he would go on to receive the Paracelsus Medal, the highest honor in German medicine), convened the Bundestag's Committee for Public Health Questions, which he chaired, to discuss the ban. Hammer's past, like that of many doctors, was complicated. He had been a member of the SA. During the war, he had served as a front-line doctor. Yet none of his technical expertise or practical experience barred him from expressing considerable sympathy for lay healers, who he believed could have an inborn, even mystical, ability to cure, one that "could be neither taught nor transmitted."[49] While many professional medical organizations remained skeptical, if not downright hostile, to lay healers, Hammer remarked that he could not easily dismiss a "phenomenon" like Gröning, someone capable of attracting "thousands and thousands of believers," some of whom he healed, a "small number perhaps even completely."[50]

The committee invited expert opinion from two other notable physicians: Viktor von Weizsäcker, who directed the Heidelberg clinic where Dr. G. H. Fischer had conducted experiments with Bruno Gröning the previous summer, and Gustav Schmalz, a psychotherapist who had trained under Carl Jung. Schmaltz, too, had a past. He had joined the NSDAP in 1933 and later worked in the German Institute for Psychological Research and Psychotherapy, called the Göring Institute for short. Its director, Matthias Göring, was cousin to Hermann Göring, among the highest-ranking members of the NSDAP and one of the most powerful men in the Third Reich. Once known as the Berlin Psychoanalytic Institute, the Göring Institute had been renamed when the Nazis came to power and all Jewish and communist doctors were ejected from it. Jung had himself worked with the institute for a time.[51]

Hammer's committee posed a number of questions to the two visiting physicians. Hammer asked whether "certain abilities to heal" could be tested. This was an important issue, because discussions of the future of the lay healer ban often concerned whether what was called a "lesser license" (kleine Approbation) should be created for lay practitioners, one that would require an independent test of their knowledge and abilities. "The most important principle of healing is Christian charity," responded von Weizsäcker, a standard that would make it "difficult to test all lay healers by the same examination procedure, the way it works for doctors." Schmaltz's response was similarly metaphysical, if less obviously religious. "Intuition," he said, "cannot be tested." A person with the right skills or gifts could heal even with the wrong methods. Von Weizsäcker concurred: "Some healers could do things and should be allowed to do them." Decisive qualities, he observed, like "talent, character and so on . . . cannot be tested by some single schema."

The conversation turned increasingly philosophical. "Where does the actual process of healing have its origins?" Hammer asked. Schmaltz responded at some length. The mind, he said, played the most essential role in healing. The right healer could access the "mysterious power" of the deep subconscious, the realm of "pathogenic disturbances." To dissolve these "unknown disturbances and expose their pathological effects," Schmaltz said, "is part of the miracle of healing." Lastly, he said, "There are mental processes that trigger physical difficulties, and there is a strange interaction between guilt and illness."[52] In the manner so common to the period, he spoke only abstractly, and not about specific sources of guilt.

This was also true of *Sickness as a Consequence of Sin*, a book published that same year, 1950, by physician Wolf von Siebenthal.[53] His stated purpose in writing the book was to "re-humanize" medicine. Like Dr. Fischer in Heidelberg, von Siebenthal did not explicitly mention what had led to medicine's dehumanization, but his book offered critiques of medical practice similar to Fischer's. Medicine that failed to look holistically at human suffering, he said, that reduced ill human beings to their diseases and malfunctioning organs, was a failed medicine. At a time when so many patients seemed to be suffering in ways that physicalist medicine could not address—paralyzed arms and legs and voices, unseeing eyes—both Fischer and von Siebenthal implored their fellow physicians to look more deeply into what was ailing them.

Von Siebenthal understood that his patients wanted to know not just *how* they were sick, but *why*. Even if a proximate cause could be identified—an infection, say, or organ failure—people still wanted to know (in a fashion reminiscent of the Azande and falling granaries) what larger, even ultimate, cause might have brought on illness. Medical science had been tremendously successful precisely by ignoring such questions, von Siebenthal wrote, but true healing required something more. He urged fellow doctors to set aside the idea that illness appeared only randomly and conformed "only by coincidence to one or another vitalist or mechanistic law." Medicine's essential task should be less instrumental than *existential*, he argued; it had to turn on questions of meaning. Sickness had an important religious purpose, he believed. It made people aware of their sinfulness and held out the possibility of redemption. Returning to health after illness required atonement, and atonement, von Siebenthal argued, was healing itself.[54]

. . .

Not long before going their separate ways in summer 1950, the ill-suited Gröning-Meckelburg trio had made a trip together to Oberammergau, home of a world-famous Passion play.[55] Situated on the banks of a sparkling river and tucked in at the foot of the magnificent Kofel, a nearly vertical peak, Oberammergau is a storybook Bavarian village. Since the time of the Thirty Years' War, in the seventeenth century, its inhabitants have regularly dramatized the trial, suffering, execution, and resurrection of Jesus. Oberammergauer began staging the Passion to thank God for sparing them the ravages of the plague, which depopulated many nearby villages but spared Oberammergau. Their descendants have continued to do so once a decade, roughly speaking, ever since.

There have been some interruptions. The 1940 season was cancelled due to the war. When Gröning and the Meckelburgs visited, the play had not been produced since the three hundredth anniversary season in 1934, when Hitler had attended it (for the second time). So the 1950 staging represented something of a revival, and drew in some half a million visitors, including US General (and future president) Dwight D. Eisenhower, German federal president Theodor Heuss, and Chancellor Adenauer.[56]

Hans Ehard, the Bavarian minister president who had been so receptive to and supportive of Bruno Gröning's healing mission, wrote an essay for the official 1950 guidebook. Ehard underscored the same themes of fortune and misfortune, judgment and redemption, sin and guilt that had led to the play's inception centuries earlier. Oberammergau's Passion play, Ehard wrote, was "meant to awaken awareness of the evil within us" and point toward its overcoming.[57]

Ehard's comments were timeless and, characteristic of the era, hazy. They veiled and smoothed over the rough facts of recent, specific evils, and the knowledge that even pious Bavarian villages had been party to cataclysm. During the war, Messerschmidt, the military aircraft producer, had moved into the village and set up a research institute. Local businesses in Oberammergau had made use of slave labor from a nearby camp.[58]

Five years after the war, the transition from past to present remained incomplete. Villagers reelected their former Nazi mayor in 1948.[59] The play itself, which had long been a deeply antisemitic spectacle, remained so—from Act I, in which Jesus expels the moneylenders from the temple (Renée Meckelburg's favorite biblical episode), to the "murder" of Jesus by "the Jews." Even the man playing Jesus in 1950, Anton Preisinger, was a former Nazi.[60]

Ehard's commentary not only finessed awful facts by failing to name them. It also gave the impression that there were things that history could not touch—things like religious tradition, devotional plays, and storybook villages. The minister president had responded to Gröning in a similar way, as many people did: as though the healer were merely the latest and greatest iteration of a traditional form—the Wunderdoktor—and not also the product of a specific, postwar and post-Nazi history. As though the outpouring of emotion in Herford and Rosenheim could have happened anywhere, at any time, and had nothing at all to do with the recent past and its legacies.

But while fears of Armageddon have surfaced and resurfaced over many centuries, to envision it in 1949 or 1950—after a war of unprecedented technological destruction, in which whole cities were annihilated from the air and atomic bombs became a reality—had a different meaning from the end-of-days prophecies that had come before. Likewise, as much as Gröning was part of a venerable landscape of folk medical practice and religious healing in Germany, in a society with such a dramatic recent history of denunciation and cruel judgment, there was a particular subtext to having a former Nazi proclaim that "evil people" were beyond healing and should be shunned. Oberammergau's seemingly changeless appeal to the deity never happened outside time: not during the Thirty Years' War, not in 1934—when it became a piece of ethnic theater par excellence—and not after 1945, when it continued in that same vein, largely unreconstructed.

Nor were obsessions with evil, sin, guilt, blame, punishment, and redemption merely "age-old" beliefs in the early Federal Republic. They were a response to the moral and spiritual catastrophe of Nazism. In the 1950s, a war of unparalleled extremity, of death squads and gas chambers, was "history" in only the barest sense. Even as the "economic miracle"—which would be widely credited with transforming German society—gained traction, and the stores filled up with goods, and the trains got running, and the chickens and geese proliferated, many people continued to feel a deep unease. We should not imagine that there is some neat separation between a modernizing country and seemingly archaic fears of divine justice and illness as a punishment for sins. The past is not superseded so much as compounded, layer upon layer, until there is indeed something quite new at the end but with the origins still, in one way or another, part of the foundation.

It would be a few more years before Israeli journalist Amos Elon, who visited the country in 1964, could describe West Germany's cities as fully "resurrected"—"brand-new, clean, sober, infinitely monotonous" and radiating "the coldly blinding glare of neon lights."[61] Some cities would be rebuilt from scratch after the rubble was cleared, appearing sleek in comparison to what had stood in their place before the bombs fell. Others, no less jarringly, were rebuilt to look just like they had before they were bombed.[62] And some cities engaged in another exercise entirely. In Essen, home of Krupp steel, the magnificent synagogue, built in the center of town in 1913 and damaged on Kristallnacht but still intact after the war, would be renovated in 1961 at a cost of two million marks. It was now used to exhibit industrial design: the stoves, dishwashers, and irons that helped fuel West German modernization and the economic miracle.[63]

Historian Jan Gross has reflected on the way his fellow Poles largely denied any role in the pogroms and mass murders of their Jewish fellow citizens after the war. What is the effect on society, he asks, of telling itself "a big lie"? "Everything that comes afterward," he writes, "will be devoid of authenticity and laced with fear of discovery." After all, he continues, "How can anyone trust people who have murdered, or knowingly denounced to their murderers, other human beings?"[64] Crimes of such magnitude, Gross suggests, inescapably seep into the very fabric, and into every strand, of life.

ARE THERE WITCHES AMONG US?

The trouble in their community could be said to have started when the innkeeper Hans and his wife, Erna, heard that Waldemar Eberling, the cabinetmaker, could maybe help with their sick baby. No one knew what was wrong with the little girl. The couple took her to the hospital, where she stayed for months. But doctors couldn't help, and she didn't get better, so eventually they took her home. This happened in October 1952, in a village in Dithmarschen in West Germany's northernmost state, Schleswig-Holstein. Eberling came to the family's home and treated the baby with *Besprechen*, medicine that relied on charms, gestures, and words. He said she would be better immediately, and she was. In the next days and weeks, Eberling came back several times to follow up on his *Besprechen* treatment. He also said that the child should take vitamin C tablets. The family were very thankful. They gave Eberling a pork roast, a jar of sausages, some cigarettes, and beer.[1]

After that, Eberling occasionally ate supper with the family. One night, as Hans and Eberling were sitting in the kitchen, Eberling revealed that Hans's family were in the clutches of an evil force, and were being shadowed by it in the form of a person. That very night, Eberling said, this evil character could not sleep, and would come around the house. The two men went outside to have a look. There was indeed someone there, who quickly took off, Hans said later. The next morning he went to the Maassens—they lived across the street—to pick up milk. Frau Maassen became very pale when she saw him, Hans said, and began to cry and seemed distressed. Eberling advised Hans that the family should never let Frau Maassen cross their threshold again. Though earlier they had all been quite friendly, now Hans's family and Frau Maassen stopped speaking. Hans began to feel that she wanted to ruin his business.[2]

Another time, Hans was at the home of an acquaintance. Eberling was there too, as it happened. The village's former mayor, a man named Claus, rode by on his bicycle. The acquaintance said to Hans, the old mayor just rode by. Hans sensed that his acquaintance was indicating to him that the former mayor was "the so-called evil force."[3] Soon, word got around that Frau Maassen and the former mayor were witches.

Herr Maassen was a tailor, and his son worked for him. One day, around Christmastime 1953, while talking with one of his father's customers, the Maassens' son learned that his mother had been accused of being a witch, and that Eberling was behind the charge. The son did not want to spoil his mother's Christmas, so he waited to tell her until after the new year. When his mother learned of the accusation, she took the news greatly to heart, becoming incapacitated. A doctor confirmed that she had been made physically ill by the rumors.[4]

Frau Maassen's son went to the police to report what was happening with his mother, and the police in turn visited the family. Frau Maassen was so overwhelmed that she broke down and could not give a statement. At first, the Maassens declined to file a formal defamation complaint, because there was a fee associated with doing so.[5] Claus, the former mayor, had no such qualms. He was not undone by the rumors now floating around—not only, it turned out, about him, but also about his brother-in-law. People were saying that both men were witches, and some thought them responsible for a number of local illnesses. Claus went around asking questions and confronted people who he heard knew something about it. He made an official statement and complaint to police.[6] Later, Frau Maassen's son would do the same.[7]

The press caught wind of the evolving story. An article in a Kiel newspaper, "Witch-Superstition in the Era of the Hydrogen Bomb," featured interviews with some of the parties involved: another woman accused of witchcraft, Frau Maassen's son, and Eberling himself. Questioned by reporters, the cabinetmaker explained his theory that people have two brains, the second brain being a kind of antenna. When this second one malfunctions, a person goes under mentally, physically, and morally. People also had three nervous systems; when one went bad, someone needed to flip the switch on a second (hitherto unused) system, to stand in for the malfunctioning first. These were the kinds of problems, Eberling told reporters, that he worked on.[8]

Police interviewed local people about their dealings with Eberling. Sometimes his treatments helped, sometimes they did not, police heard people say. With the exception of Frau Maassen, and Claus and his brother-in-law, they could not find anyone else who would admit to having been accused as witches.[9] In fact, Eberling generally had a good reputation as a healer, and a great many people sought out his services.

He did not always mention witches or an evil force. Sometimes he prescribed nothing stronger than buttermilk, salted herring, or mustard seeds, told his patients not to smoke or consume alcohol, and had them make a tea out of gentian root. Sometimes he recommended they whip their limbs with nettles or rub them with alcohol and formic acid.[10] He cured people's headaches and got children who had been sick to eat properly again. He often had his clients burn a foul-smelling powder known as devil's dung (*Teufelsdreck*) and use it to smoke out their homes. Also known as asafetida, this powder, made of the dried sap of certain herbs, was available in every pharmacy.[11]

At other times, though, Eberling's interventions were more elaborate. Around December 1953, for example, he was called to the home of Frau Pieper, who had two small children. The younger one, a girl, cried all through the night. Her older brother had done the same when he was small. Doctors had given the older child drops, but now the mother was ready for a different approach. In the Piepers' apartment, Eberling performed *Besprechen*, and went around touching everyone on the head. "What he murmured, I couldn't understand," Frau Pieper told police. Herr Pieper was asked to go outside and gather nettles, and these and a pair of open shears were laid on the Piepers' daughter's bed. All the keyholes in the house were stopped up with cotton wool and sewing needles. Eberling wrote out messages on slips of paper—they looked like Bible verses—and gave them to the children to pin to their clothing. He also gave the family a note to give to the pharmacist for some medicine. Finally, he told them to look at the children's featherbeds: were the feathers forming themselves into shapes, like wreaths or crowns?[12] These feather shapes could indicate the source and nature of an illness.[13] Eberling also gave the Piepers a piece of advice: a person asking to borrow something from them would be the one who had made their child sick. Eberling did not ask anything for his services, but Frau Pieper gave him five marks and five cigarettes.

As it turned out, Frau Pieper and her family were quite lucky. They did not find any shapes in the children's bed feathers that might have indicated that an evil force in the neighborhood had stealthily assailed their children and made them sick. The family unstopped their keyholes and did not pick up the prescription.[14] In general, while Eberling's patients found many of his procedures good and right, they also declined others as superstitions.[15] Still, people kept finding themselves getting somehow pulled into the drama around him: someone who was sick would meet with Eberling for treatment and soon stop greeting neighbors, or begin avoiding them altogether.[16]

When Eberling did find shapes in people's featherbeds, like nests or birds, these could be an important sign, he said, that one had enemies, people who harbored ill will against them. One woman, Frau Heesch, found three heart shapes in her family's bed feathers, one large and two small ones, which she described as "partially still sticky with blood." These, she was given to understand, represented "[her] heart and the hearts of [her] small children." Eberling told Frau Heesch to burn these hearts and asked whether she and her family had any enemies in the village. Yes, she said, and told the following story. Her father-in-law had been the mayor of the village and "also held other offices" in the Third Reich, until what she called the "downfall"— that is, the end of the Nazi dictatorship. People treated him very badly afterward, she said, and "we must view them as our enemies." She named Claus, the one who had become mayor after her father-in-law—the one who had gone by that day on his bicycle, and who Hans felt had been identified as "the evil force." After the war, it had been Claus, Frau Heesch told the police, who had made decisions about "the handovers." By this she seems to have meant that he had been in charge of redistributing property during denazification.

After Eberling's treatments, Frau Heesch and her children were tremendously better off and could sleep at night. People noticed how much better they seemed. "I am often asked," she said to police, "who was to blame for our sickness." She thought that Claus was to blame. Claus had filed his complaint with police against Eberling, she believed, because "he was plagued by a bad conscience, because he had wanted to destroy us."[17]

After the police took down many such statements—from Eberling, Frau Heesch, Hans and his wife, the Maassen family, the Piepers, and a number of others—they wrote a synopsis of the case. The village where these events transpired, in their view, was "prone to these kinds of intrigues." "Witch mania" had "always moved the feelings" of people there, they said. But that also made the police's investigations difficult. People "held back conspicuously" from discussing the whole affair, "as though they were afflicted by a certain fear." The police also noted that a recent newspaper article on the story had led people from outside the town to come looking for Eberling, hoping he could help them. Whether the arrival of these newcomers would produce additional complications was anyone's guess.[18]

The police thought it quite clear in any case that Eberling had broken the law—the lay healer ban. In the course of their investigations, they questioned everyone they interviewed about whether he had asked for payment: if he was treating the sick for money, as a professional, he had definitely broken the law. They also noted, though, that he tended to charge money only of those who could afford to pay. One of these people, as it turned out, was Frau Heesch, the mother who found the heart-shaped clumps of feathers with blood on them. Without further comment, the police inspector remarked in his report that her family were the "most financially powerful farmers in the village."[19] Under Nazi rule, the Heesch family had been significant, but not just financially: they had been in charge.

The police reports and files concerning Eberling's case sit today in the state archives in Schleswig, a small, sleepy city on a slender inlet of the western Baltic called the Schlei. The documents are circumspect concerning any relationship between this case and the "most recent past." They show no obvious evidence that history mattered much to how police and other officials viewed the case. In fact, if the police thought about history at all, it was only in terms of their perception that a timeless "superstition" had forever ruled the minds of locals. But then again, drawing out connections between past and present is not the police's job, but the historian's.

• • •

People accusing each other of being witches—as Eberling had tacitly accused Frau Maassen and Claus, the former mayor—was not an unknown phenomenon in modern German history. People had worried about it for decades. In 1908, a criminologist named Albert Hellwig published a book identifying witchcraft beliefs as a genre of what he called "criminal superstition." An anticlerical, Hellwig deemed "the dogmas of the church, especially the Catholic" responsible for cultivating witch beliefs.[20] But clerics themselves, including Protestant clerics, were concerned about witch beliefs among their parishioners, too. In the early 1930s, the Lutheran state church in Hamburg observed in its annual report, "Some people—old women—are called witches, even though they go to church sedulously. When people or livestock get sick, a witch banisher is hauled in from the country or a wise woman is called in to say some charms!" This was happening, the report continued, "within a few kilometers of cosmopolitan Hamburg."[21] A few years into the Nazi dictatorship, in 1935, Eduard Juhl, a Protestant pastor in Hamburg, called "superstition and magic" an "epidemic amongst the people," a pestilence, a poison, which had "not ebbed away in the new Germany" (by which he meant the Third Reich). For Juhl, this "dark flood" of superstition and magic was a product of "demonic seduction."[22]

But after World War II, especially in the 1950s, there was a clear spike in witchcraft accusations. They became an issue of enough concern that a minor scholarly field grew up to address them. Articles and books were written—by a PhD-credentialed criminologist and several clergy members, among others. Conference papers were presented, editorials written, and state governments issued directives to local health offices and police departments to gather information about the matter. Countless newspaper clippings from the day's popular periodicals told stories of bewitchings and fears of bewitchings. The publisher of a popular magic book was repeatedly taken to court to stop further distribution, because it was said that the book incited fears of witches. And in dozens of trials, the witches' accusers were taken to court on charges of slander, defamation, and violence, including assault and even murder. This news was reported not only in East and West Germany but abroad as well.[23]

A study published in 1959 showed that while the interwar period had witnessed eight "witchcraft trials," and the Third Reich eleven, the immediate postwar era—or, more precisely, the years between 1947 and 1956—saw seventy-seven of them.[24] Yet even this figure may underestimate the phenomenon's scope on two counts. First, official agencies and national and local press reported much higher numbers. In the mid-1950s, the German Medical Information Service reported that some seventy witch trials were held in Germany annually.[25] One newspaper claimed that in 1950 there had been sixteen such trials in the small city of Lüneburg alone.[26] Another paper reported that there had been "sixty-five modern witchcraft trials" in 1952, "mostly in northern Germany."[27] Yet another paper, the *Welt am Sonntag*, indicated that "in 1952–53 over 130 witchcraft trials had taken place in Germany."[28] Perhaps varying ways of constituting a "witch trial" lay at the root of these divergent numbers, and in any case, given the exaggerations of the postwar press in other instances, we should treat these estimates with some caution. It's also important to note, though, that the vast majority of witchcraft accusations never made it anywhere near a court. Being accused as a witch brought with it serious social repercussions. It was often enough to transform whole families into pariahs—the fate that befell the Maassens and made Frau Maassen so ill. People's businesses might fail; they lost community support and could no longer depend on their friendships and neighbors. So people often kept quiet, fearing worse trouble.

Compounding the phenomenon's relative invisibility for those who aimed to put a stop to it was the fact that those who feared witches never actually used the term "witch." Eberling, for example, spoke of an "evil force." Sometimes, people became known as witches through nonverbal communications or by simple inference. Frau Maassen just happened to be outside at night after Eberling said he sensed the "evil force" around Hans's house.[29] And when Frau Heesch named Claus as an enemy of her family, Eberling had nodded.[30] Two psychiatrists to whom the court later assigned the task of interviewing Eberling and assessing his mental capacity and legal responsibility were puzzled that he attributed to "evil people" everything that "since time immemorial" had been ascribed to witches.[31] What the psychiatrists failed to understand was that the two terms were synonymous; both indicated those with the desire and the supernatural ability to do harm. Bruno Gröning, of course, used the same language, speaking of "evil people" who conspired to make their neighbors ill or kept them from getting well, or those whose wickedness marked them as "slaves to Satan."

Witch trials were held in tiny localities, like Leck, near the Danish border, and Türkheim, far to the south. There were also trials in larger towns (Bremerhaven, Gifhorn, Celle, Hildesheim) and in big cities (Berlin, Hamburg, and Kiel). Some places, such as Vilshofen and Braunschweig, seem to have had only a single incident, while others— including Lüneburg, Hameln, and Uelzen—saw a recurring spate of them. The northern states of Schleswig-Holstein and Lower Saxony were notably overrepresented in the statistics.[32]

Scholars of witchcraft—contemporary and historical—tell us that it is a nearly universal phenomenon. A murder in 1920s Pennsylvania, to take just one example, was precipitated by a man's belief that his neighbor had put a hex on him.[33] In his global history of witch-hunting, Wolfgang Behringer writes that, in societies all around the world, "witchcraft is often a synonym for evil."[34] Beliefs that neighbors might secretly conspire to do harm to other neighbors (or to those neighbors' families or farms or livestock) could be found at more or less the same time as Eberling's case in France, Italy, England, Hungary, and Poland.[35]

Yet though witch beliefs have existed and do exist in many parts of the world, they can take quite different forms, and they often erupt in response to abrupt social change and unrest. What links them, scholars say, is their relationship to matters of intimacy and mistrust. Witchcraft "conjures up the danger of treacherous attacks from close by," anthropologist Peter Geschiere writes, and it warns that "seeds of destruction are hidden inside" human relationships. Fears of witches—and thus witchcraft accusations—are more likely to surface in moments of instability, insecurity, and malaise, moments very much like the one that followed World War II in Germany. They prevail in situations where dramatic change has caused the familiar suddenly to appear strange, and even ordinary occurrences—illness, bad luck, accidents, injuries—to gain graver meaning. A death or injury, coming on the heels of other setbacks, can be perceived as having

been not merely accidental but orchestrated by someone, or a conspiracy of someones, in secret, behind the scenes. To be sure, even in
times of heightened calamity, not every misfortune will be perceived
as resulting from witchcraft. But widespread mistrust may make it
more likely.[36]

In this sense, witchcraft fears can be seen as a cultural idiom of interpersonal and communal conflict, a way of seeing the world and inter-
preting what happens in it, a search for causes behind causes. Just as
the Azande asked what larger meaning might be behind a granary
collapsing in a particular moment, West Germans in the 1950s asked:
Who caused my child to become ill? Who is responsible for my hogs
dying, my cows not giving milk? Accusations of witchcraft were a
language and logic of laying blame when misfortune could not be
otherwise clarified.

The spate of witchcraft accusations in early West German history constitutes an almost entirely unremembered history. Only a
handful of specialists have written anything about it. Writing in the
mid-1960s, the folklorist Leopold Schmidt offered a single theory to
explain the era's uptick: the flow into the country of millions of German refugees who fled or were expelled from Eastern Europe had
created social tensions that resulted in accusations of supernatural
evildoing.[37] It is certainly true that there was a dramatic surge of refugees into Schleswig-Holstein, which absorbed a larger percentage relative to its indigenous population than any other federal state, in the
postwar years. Village life underwent massive structural changes.[38]
But most witchcraft cases clustered around the mid-1950s, almost a
decade after most refugees had been resettled. And Eberling's case—
possibly the only one for which significant documentation still exists—
involved people who had known each other for years. This suggests
that the 1950s witch scare may have had less to do with the presence
of strangers in settled communities than the strange and ambivalent
ways in which lingering mistrust and resentment got worked out at
society's grassroots after 1945.[39]

In the fifties, a genre of movies called *Heimat* films, or "homeland" films, depicted West Germany's rural landscapes as places of untouched beauty, timeless values, and sweet sentimentality. Picture books showcased half-timbered houses, wildflower-strewn Swabian hillsides, and medieval castles, conjuring up a world unchanged not only by fascism, war, and genocide, but by modern life altogether.[40] But something quite like the opposite of "untouched" and isolated was true of rural West Germany in the years after Nazism.

The region where the drama of Eberling and his clients unfolded is called Dithmarschen, and it lies between the North Sea and the Elbe River. Over centuries, land in Dithmarschen had been reclaimed—or, maybe more accurately, incrementally wrested—from the sea through the arduous labor of constructing dikes. Germans from this part of the country sometimes describe the stark beauty of the terrain as öde—a word that implies something monotonous, desolate, and solitary. Even now, Dithmarschen remains one of the more rural parts of an overwhelmingly urbanized country, a singular and sometimes uncanny landscape of tidal flats and heaths and bogs. But there is nothing isolated about this region, nor was there in the 1950s. It had long been fully integrated into the wider national, regional, and indeed global economy. It had also been a part of the political turmoil of the preceding decades. In the 1920s and early '30s, the western marsh plains and moorland had been the home of the militant, bomb-throwing, viciously antisemitic Rural People's Movement (Landvolkbewegung).[41] Later, this movement would be co-opted by the National Socialists, who gained a majority in the parliamentary elections in Schleswig-Holstein before any other state. Ultimately it had more Nazi Party members per capita than any other state in Germany, one in eighteen.[42] In some parts of Dithmarschen, more than 90 percent of property owners had been in the party.[43] The state with the most former party members was also the site of a significant postwar witch scare.

. . .

Eberling's biography, as revealed in interviews he gave to police and psychiatrists, was very much a twentieth-century German life, one that unfolded over some of the most turbulent years in German history and intersected with politics and war at every turn. The future *Hexenbanner*, or witch banisher, was born in Schleswig-Holstein in 1908, making him Bruno Gröning's close contemporary. His parents came originally from Pomerania and West Prussia. He would later say that they were very strict—they did not allow him "to go out for the first time" until he was nineteen and a half, and only then with his older sisters. Eberling's older brother became a postal official in Cologne; an artistically inclined older sister married a chamber musician.[44] Eberling attended school until he was fifteen, after which he followed his father into carpentry; he had a four-year apprenticeship as a furniture maker.[45] In 1928, having achieved journeyman status, he went to the Ruhr region, to Dortmund, a Westphalian city of steel mills and coal mines. He worked as a mines carpenter and also briefly in a furniture factory. In 1929 came the stock market crash and then the Great Depression. Eberling returned to Schleswig-Holstein. A few years later, in the Saarland, he took part in constructing the Siegfried Line, a military fortification extending from Switzerland to the Dutch border. By then, Eberling's father, supervising barracks construction on the North Sea island of Sylt, was able to bring his son back north to work again. From 1940 to 1945, Eberling worked on Luftwaffe construction sites. He was briefly a British prisoner of war. Finally, he returned to his hometown to work in his father's carpentry shop. He and his wife had six children.[46]

From the start, Eberling's career as a healer was a religious undertaking. Just before he finished school he started having prophetic dreams, which gave his life a new direction. On this issue, Eberling's family was split. His father, whom Eberling described as a socialist, "read scientific books, and after the First World War declared that there could not be a God." His secular point of view made him contemptuous of Eberling's healing practices. Eberling's mother, by contrast, was quite religious, and always had an understanding for her son's "efforts to heal sick people."[47]

During the Second World War, Eberling continued having visions.

Some foretold death in the war: "I saw soldiers running over the field, ships, fire falling from the sky, and the women hiding themselves. I saw how people were crushed, and the houses burned." Eberling also predicted that Germany "would lose the war, and . . . on a fifth of May it would be over." (The Allies formally accepted the German declaration of surrender on May 8, 1945.) Other visions predicted losses closer to home. In 1946, he saw an earthworm lying out, after a rain. He always picked up worms and put them back in the ground, so they did not dry up in the sun or get eaten by birds, but this time he didn't. Then, suddenly, he had a vision of his daughter in a coffin. Terrified, and overcome with a bad conscience, he ran back to where the worm was to put it in the ground. It was gone. Two days later, Eberling was called in from the fields because his daughter was sick. As soon as he got inside, he said: "she has diphtheria." He could smell it, he said; he had smelled it before. This time his healing talent and clairvoyance did not help. His daughter died a few days later.[48]

Eberling had begun learning about healing arts in Dortmund, in the late 1920s. He had rented a place to sleep from an old woman. A group of workers lived in her house, "four or five to a room." The woman offered him a book, containing "advice for healing charms," so he "would have the ability to help other people." This might have been a magic book, a grimoire, of which several popular titles were commercially available. Eberling rejected the woman's advice; he believed her to be a witch. He "only treated people with the help of God," not magic, he said. But Eberling did say he learned from watching the old woman secretly that people were especially vulnerable to devilry in their sleep or when they were in a weakened state. He also learned that the feathers in people's beds would form themselves into shapes, like birds or hearts. "If there are crown shapes in the bed, for example, that points to a stomach ailment." Mostly, Eberling said, he helped people who were weak in a *seelisch* sense—weak in their souls or minds.[49]

For a while, Eberling seems to have healed people without raising official ire—that is, until a few years into the Nazi dictatorship. He was arrested and detained, more than once, as an anti-Nazi, and labeled a Jehovah's Witness.[50] As pacifists, Jehovah's Witnesses were reviled by the Nazis and thrown into concentration camps. In 1936, Eberling was hauled into court and found guilty of deception (*Betrug*). In the extreme language characteristic of Nazi jurisprudence, the court urged "every member of the national community" to "work together toward exterminating" the kind of "questionable superstition" Eberling represented. He was sentenced to thirteen months in jail and deprived of his rights as a citizen for three years.[51]

Eberling's own account of the 1936 court case suggests how personal intrigues could intersect with political power at the local level in Nazi Germany. Eberling knew a married woman who was having an affair with an SA man, he explained: "he hated us." (A lot of local Nazis, Eberling said, despised his family, who had always been Social Democrats.) Eberling did not want to have anything to do with the woman, he said: she was having affairs with a number of men, including her own father-in-law. But he had helped her when her child was sick. This led to his arrest for fraud and an unnamed "crime against morality." Though the latter charge was dropped, Eberling was convicted and sentenced to jail for fraud. His lawyer told him to say in court that "there is no such thing" as witches, hoping the judge would go easier on him. Later, Eberling claimed, the people who conspired against him were repaid in kind. The woman went to jail for "black slaughtering"—illegally butchering animals during postwar food rationing—and her husband died. The guard at the prison got fifteen years for "homosexual activities." [52]

After the war, Eberling's father, whom Eberling described not only as a socialist but also, like himself, anti-Nazi, served as a local political representative (*Kreisabgeordneter*) and mayor, as well as an arbitrator. He also held several honorary offices and was involved in local denazification proceedings. Eberling, meanwhile, worked in his father's carpentry shop. In 1947 he sat for the exam that would have earned him the status of master carpenter, but failed part of the test. The examiners, he said, had been political enemies of his father.[53]

Yet Eberling's story is not a simple one about good and evil, about Nazi-era crimes and post-Nazi punishment. Nor is it a folk morality tale in which those who suffered under dictatorship found postwar redemption or got revenge. By his own account, Eberling had been persecuted and jailed under Nazi rule, and as an anti-Nazi, stripped of his rights as a citizen for plying his brand of spiritual medicine. The exam that might have helped him secure a better economic future was prejudicially misgraded. Yet Eberling had identified Claus, the first postwar mayor of their locale, to Frau Heesch, whose family had been prominent under the Nazis, as a person "ill-disposed toward" her.[54] Denazification records suggest that Claus's brother-in-law Adolf had indeed been a powerful local Nazi, a *Blockleiter*: a person whose job it was to supervise the neighborhood and motivate ideological conformity. There are no such records concerning Claus himself.[55]

Nor is it quite right to see Eberling as a man of purely pious intentions in the clutches of an authoritarian state and small-town stratagems. During their investigations, police talked to a man named Walter whom Eberling had treated.[56] The state had forcibly sterilized Walter in 1939 for being "slow-witted."[57] After using *Besprechen* on him, Eberling told Walter he would be fertile again. About eight weeks later, his wife, Käthe, stopped having her period. The charm seemed to have worked. But later, Käthe claimed that it was Eberling who got her pregnant. She had been visiting her parents; Eberling had also been present. The two had taken the same route home. Suddenly, she said, Eberling grabbed her and "had sexual intercourse" with her "standing up against the wall of the savings and loan." The sex was consensual, Käthe said; she had not been threatened. But she wondered if Eberling's intention had been to get her pregnant to create the impression that he had cured Walter's infertility.[58]

Nothing about this story of small-town magic and fears of secret malevolence in Dithmarschen is unequivocal. Though voluminous, the evidence can't answer all the questions one wants to pose, and what is available can be interpreted in more than one way. But that's how witchcraft works. By its nature, it is ambiguous, and driven by context, as Jeanne Favret Saada, a psychoanalyst and ethnographer who has written elegant studies of witch beliefs in northern France, explains. Who is evil, and who is performing acts to counteract evil, in a given set of circumstances? Who is healing, and who is bringing sickness? In times of heightened fear and mistrust, one cannot necessarily know who is an ally and who an enemy.[59] And it is that very ambiguity that allows accusations to catch fire, and for a "belief in witches" to become a full-scale witch scare.

Eberling's story also hints at the intimate and ambiguous ways that local power worked in people's lives before and after 1945. In a state like Schleswig-Holstein, with so many former Nazi Party members around, it is perhaps unsurprising that there was little popular or official appetite there for opprobrium or condemnation of Nazis after the war. According to one account, not a single person in the entire state was found to belong to the categories of "offender" or "major offender," and more than 99 percent of those processed through denazification courts were "fully rehabilitated or given small fines." In general, officials in Schleswig-Holstein behaved in a "bureaucratic and miserly way" toward victims of the Nazis, while offering former Nazi elites avenues toward social reintegration.[60]

In the intimacy of communities, in local settings, those who got power in 1933 and then lost it in 1945 lived side by side with others who had lost power in 1933 and then regained it after the war. Many villagers in the 1950s would have remembered how the Nazi new order had settled in when the dictatorship took hold—the way property, power, and position had been seized by the new masters and handed out among friends and allies. After 1945, those same friends and allies sometimes lost their ill-gotten gains. It was denazification committees, formed of politically "unburdened" community members—often Social Democrats like Eberling's father—who took charge.[61] To these committees fell the task of interviewing fellow community members and examining their documents and records and handing down verdicts, often on people they knew. Those found to be "compromised" by past associations were not considered when new plots of land were handed out, or had to wait in line behind those deemed politically untainted.[62]

In Schleswig-Holstein, former Nazis were almost never stripped of their property after 1945.[63] But this sometimes happened, as it seems to have for Frau Heesch's family. She said that Claus had been in charge of the "handovers." Her conviction that the former mayor was a witch responsible for her child's sickness shows one form that animosities and unresolved grievances could take in these communities where witchcraft beliefs served to explain the causes behind causes.

In another Schleswig-Holstein community, Social Democrats running a local denazification committee tried to levy a fine against former Nazis who had managed to skirt any sanction.[64] Their attempt went nowhere, but the very fact that it was made is significant. In a small community where there was no place to hide, the impact of even failed gestures at punishment—let alone actual judgments and more powerful reversals of fortune—may have been remembered as a special, intimate affront. How capricious fate might have seemed to them, the winners and the losers alike, in those days.

A pointed example occurs in Hans Fallada's 1947 novel *Nightmare in Berlin*. The novel recounts the story of Dr. Doll, living in a small town in the Russian zone just after the war. Doll is generally disliked. He is an outsider from Berlin and not a Nazi, and as such is the subject of a great deal of spiteful gossip. Red Army officials set him up as mayor essentially for those reasons. He has no connections and no loyalty to anyone in the town, where "former" Nazis now falsely grovel and scrape before the occupiers. It becomes Doll's job—as it became Eberling's father's—"to classify these Nazis as harmless fellow travelers or guilty activists, to root them out from the bolt holes where they had been quick to hide themselves, to kick them out of the cushy jobs they had cleverly and shamelessly landed for themselves . . . to strip them of the possessions they had acquired by fraud, theft, or blackmail, to confiscate the stocks of food they had been hoarding, to quarter the homeless in their big houses."[65]

However equivocal, Eberling's story hints at how Nazism's pernicious legacies—the shame of sterilization, destroyed reputations, thwarted ambitions, retributions and recriminations—continued to churn through everyday interactions in communities and individual lives. The most commonplace image used to evoke postwar Germany is the rubble that littered the cities. But there was a kind of rubble plaguing the smaller towns and the countryside, too: the rubble of social relations. It could not be measured in cubic tons, but maybe it was heavier, because it could not be picked up and carted away. The unprocessed past—not just the Nazi past, but also the period of denazification—left behind a climate of bitterness and insecurity in places where witchcraft was an available logic of social relations, a way of working out who was whose ally in a shifting landscape of loyalties.[66] In this sense, Eberling's story might be Schleswig-Holstein's postwar struggles in microcosm, framed as a battle between the godless and the righteous, "evil people" and the innocent. Given the terms of debate, it was probably hard not to choose a side.[67]

In communities like the ones where Eberling worked as a healer, almost everyone might have known something that someone else did not want them to know, might have received goods they were not due, might have kept property that was not rightfully theirs. We can only imagine how much distrust this sowed. Some had aligned themselves willingly with outsiders—the British occupation—to help bring down other members of the community. No one would have soon forgotten that. And, as an idiom of social conflict and suspicion, witchcraft was part of a wider culture of denunciation—such as reporting one's neighbors to the authorities for all sorts of transgressions, a practice that, as noted earlier, outlived the Third Reich.

In other words, the trouble among people in Dithmarschen in the early 1950s could be said to have started when Eberling helped Hans and Erna's sick baby. Or it could be said to have started much earlier—in 1933.

• • •

When Eberling's case came to trial in late 1954, it was a media event. Reporters from dozens of newspapers attended.[68] The Hexenbanner was charged with fraud in connection with violating the law on lay healing, defamation, and negligent bodily harm.[69] Whether or not they could prosecute him for it, state's attorneys said, he had set "families who had been friendly up to now" against one another. He had sown disharmony, and practically caused Frau Maassen to have a nervous breakdown.[70] The proceedings were held in the dancehall of a local inn. The location helped accommodate spectators, though holding court in a tavern made certain improvisations necessary. A table re-purposed as a judge's bench had as its backdrop a curtain featuring elves and angels playing musical instruments. Onlookers brought candy and sandwiches for the occasion, packing the courtroom for eight hours, and listening as some twenty different witnesses took the stand.[71]

As the proceedings commenced, letters trickled in from surrounding towns, addressed to the court, attesting to the significance of these matters for members of the local community. One man wrote: "It's true that there are evil influences from the other world at work on people in this world." The solution was redemption and forgiveness: the people in the village needed "to see the good, the just, the true and the peaceful and not the evil . . . in their neighbors." To blame for the witchcraft in the village? "The villagers themselves!"[72] Another man wrote several lengthy longhand letters in which he suggested, among many other things, a relationship between the accused and "the well-known Gröning."[73] A third man—who said he'd had "unusual qualities" since birth—wanted to relate a vision he'd had, of Eberling standing in court and raising his finger to heaven, "in the name of the Father, the Son, and the Holy Spirit." "I am innocent of all charges," Eberling said in the man's vision. And at the end, everyone in the room rose and sang a hymn together, "Now Thank We All Our God."[74]

As important as many locals perceived the case to be, the proceedings in the dancehall courtroom ended abruptly when the defense unexpectedly called for an adjournment.[75] A few years earlier, it seems, before the trouble with Hans and his family began, Eberling had seen a doctor for a work-related accident and injury.[76] Had it possibly damaged his brain? Eberling's lawyer requested that his client's mental state be assessed, to see whether he could be held responsible for his actions under German criminal law.[77]

It was a chilly winter day in early 1955 when Eberling walked into the examination room at the University of Kiel's Psychiatric and Nerve Clinic, looking "assured and unselfconscious." He made a "friendly, confident" impression on Professor Dr. Gustav Störring, director of the clinic, and a Dr. Völkel, who would together later write a report about him for the court.[78] For an entire month, from January to February 1955, Eberling would reside at the clinic and submit to various examinations under a variety of conditions: sometimes with Drs. Störring and Völkel alone, sometimes with a stenographer present. On at least one occasion, he seems to have been examined in a lecture hall by a larger group that included doctors from Kiel's Institute for Forensic Medicine.[79]

Doctors sought information about not only Eberling's physical and neurological health, but also his mental fitness and intellectual abilities. They quizzed him to determine his "base of knowledge"—how many tropical fruits could he name? Who was Friedrich the Great? They tested his ability to think abstractly: He was given a list of items and asked to identify their relationship. "What are roses, tulips and carnations?" "Peas, beans, lentils?" Or he was given lists of words and asked to put them in a sentence: "mother, bouquet, child, colorful, picked." He was shown and asked questions about "Binet pictures"—cards from the Binet-Simon intelligence test.[80]

Doctors found Eberling had command of book learning—in math, geography, natural science, and history—in keeping with his "education and origins." He also had an active imagination. When asked to order random words into a sentence, his thought processes were "largely determined," the doctors asserted, "by figurative associations unconnected to the words given." Eberling had a tendency toward "confabulation." He possessed quite a vivid memory—"an above-average ability to remember in graphic terms." A memory like Eberling's, Dr. Störring remarked, was often seen among the artistically gifted. Physically speaking, Eberling was a "leptosomatic constitutional type," which, according to the then-current theory of somatotype, meant he was inclined to be anxious and introverted. Neurologically doctors found him in order. His hands, feet, and armpits seemed to sweat a bit. His hands also shook lightly when he stretched out his arms. But an electroencephalogram found nothing unusual.[81]

In terms of Eberling's "general worldview" and "religious perspective," the most central aspect seems to have been the idea of two warring forces in the world: God and the Devil. Of them, Eberling said, "God is the most powerful." Some people served both these forces—"for example, when they do *Besprechen*," a practice that could be used for good or ill. "God tests people, to see if evil drags them down or if they are steadfast."[82] Like Gröning, Eberling saw God and the Devil as personified beings, dueling cosmic personalities.[83] The Devil could come in through a keyhole, Eberling said. Also like Gröning, Eberling said he could *see* when people were evil. They were uneasy and could not rest at night, and got up to mischief. Whole families, whole villages could be evil; evil people made up a kind of army of the Devil on earth. Though "we could have heaven on earth if we could all just get along," that seemed unlikely to Eberling. "If Jesus came back, people would crucify him again."[84]

After a month of interviews, questions, tests, exercises, and stories, Störring and Völkel wrote their report. They found Eberling's personality complicated. He was "polite" but eager to dominate conversation, despite having, in their view, "no clear train of thought." He had, the doctors wrote, an "astonishing lack of critical faculties."[85]

Just as had been true of the police who first investigated Eberling at the Maassens' instigation, doctors placed no apparent weight on what Eberling said about his experiences under National Socialism or after. Relying on their medical and psychiatric tools, they provided information of a kind, but in a generalizing professional jargon. Eberling could have been almost any man, anywhere, anytime. He had a need to feel important in order to mask feelings of inferiority, doctors said; to seek the causes of any failure or accident in the external world, rather than within himself. The doctors' opinions often had quite a bit to do with their own ostensibly superior cultural values. They focused on Eberling's alterity: he was in the grip of "superstition" and came from a "primitive" place. He was "an anachronism," someone who had somehow remained fixed in an "earlier mental-spiritual stage of humanity." Like a child, they continued, Eberling "projected onto the outside world an uncanny and mysterious feeling and the anxiety connected to sickness, death, and natural catastrophes."[86]

These diagnoses betrayed considerable class and status prejudice to be sure. But more significantly, they lent no credence to—nor sought any meaning in—Eberling's intimations that political and social resentment might have been part of the local troubles in which he had been involved.[87] They never inquired into how his career might have been shortchanged by former Nazis who were enemies of him and his father as Social Democrats. They never asked whether these enmities were connected to his arrest in 1936 for plying his healing trade. Given the circumspection about the Third Reich in the 1950s, the avoidance of this line of questioning is in one sense unsurprising, and psychiatry has generally purported to be a universal science. But the episode also fits a larger postwar pattern: playing down specific nasty facts in favor of broader, less harmful generalizations.

As it happened, one of the doctors who examined Eberling—Dr. Störring—had just published a book. In it, he discussed the case of a schizophrenic man, Paul D. In the mid-1930s, Paul D. started having ideas that got him into trouble. He was being followed by the SA, he said, and by Hitler—whom he identified as "the Devil" and "the enemy." Hitler, according to Paul D., had it in for him. "Die, Hitler!" Paul D. had been heard to shout in and around his house. In 1936, Paul D. was sterilized by the state. Three years later, he was diagnosed with "dementia paranoides"—dementia with paranoid features.[88]

According to Störring—and this was really his reason for discussing the case in his book at all—as long as one restricted conversations with Paul D. to "purely factual things and posed themes for discussion with strict instructions to stay on topic," Paul's "schizophrenic delusions . . . were mostly not noticeable." For example, when asked to talk about banalities like the seasons or forms of transportation, Paul talked about them. When asked to make a sentence out of a group of words (cat, mouse, cellar)—as Störring and Völkel had also asked Eberling to do—Paul did: "A cat went in the cellar to follow a mouse." Störring liked Paul's D.'s case because it helped him advance a theory about how schizophrenic patients thought. He believed Paul's thinking only showed "defects" when he was asked to "take a personal stand" about something. Questions about plain facts within his sphere of knowledge did not "impair" Paul's thinking.[89]

Whatever the scientific value of Störring's argument for the study of schizophrenia may have been, what seems striking now is the diagnosis of a man as paranoid after he had been forcibly sterilized in the Third Reich. Even if this man was, strictly speaking, delusional about Hitler following him around, he was also sterilized by an overwhelming power he likely had no means of resisting, a power Hitler represented and embodied. In other words, context matters. Psychiatric diagnoses are made in time and space; they are influenced by changing cultural and political conditions, ideas about the self, changing social norms, what we take to be natural, or to be real. Behavior has social meanings, and these meanings change. Störring himself seemed to concede something similar. "I am convinced," he wrote, that many "misunderstandings about . . . existential questions" emerge when people don't pay enough attention to complex differences in "social, social-ethical, religious, and aesthetic values."[90]

Even as his doctors avoided commenting on the more specific, historically conditioned aspects of Eberling's biography, they were also convinced of the Hexenbanner's utter sincerity. Like Gröning, he said that he could only heal with God's help, and sometimes felt that his ability to heal was a burden. Still, Eberling said, "God has always helped through me." He believed "fanatically in the superstitious world he inhabits," his doctors wrote, one in which evil flourished with tangible effects on people's lives. He also believed that it was the solemn duty of those who became aware of evil's presence to extirpate it. A professor from the Institute for Forensic Medicine asked Eberling what he thought of a man who had beaten to death a neighbor whom he believed to be a witch exercising influence over his mother. Eberling responded that punishing the man would not be justified. "He defended this conviction" even when a Professor H. from the institute tried to unsettle him, by "remarking emphatically, 'but that is just plain murder.'"[91]

Störring and Völkel expressed surprise that "in our century and in a country at our cultural standard," a person might appear "suggesting that health and wellbeing, sickness and death, accidents and catastrophes occur not in accordance with natural laws but are instead determined by demonic, irrational forces, whose bearers are people in the service of the Devil." Still, in their view, "there was no evidence of any real mental illness in the sense of a psychosis," nor was there any "organic illness of the central nervous system." The doctors found no evidence of brain trauma or any mental damage, or any change in personality resulting from Eberling's earlier injury.[92]

Thus, his doctors concluded, Eberling was childlike, "undisciplined and autistic" in his thinking, and suffering from weak critical faculties. But otherwise—perhaps a little like Paul D. when talking about "purely factual things"—he was quite normal. At least, normal for the place where he grew up. Again the doctors generalized, casting Eberling's world as a timeless place that history and change never penetrated. In Eberling's region, "superstition still had deep roots in people's consciousness," the doctors averred, and one could easily get an "unintentional education" in superstitious thinking from all the "witch and fairy stories" one heard from early childhood on. Then again, they speculated, maybe Eberling was simply in an unconscious state of rebellion against his freethinker father. In any case, he was not mentally ill, though he was "in the psychiatric sense" a psychopath: a person whose "mental makeup fell outside the normal range."[93] His trial could resume.

. . .

Eberling went back to court in May 1955, this time in another unlikely location, a local tavern called Jochen's Inn. On Saturday nights, reporters explained, youths packed the ballroom to "dance boogie-woogie." On this occasion, too, the extemporized courtroom was filled to capacity. Film cameras and Northwest German Radio set up to record the proceedings.[94] Three entire tables were reserved just for the press, who listened as scores of witnesses described their dealings with Eberling.[95] Journalists seem to have found the affair by turns baffling, colorful, and sordid; they tended to contrast "the Middle Ages" (supposedly represented by Eberling and his cohort) with "the atomic age." Thus a typical headline conjured an image of Satan arriving at court in an oxcart, against a backdrop of sleek, modern, "blindingly chromed" sedans lining the streets outside the inn.[96] One witness, whom newspapers referred to as Grandma C., produced a bottle of a stinky red powder—"real German witch powder," no doubt devil's dung. She'd bought it from a pharmacist for treating people who were "sick, and not normal sick."[97]

Not all the drama in the court over those two days was verbalized. Mistrust seemed to permeate the assembly. When a certain witness went to take a place on the bench where witnesses customarily sat, those already seated there threw their hands up "in a defensive gesture" and stopped her. Perplexed, she went off in search of another place. Finally, someone else offered her a seat.[98]

Those attending the trial heard details of village gossip, misdemeanors, and intrigues. Some of it may have been petty, but it was hardly victimless. Frau Maassen, as we know, suffered crippling anxiety from her ostracization. She had been unable to attend Eberling's trial earlier because her doctor feared she would fall back into the same severe depression that had caused her to lose ten pounds since she learned of the accusations against her.[99]

There was more. The court believed a man who accused the Hexenbanner Eberling of having threatened to "break every bone in his body" if the man talked to police investigators. Eberling may also have intentionally given people the impression that he had some kind of medical credentials. And there was little reason to doubt that Käthe's story about sex up against the savings and loan bank was true, because "a comparable allegation" had been made at the time of his 1936 trial.[100]

Still, it is difficult to know who was telling the truth about Eberling, or whose truth they were telling. Many of the people who testified were almost certainly dissembling. Eberling would claim again and again never to have mentioned witches, and he was probably being honest about that. No one admitted in court to believing in witches per se, but many involved in the affair spoke of "the evil power." When Eberling said the phrase, everyone knew he was talking about witches.

Eberling's lawyer, Kremendahl, used this tendency not to want to speak directly of witches to his client's advantage. Eberling merely performed "hocus pocus," he said—empty rituals that had nothing to do with healing in a sense that might contravene the lay healer law. Eberling, his attorney contended, was merely a "child of his region," a place where "witch beliefs were still at home." All his client had done was to "sell superstition" to people who, like himself, were superstitious. He had not, therefore, cheated anyone.[101]

The court did not find this defense legally sustainable. Eberling "sought with his occupation," as the court put it, to alleviate suffering. He had done so without a license, and if not always for monetary remuneration, then for some form of commercial gain (if only cigarettes and jars of sausages). He had not demanded payment, but had taken anything offered to him. Nor was fraud an untenable charge, the court held. The services he offered—to shield his patients from evil—were "objectively impossible." What Eberling himself believed made no difference. But what of the fact—a point raised by Eberling's lawyer—that no one whom he treated felt cheated? No matter. "Injury," the court declaimed, "is what can be measured by a general standard of injury."[102] The logic was circular, perhaps, but there it was.

There were a couple of specific instances in which, the court held, fraud had not been proved: those in which Eberling's clients had *not* believed in his methods. If it could not be shown that he had "provoked falsehood," then there was no fraud. In other words, his clients' thinking that Eberling's methods were bogus was evidence that he had *not* committed fraud in those cases. But he was found guilty of other instances of fraud, of violating the lay healer ban, and of harming Frau Maassen. Maybe he had not said she was a witch, the court ruled, but in a region where "a long-standing, traditional belief in witches" obtained, no one had to say "witch" or "witch master" to mean it. If Eberling referred to "the evil power," or said that someone's stall "needed smoking out," he was speaking in code about something dangerous that could not or should not be said aloud. Everyone knew he meant that a witch was afoot. Eberling had caused Frau Maassen to become ill, and he was therefore guilty of negligent bodily harm. He had "agitated an entire region and disturbed village social life." He was sentenced to a year in jail.[103]

Again letters flowed into the court from concerned citizens. One woman wrote that she "would not be a Christian if she remained silent and left" Eberling "to march blindly into hell" by accusing people of witchcraft. She urged him to "take up the Bible!"[104] But others seemed to see that more temporal issues, in some constellation, might be at stake. Eberling's former neighbor, a man named Ehrenberg, wrote to the judge to support his friend, who had endured many trials and neglected his own work to help others. Unlike so many people, said Ehrenberg, Eberling had not genuflected to the "Nazi power" or altered his "social attitudes" in the face of it, nor had he used "his own power to the detriment of 'former Nazis' after the collapse."[105] Ehrenberg presumably placed the term "former Nazis" in scare quotes to make sure that whoever read his letter would know—as everyone no doubt did—that many were only technically "former." Eberling had been taken down by the Nazis, wrote his defender, but he had not used his talents or abilities to come back at them.[106] And now, after all he'd been through, Ehrenburg suggested, the court was persecuting him. The Nazi power had come and gone, but not much had changed.

. . .

Ultimately, Eberling's case went up to the highest criminal court in West Germany, the Bundesgerichtshof. After his client's conviction, Eberling's lawyer had quickly filed an appeal on various grounds. Eberling could not have violated the lay healer law, Kremendahl argued, since his methods "stood outside the standards of any medical science." The law on lay practitioners had not been intended to apply to *Heilapostel*, or "pure faith healers," who sought to counteract "bad forces, or however one wants to name such phenomena, through prayer, *Besprechen*, and other similar procedures." The conviction for fraud was also legally unjustified, since that would require the court to have proved that the "promise of healing" among those who went to Eberling for treatment was any different from the expectations people normally had when they sought the "kind of magical treatment" his client provided. The German Criminal Code defined fraud as being perpetrated when "the property of another is damaged through the presentation of falsehood or through the distortion or suppression of true facts, thus awakening or supporting error." The Schleswig-Holstein court had claimed that because Eberling had already been convicted of fraud in 1936, he should have known that his activities fell into that category. Yet the court itself quoted Eberling's doctors as saying that he had a "fanatical" belief in his methods.[107]

The Bundesgerichtshof heard Eberling's appeal in fall 1955 and overturned his conviction. They agreed that procedural errors had been made in his trial. Fraud had not been proven. Eberling would have to have known that "his methods were useless," yet the state's lawyers suggested precisely the opposite was true. The high court did, however, find Eberling guilty of violating the lay practitioner law.[108] His case went back to the district court in Schleswig-Holstein in April 1956. Eberling was convicted of violating the lay healer law and of one count of defamation; he was sentenced to four months in jail and a fine of four hundred marks.[109] Despite having "seen the world," the court declared, Eberling "had stayed stuck" in the "medieval beliefs" of his home region.[110] This verdict and judgment did little to harm his local reputation. In fact, he now became something of a "little Gröning." Cars and whole buses, "often with Danish license plates," came calling at his house, bringing people seeking the Hexenbanner's expertise.[111]

The court and the psychiatrists who interviewed Eberling had both puzzled over the fact that he did not use (or claimed not to use) the word "witch."[112] But as Eberling and his lawyer knew, one did not lightly use loaded language. Under National Socialism, a simple word to the right person suggesting that someone's neighbor listened to the wrong radio program or told the wrong joke in a bar the night before could get that neighbor sent away, or worse. In court in 1956, Eberling said he had denied believing in witchcraft at his 1936 trial not because he thought the court would go easier on him, but because he feared that his unorthodox views might be taken as a sign of mental illness. And that could easily have led, as it did in Paul D.'s case, to his sterilization. The district court that convicted Eberling in 1956 concurred that this was a distinct possibility. Eberling's assertion, the court concluded, "stood to reason."[113]

KRUSE'S CRUSADE

When they thought about mounting witch accusations in the 1950s, doctors, the courts, and the press mostly dismissed them as examples of rural primitivity and a lack of enlightenment. As *Der Spiegel* loftily stated in 1951, rural people's isolation—in the country's mountains, heathlands, and moors—made them susceptible to "con artists" and "inbreeding."[1] Members of the public agreed: witch fears represented a "great nadir of culture," as a man opined in a letter to authorities in Lower Saxony in 1955.[2] Other observers saw witch fears as little more than colorful folkloric relics—harmless because timeless, "traditional," and confined, they imagined, to places they did not care to think about much.

As this book suggests, by contrast, the uptick in witchcraft accusations cannot be ascribed to a supposedly "timeless" superstition. Instead, it should be considered as resulting from a specific set of post-1945 social conditions: potent animosities left over from the Nazi era that lingered into the 1950s, especially in small, face-to-face communities. In such places, witchcraft acted as a language of social conflict.

Now, that is a historical perspective, gained with a distance of many decades and a good deal of archival and secondary research. It would not have been at all obvious to those living through that time. Still, at least one man, a native of the same region as Eberling, did see the increase in witchcraft accusations as a social problem linked to the past. In fact, he regarded witchcraft accusations as *the* social issue of his lifetime. That man's name was Johann Kruse, and he was a retired schoolteacher. From his perspective, what was most important and most frightening about the sudden increase in witch accusations was the way they reverberated with earlier "witch hunts"—that is, with the scapegoating of Jews that had culminated in the Holocaust. Throughout the 1950s and '60s, he committed himself to vigorous activism on behalf of those charged with being witches, and the unspoken subtext of all his work was the Holocaust.

Given the era's evasive and uneasy silence concerning the Nazi past and the Nazi genocide above all, that made Kruse an outlier. He was also a tenacious, if unlikely, protagonist. He had a way of popping up almost anywhere that witchcraft accusations surfaced. He was in the courtroom at the first nationally publicized "witch trial," in April 1951.[3] He advised Claus (the former mayor who had been accused by Eberling) to file a complaint against the Hexenbanner, whom Kruse had already known about since Eberling's trouble with the law in the 1930s.[4] Kruse loudly and publicly expressed his disgust after the federal high court overturned Eberling's conviction, proclaiming the decision "disconnected from local realities" and calling for Eberling to be punished "severely" for his misdeeds.[5] (Eberling's response to Kruse in the press is worth mentioning: "those who wanted to drive him out into the open and hunt him down" might more usefully muster their energies against "those who contrive and build weapons to kill whole groups of people." The "really dangerous superstition," Eberling said, was that the spread of atomic weapons could be "regarded as normal and irreversible.")[6] Kruse knew the accusers and the accused, made himself available to the press to explain what he knew about individual cases and the phenomenon of witch accusations more generally, and freely offered his opinions about it all to anyone who would listen. So renowned did he become as a bearer of special knowledge about witchcraft matters that some people interpreted his zeal as evidence that he himself must be an especially good sorcerer.[7]

Over the course of the 1950s, Kruse became the go-to expert on witchcraft beliefs and the trials that sometimes followed the accusations. He wrote so many letters to government officials that they knew him by name. Eventually, his efforts led lawmakers and police to hold meetings to discuss popular fears of witches based on evidence Kruse provided. His name was in the headlines, and his research was discussed on West German radio and quoted by "anti-superstition" activists in both East and West Germany. He gave lectures hither and yon, was mentioned in American newspapers, shared information with an Amsterdam professor working in the field of mass psychology, and was cited by a Danish folklorist at an international ethnography congress in Moscow.

From Kruse's perspective, while the wave of witchcraft fears that crashed over West Germany in the early- to mid-1950s did represent an eruption of irrationalism, that was not their greatest threat. Far more ominous was the way such fears inspired a search for enemies— the way they made outsiders out of community members, and then encouraged the rest of the community to train a suspicious gaze on these "others," now regarded as the cause of their various misfortunes. In this, he believed, the witchcraft fears bore clear similarities to the scapegoating and persecution of Jews in Nazi Germany. Yet so powerful were the taboos surrounding talking about that all-too-recent history in the 1950s that Kruse would only address those similarities tangentially or by proxy.

As a result, and despite the attention he garnered, the public and relevant authorities remained largely impervious to the notion of any underlying social danger in witchcraft fears—they could and did chalk

them up, however vaguely, to village intrigues and "age-old" superstition. Some officials claimed that Kruse (along with the press) exaggerated the problem. Others said they found the matter too foreign,
too far outside their ken to make much sense of. There is an irony
in this, of course, given how very recently Germans across every part
of the country—not just in supposedly "unenlightened" and remote
villages, but in every urban center and town—had been willing to
ascribe to their Jewish neighbors just about any evil under the sun.
Then again, turning away in reticence and feigned incomprehension
might have been precisely the point.

• • •

Johann Kruse was born in 1889, an era of extraordinary change in
largely agricultural Dithmarschen, the region of his (and Eberling's)
birth. A revolution in farming had come in the form of fertilizers and
new forms of machinery and livestock breeding techniques.[8] Canals
and railroads began to connect the region ever more densely to the
world outside. As it drew in the workers who built the canals, bridges,
and railroads, Dithmarschen also became more urbanized. These transformations spoke to Kruse. He became fascinated by working-class
politics from a young age and would later join the Social Democratic
Party. He developed a strong orientation toward social justice, and a
desire, from his youth, to help the oppressed and the misunderstood.
In the 1920s he even published an agitprop novel, *The Shame of Our
Times*, which dealt with the exploitation of workers on Germany's
North Sea dike-building projects.

Though he continued to be affiliated with his local Lutheran church
well into the 1920s, Kruse was also much influenced by freethinking—
especially the monistic philosophy of Ernst Haeckel, the great biolo-
gist who helped promote Darwin's ideas in Germany. Monism, which
posits the unity of all things in the universe, served almost as an
ersatz religion among many freethinkers in early twentieth-century
Germany. After training as a teacher and doing some traveling, Kruse
fought in World War I—an experience that turned him into a lifelong

pacifist. The revolution that ended the war in 1918 made him a fully convinced supporter of the new Weimar Republic. After the war, he had some unpleasant run-ins with a local pastor whom Kruse perceived to be more interested in nationalist agitation than in preaching Christian charity. This conflict prompted him to leave the church in 1926. He went to live in industrial Altona, near Hamburg, historically one of the most tolerant and freethinking places in all of Germany.[9]

If Kruse was motivated throughout much of his life by the tenets of antimilitarism, a mild socialist internationalism, and scientific enlightenment, some people would nonetheless accuse him of having a tendency toward paranoia. The potential sources of this trait are not hard to imagine, given the times in which Kruse lived. He saw some of the twentieth century's worst, close-up: war, defeat, economic dislocation, and fascist terror. He watched the workers and farmers of his region go from being socialists in 1919 to becoming some of the earliest and most passionate Nazis. He watched the shadows descend as the red, black, and gold flags of Social Democracy that once fluttered in Altona windows turned communist red and then Nazi black, and the clergy enthusiastically embraced fascism. He saw his brother and his son locked up by the Gestapo, mostly for refusing to look the other way about local party machinations. On one occasion, for instance, his brother had opposed a party headman enriching himself by appropriating communal land.[10]

Kruse once described the behavior that accompanied the Nazis' seizure of power. "All of a sudden, overnight," he wrote, "on our block like all over Germany, arrogance, conceit, and stupidity spread out in all directions. Perfidy and malice ruled and anyone who didn't want to get in line became the subject of infamous intrigues and more or less open threats." Under Nazi rule, Kruse found himself transferred again and again from school to school because he showed too little zeal for the NSDAP and its organizations, like the Hitler Youth.[11] In the Third Reich, "paranoia" might just have been another word for good common sense.

But maybe the origins of Kruse's unease went back even further.

When he was a child, a laborer's wife had paid a visit, in great distress, to Kruse's mother. It seems the woman's neighbors had accused her of being a witch.[12] This experience stayed with Kruse a long time. Especially after World War I, heightened antisemitism began poisoning social life—in Schleswig-Holstein, with its tiny Jewish population, even more vociferously than in other regions.[13] Kruse came to believe that popular terrors about witches and antisemitism were linked. In 1923, long before the Nazis represented anything more than the most radical-right fringe of German political life, Kruse wrote: "If a farm's livestock gets sick or dies, or the children in a family don't turn out well, or a farmer doesn't succeed in business, he won't look long for the . . . causes of his misfortune, because then he would have to confront the uncomfortable knowledge of his own ineptitude and negligence. And to avoid such thoughts . . . it is . . . pretty easy . . . to suspect someone, out of jealousy or desire for revenge, of having used witchcraft to cause his bad luck." In the '20s, Kruse saw his fellow citizens increasingly "pushing blame off onto someone else." It was related, he was sure, to what he called *Judenhetze*, or "Jew-baiting."[14] Kruse identified this problem and watched it take shape long before the first boycott against Jews in Germany was ever imagined, let alone the first concentration camps built or roundups and deportations organized. What he realized already in the 1920s was a powerful pattern coming into view: looking for someone to blame when something went wrong. When people asked *why me?*, all too often the answer was *because of them*.

And so much had gone wrong in Germany in those post–World War I years: the deaths of millions of young men; the aftershocks of a lost war and a collapsed empire; frequent political instability; hyperinflation that erased lifetimes of careful saving, followed, only a few years later, by total economic collapse. Much more clearly than many of his fellow citizens, Kruse understood the sinister desire to blame someone for misfortune, rather than try to understand its true sources. Those who fear witchcraft fear hidden evil, murky conspiracies, and demonic alliances. Antisemites had similarly insisted that Jews were secretly behind every problem, every trauma, every loss. They believed Jews had influence out of all proportion to their relative numbers in German society, derived from an international plot working remorselessly, in stealth, to control the levers of global power. Not only did witchcraft accusations and "Jew-baiting" work the same way, by casting blame on "others"—who might appear outwardly innocuous, but were surreptitiously in league with nefarious, world-dominating forces—but the two beliefs also had structural similarities.

. . .

Nevertheless, after the Third Reich, after Nazi terror and the vilification and persecution of Jews that culminated in the Holocaust, Kruse dropped that line of argument. Over the course of the 1950s and into the late 1960s, he corresponded with cultural, interior, justice, and social ministers in several German states, commented in the press, and even published a book on witch beliefs. In none of these documents did he draw any explicit parallel between witch accusations in Germany and the recent persecution of Jews. He followed, in other words, a pattern that held true in the Federal Republic generally. He forswore dangerous words. He abandoned any references that might overtly connect the present to the past. It's not that he forgot those parallels he had earlier identified between witch accusations and *Judenhetze*—for he would write about them again. In a 1967 manuscript, he would assert that between the "two most shameful chapters in German history"—the "time of the witch burnings and the time of the Jewish genocide under Hitler"—ran a "straight bloodline of hate and cruelty."[15] But that manuscript went unpublished.

Yet even as Kruse withdrew from making such arguments publicly, he obsessively, doggedly sought to inform officialdom and the public about the social problem of witchcraft fears—the vilification of one's neighbors as agents of evil. If anything, he pursued this aim with even more vigor than he had done in the past. His lengthy letters turn up over and over again in archives from Munich to Hamburg.

When he did not get satisfactory answers swiftly enough, he wrote follow-up letters, his tone demanding to the point of exasperating. And sometimes, subtly, even as he avoided putting too fine a point on things, he feinted toward a larger picture. The title of his 1951 book, *Are There Witches Among Us?* strikingly parallels *The Murderers Are Among Us*, a 1945 film that dealt in an unvarnished fashion with the postwar legacy of German war crimes.

What motivated Johann Kruse? Foremost seems to have been his genuine desire to help those who, like Frau Maassen, suffered the terrible burden of being labeled witches, and this was a consistent theme in his correspondence with state officials. Though Eberling's case showed that men (such as the former mayor Claus) were also sometimes accused, Kruse fixated on how witch fears victimized women in particular. It was as though women stood in, if one will, for Jews in his conception of the larger meaning and threat of witch fears. Kruse was also convinced that he was talking about something that people

HEXEN
UNTER UNS ?
JOHANN KRUSE

did not want to hear about, and that inspired him, too. It's hard to know to what extent the "paranoia" he had justifiably developed over several decades was to blame for this feeling, or if he simply had a fractious personality (as some who had dealings with him would assert). The publishing history of *Are There Witches Among Us?* may help to illustrate the issue. Within six months of its appearance, the initial print run of some three thousand copies was scheduled to be pulped. Kruse suspected foul play. His book was being pulped, he became convinced, not because it failed to connect with the public, was too expensive, or got poor distribution, or for any number of other plausible reasons. After all, the book had a catchy title, and he was a seasoned writer with several publications under his belt. Rather, he deduced, certain institutions of the state, the church, and academia did not want witchcraft to be talked about.[16]

And yet: people, and especially the press, *did* talk about witch fears in the 1950s. In fact, judging by the volume of newspaper clippings in various archives, they talked about it more and more as the decade wore on. In part this was Kruse's own accomplishment. On the heels of his book's publication, the former schoolteacher founded the Archive for Research into the Modern Witch Craze to house materials he'd gathered over three decades traveling around Schleswig-Holstein by train, on foot, and by bicycle.[17] The archive came in handy when reporters came calling, seeking expert knowledge on witch accusations, as *Der Spiegel* did concerning the 1951 "witch trial" of a man the press referred to as Farmer Bading. *Der Spiegel* quoted Kruse liberally about the case, mentioned his archive by name, and even published his photograph. The exposure made Kruse's archive national news, and him famous. He became the Federal Republic's chief authority on an aspect of popular culture otherwise unfamiliar to many people.

Unfortunately, though, despite all of the attention he received from the press, reporters generally failed to fathom the message Kruse practically shouted, over and over—that witch beliefs did real harm to the accused—let alone his proxy message about the dangers of

scapegoating. Instead, reporters once again chose to focus on ste-
reotypes about rural backwardness and lurid details. (*Der Spiegel's*
article on Farmer Bading, for example, was called "Until the Blood
Comes," a reference to witch banishers' recommendation that to de-
hex a bewitched child, one should beat the child bloody.)[18] Needless
to say, no connections were made between "superstition" and Nazi
persecution.

State officials were similarly resistant to enlightenment, Kruse
found. In May 1952, he mounted an outspoken letter-writing campaign, first addressing the cultural ministry of Lower Saxony, the state
bordering Schleswig-Holstein, demanding it do something to combat
the "spiritual plague" of "witch madness."[19] While Kruse conceded
in his letter that the press—foreign and domestic—had covered the
issue, he nonetheless lamented that his "petitions, newspaper articles,
and lectures" had gone "unheeded" by his real targets: "government
authorities and academic institutes." In the hopes of drawing their
attention, he went on to describe in his letter a litany of baleful cases,
including that of "a nineteen-year-old who had killed his . . . grandfa-
ther with an axe because from his youth he believed the old man had
bewitched him, making him sick." Kruse also told of a woman who
had recently suffered the deaths of her son and husband only to find
herself accused of witchcraft. In the "throes of witch mania," Kruse
warned ministry personnel, "people are murdered . . . or kill themselves in a panic of anxiety."[20]

In response to Kruse's letter, the cultural ministry thanked him
for "the no doubt worthy material" that *Are There Witches Among
Us?* had provided "for battling superstition." But perhaps the former
teacher's "meritorious work" exaggerated the problem?[21] For example, Kruse had claimed in his book that teachers were instructing
pupils in superstitious beliefs, whether wittingly or not, by teaching
them folklore and fairy tales. These stories, he wrote, gave "children, especially those in elementary school . . . ideas about the Devil,
witches, and ghosts." Even the "seemingly harmless tale of Hansel
and Gretel," the retired schoolteacher argued, "had caused plenty of

damage." That story, after all, "dealt not only with witchcraft, but also cannibalism."[22] Ministry officials understandably felt this warning "went much too far." Nevertheless, they did offer Kruse support in his "enlightenment work," if he wished to take his case on an instructional radio program used by schools or wanted to present his materials at local teacher conferences. They also suggested that perhaps a regional heritage association might be the right audience for his message—apparently still convinced that witchcraft beliefs were more of a historical artifact than a contemporary and expanding phenomenon.[23]

Officials in Lower Saxony also criticized Kruse's methodology. *Are There Witches Among Us?* "suffered a great deal," ministry correspondents chided the schoolteacher, "from the use of anonymous sources."[24] As Kruse himself explained in the opening pages of the book, however, there was a good reason for the anonymity. "In relating the facts here," he wrote, "I could not always name the people involved personally, because most are still alive." He kept silent as well about specific place names, and for the same reason: to protect anyone "ostracized and persecuted" and labelled a "servant of the Devil."[25] "Why would I publicize the names of people accused of being witches," he retorted to Lower Saxon authorities, "who already suffer ostracism in their villages?"[26] The following year, Kruse described to reporters his experiences of visiting and trying to comfort the accused. Some kept a clutch of newspapers like talismans, he said, because these bore headlines declaring in print—and therefore authoritatively—"there are no witches."[27]

Even as state officials minimized the problem, Kruse found other ways to advance his agenda. He began to attract disciples, among them Herbert Schäfer, a criminologist with a PhD from the University of Bonn. Strings of footnotes in Schäfer's 1955 book, *Witch Power and Witch Hunt*, attest to the schoolteacher's influence. Kruse also formed alliances with a diverse collection of organizations and partners, including the World Organization of Mothers of All Nations (WOMAN), the German Animal Protection Society, the Working

Group of Bonn Scientists, and the president of the Hamburg Chamber of Apothecaries.[28] Kruse also joined the Deutsche Gesellschaft Schutz vor Aberglauben (DEGESA), the German Society for Protection Against Superstition, which formed in 1953. DEGESA seems to have labeled as "superstitious" almost anything its members—most of them academics, many physicians—deemed insufficiently aligned with medical and scientific norms. It railed against everything from card reading and parapsychology research to yoga and acupuncture.[29] These phenomena were hardly the same as fears of witches, but Kruse brandished connections to such organizations strategically in correspondence with state agencies as evidence of a growing reputation and the integrity and significance of his work.

. . .

What ultimately gave Kruse's cause traction with state governments, however, had less to do with his various institutional affiliations and industrious activism than, ironically or not, with Eberling. In 1955, the Hexenbanner's trial became national and international news. Newspapers far outside Germany picked up the story.[30] Northwest German Broadcasting responded by offering a four-part radio series called "Witch Mania in Our Time."[31] A few months later, Eberling became the subject of a *New German Weekly* newsreel.[32] With this increased level of publicity, Kruse's confrontational missives began to produce better results. "I permit myself to pose the polite question," one of his letters demanded of Lower Saxony's interior ministry in late 1955. What "measures" had the "ministry . . . taken," he asked, "to ensure that women and mothers in Lower Saxony are not persecuted, mishandled, or murdered as witches?"[33] The letter was forwarded to the cultural ministry with a request to "look into" it.[34] From there it went on to state police, whose officials explained to their colleagues that it was not clear what if anything the law could do. "If occasionally reputed acts of witchcraft lead to criminal proceedings, they usually deal with cases of defamation or instances of bodily harm," officials wrote. (It was true: Eberling, after all, would ultimately be convicted only of violating the law on lay healing and a single count of defamation, not of inciting Frau Maassen's neighbors against her.) But state police agreed nonetheless to investigate eight specific cases Kruse had inquired about.[35]

Three months later, the investigation concluded. There was no cause for concern, state police reported to the interior ministry. The problem was not a "serious danger." The cases Kruse had indicated as instances of witch persecution had involved nothing more than faux healers bilking people out of their money, and had "nothing to do with superstition in the actual sense." Here again, it is not at all clear that police or other officials quite understood just what they were investigating. Of the eight cases Kruse brought to their attention, six clearly involved fears of witches, several involved violence, and one resulted in murder.[36] Maybe investigators could not take seriously that these cases had at their source imputations of witchcraft, or could not imagine that the people involved in them "really believed" they were being pursued by witches (if this is what was meant by "superstition in the actual sense").

So while it was true that authorities were more willing to look into these matters following Eberling's trial, they still failed to comprehend the core problem as Kruse perceived it: that witch fears led to social ostracization and scapegoating. Even when confronted with a specific instance of persecution, authorities largely failed to grasp its social meaning and potential threat. An official in Lower Saxony, for example, referenced a case in which neighbors had accused a "quarrelsome and litigious" woman of bewitching a child. The woman had contemplated suicide and had to be placed under a doctor's care. Yet the official was confident nonetheless that local citizens took no notice of ongoing "battles" between the accused woman and her neighbors. The problem among them was "more or less internal." He saw no larger or more significant social problem in play.[37]

When officials considered intervening, it was against particular offenses covered by the law: fraud, threats to public health, violations of the lay healer regulations. "Superstition," to them, was a generic problem that could contribute to those offenses. Some officials simply misunderstood the issue, or, in their ignorance of what to many people were no doubt quite exotic strands of popular culture, mixed up different varieties of "superstition" that had little to do with fears of covert evildoing. Lower Saxony's interior minister, for instance, seems to have thought that the problem was fortune-telling, a practice that, he noted, all the districts in the state already regulated.[38]

Even if officials remained confused about what witch fears meant, though, they did acknowledge that the phenomenon seemed to be expanding. In 1956, Lower Saxony's minister for social policy, Dr. Heinz Rudolph, put the heads of local administrative districts on notice to report any instances of witchcraft-related matters. Rudolph wanted to determine whether "measures to protect the health of the . . . population" were warranted.[39] The results of this initiative, according to internal correspondence, were "not unambiguous." In "certain parts" of the state there were "witch-mania cases," but tabloids "hunting sensational headlines" tended to "exaggerate" them. Still, among themselves, officials cautioned against discussing the matter publicly, for fear of fueling witch scares. A "big discussion of them would cement them in people's consciousness," predicted one high-ranking civil servant in Lower Saxony's social ministry in a letter. Precisely the "opposite effect" to the one desired "would be achieved if we sound the alarm."[40]

Whether the issue was exaggerated in the press or not, Lower Saxony took the matter seriously enough to place "fighting witch mania" on the agenda when nearly two dozen leading police officials, commissioners, and senior civil servants in the state's interior and social ministries conferenced for two days in October 1956. Here again, a consensus prevailed among them that the problem of witch beliefs was the result of a generic "lack of enlightenment" that might be spreading, but in which they perceived no larger social meaning. And in any case, individual instances in which "witch mania had played a role" had been largely of "local significance," and so were not "generally" threatening.[41]

At the same time the gathering did recognize that once a community turned against a neighbor, witch beliefs could lead to ostracism and violence. In a report produced at the conference, officials attempted to sort out legal remedies in various cases stemming from witch fears. For those who claimed to be Hexenbanners, officials noted, the lay healer law provided the state a legal remedy. As for helping those denounced as witches, there, too, was legal recourse: bodily harm and defamation carried criminal penalties.[42]

Finding legal solutions for the cultural *beliefs* that prompted accusations was a murkier business. Officials recommended more education: when legends and fairy tales were discussed in school classrooms "and the discussion naturally turns to [witches]," teachers could make a few comments in passing about "witch madness" being "nonsense." Pastors and institutions dealing with local history and culture could also raise critical voices.[43] Presumably moved by the light Eberling's court case had shone on the issue, officials called on "all agencies and offices" to be more watchful, and asked that the justice ministry encourage prosecutors to ask for higher penalties when such cases came to court. When no legal penalty could be exacted, but people had "suffered particular public abuse," the interior ministry should be informed.[44]

By 1956, the tide of opinion among state officials seemed to be turning in Kruse's favor: even if their conclusions were sometimes less than satisfying, officials saw fit to investigate his claims. That same year, another front in his campaign also began to yield victories. For years, Kruse had unsuccessfully brought complaint after complaint against an outfit called Planet Publishers, in Braunschweig, that produced a pulp magic book called *The Sixth and Seventh Books of Moses*.[45] Kruse had long been convinced of the book's role in promoting witch beliefs and violence against those labeled witches, as he explained to a journalist.[46] In one of his battle-ready letters, Kruse had demanded in 1954 that Lower Saxony's government take measures to prohibit the sale of all magic books, including the Moses book.[47] Authorities had been initially unmoved by these appeals. A

senior prosecutor explained to the press in 1955 that the book—
which offered, among other things, various folk-medicinal recipes—
was merely a "literary product without medical value." The publisher
had made clear enough, officials felt, that the book was no replacement for being under a doctor's care. (It is true that a "Publisher's
Comment" on page 101 urged readers "in case of illness absolutely to
seek a doctor's advice.") The state's attorney and the upper regional
court in Braunschweig agreed.[48] No one, state authorities were convinced, would take this book seriously.

But after Eberling's case went to the Federal High Court, perceptions began to shift. Soon, Planet Publishers would stand accused of
fraud and dishonest business practices (the Moses book was said to
make false claims); inciting the public to commit criminal offenses
(including cemetery desecration and the mishandling of animals for
use in magical recipes); and violating the Federal Republic's 1953 Law
for the Control of Sexually Transmitted Diseases (the book provided
advice for treating syphilis). In support of the case, Kruse supplied the
court with pages of documentation testifying to what he saw as its
harmful social effects—not least, the information it provided about
how to unmask witches.[49]

Leafing through Planet's 1950 edition of *The Sixth and Seventh
Books of Moses* today, it's not hard to understand why authorities
initially saw it merely as a novelty, rather than any kind of serious
threat to public health or an incitement to criminality. But appearances can be deceiving. There was a secret history lurking behind the
pages of that little volume—a history Johann Kruse probably knew
more than a bit about, in one way or another. Deceptive advertising
and cemetery desecration were surely among the least harmful aspects
of the book, which deserves some attention of its own. It was there, in
that 1950 edition, that we can begin to perceive the connection that
Kruse saw—but no longer explicitly mentioned—between the post-
1945 history of witch accusations and the vilification of Jews in the
decades before.

. . .

A magic book is an instruction manual. It contains knowledge of rituals, spells, and incantations. It tells readers the procedures through which to appeal to supernatural entities. Such a book can offer methods and recipes to secure wealth, love, or good fortune; to achieve power; to do harm or ward it off. The authorship of magic books is generally attributed to a powerful, profoundly wise, and legendary figure—King Solomon, for example—whose secret knowledge (and it is always secret knowledge) is revealed in the text.[50]

The Sixth and Seventh Books of Moses was the most popular of all magic books in the twentieth-century German-speaking world. It was first published in Stuttgart in the mid-nineteenth century.[51] The supposition behind it is that God gave Moses more wisdom than what got set down in the five books of Moses in the Torah—Genesis, Exodus, Leviticus, Numbers, and Deuteronomy. Since an apocryphal eighth book of Moses survives in papyri from around the fourth century CE, people have reasoned over the years that there must have been sixth and seventh books, too.

The Sixth and Seventh Books of Moses is not a "fixed" text. It has been published and republished, reworked and rearranged in various collections and editions many times over.[52] In the Weimar era alone, at least five different publishers produced editions.[53] Under National Socialism, the production and distribution of esoteric literature was sometimes suppressed, though unevenly and inconsistently.[54] In 1950, Planet Publishers—whose catalog in the decade also included joke compendia, advice books for women on pregnancy and for couples on marriage, and such pulp classics as *Sun Koh: Heir of Atlantis*— brought out its edition.[55] A small, hardcover book bound in black with red-edged paper, it looked, more than anything, like a weird hymnal, if a hymnal also contained chapters on selecting and preparing a divining rod, the proper times for calling on the spirits, and how to summon Lucifer, "protector of the souls of the damned." It explained how one should correctly prepare oneself before engaging in ritual activity: by eating only twice a day, and then only at midday and midnight, and by abstaining from "relations with any woman." Only by scrupulously adhering to these and other instructions might one enter "dangerous battle and emerge the victor."[56]

The 1950 Planet edition was a minor bestseller. An initial print run of nine thousand copies suggests how confident the publishers were in potential sales, and this print run was followed by others. The book generated nearly 100,000 DM in sales between 1950 and 1954. It would continue to sell into the 1970s.[57]

The Sixth and Seventh Books of Moses was known to many people in Germany, whether or not they actually bought or used it. It was said that mass murderer Fritz Angerstein had been motivated to kill his wife and various other family members and employees in 1924 by the Moses book.[58] After the Second World War, folklorist Adolf Spamer described encounters he'd had related to his work on magic and specifically the Moses book. A woman he knew was convinced she'd had bad luck all her life because in her youth in the 1920s, having money to buy only *The Sixth and Seventh Books of Moses* or a corset, she'd chosen the corset. In the Prussian State Library in Berlin (today's Staatsbibliothek), Spamer tried to get a look at available editions. Every request he placed came back with the comment "cannot be located." Copies of the Moses book were routinely stolen, replaced, and stolen again. When Spamer lent his students his own copy of *The Sixth and Seventh Books*, he got it back but with some of the healing charms and talismans cut out. When he asked his students about it, they denied having any "interests in or dispositions toward magic."[59]

People may have denied interest in the Moses book because they did not want to expose themselves to ridicule, or because their priests or pastors told them to avoid it.[60] But others surely denied knowledge of the book for some of the same reasons that they tended to speak in code about witches: it was by reputation a source of harmful magic. Herbert Schäfer, the criminological researcher who followed in

Kruse's footsteps, found in the late 1950s that, as was true of witches, people spoke of *The Sixth and Seventh Books* only with trepidation. No one would readily admit owning or using it, though they sometimes accused those whom they suspected of witchcraft of using it.[61] In May 1953, the Munich tabloid *Abendzeitung* reported that Bruno Gröning was suing his estranged brother Karl for claiming in a manuscript he was shopping to publishers that Gröning used the book.[62] Herr C., whose story introduced this book, claimed to have spied Frau N. through a window using the *The Sixth and Seventh Books*. This was proof, for him, that she "worked with the Devil."[63] And during the proceedings against Eberling, a man had directed a letter to the court in Dithmarschen denouncing the Moses book, apparently assuming it must be connected to the case. Anyone who "read it," the man wrote, "has already fallen to Lucifer."[64]

On various occasions, Eberling himself said contradictory things about the sources of his medicine.[65] He recalled that when he was working as a mines carpenter in Dortmund, the old lady he lived with had offered him a book that she said would make him powerful. He had rejected it, he said, because "the Devil was in there." He also insisted that the old lady's book was not *The Sixth and Seventh Books of Moses*.[66] Still, when he was sentenced at trial in 1936, the court noted that he had appeared at the home of a family under his treatment "with some books, some of which were religious, and some of which had a Cabalistic content." It was said that Eberling transcribed things from these books onto slips of paper.[67] Whether he used the Moses book or not is unclear—but then again, people did not usually admit such things.

The court's statement about books with a "Cabalistic content" is worth lingering on. Past editions of *The Sixth and Seventh Books* had often used Hebrew words and characters and names for God, and Jewish (or pseudo-Jewish) symbols. In other words, those editions associated Jews, Jewish cultural and religious forms and symbols, Hebrew words, and "secret" Hebrew names for the divinity with magic—even harmful magic.

The idea that Jews had magical power surfaces in a variety of German cultural artifacts, before and during the Nazi period. *The Dictionary of German Superstition*—a massive, ten-volume compendium of all manner of "popular beliefs"—is a good example. Published between 1927 and 1942, it featured work by some of the most prominent folklorists of the era. One of the lengthier entries is for "Jew/Jewess." Among many other things, it notes that "Jews have always been presumed to be magicians," and that Jews read "magic books like *The Sixth and Seventh Books of Moses*." The "Jew/Jewess" entry, which appeared in a volume published in 1932—before the Nazis took power—continues in this vein, recording the enduring idea that "objects of Jewish provenance have magical power." In light of the long history of such notions, the entry explains, "it is understandable that people still ascribe magical power to Jews today."[68]

After the Holocaust, such ideas became taboo. Nonetheless, it is possible to find various hints that some Germans continued to associate Jews with occult power—sometimes for good, mostly for ill. The exorcist at the site where the Virgin Mary appeared in Heroldsbach, as we have seen, referred to the Latin "Sator Arepo Tenet Opera Rotas" incantation as the "Hebrew Our Father."[69] Near the same apparition site, one could find self-published pamphlets for sale in local shops. Some claimed that what they called a "trinity triangle" would forge a mystical link between Heroldsbach and a pair of other pilgrimage sites and bring the Devil's power on earth to an end. This was being prevented by Satan, however, with the help of the French and the Jews.[70] And, of course, Moses was in the very name of the magic book itself.

The 1950 Planet edition of the Moses book continued this tradition of associating Jewishness and magic, if in what we might call a chastened form. Some earlier German editions had attributed the seventh book to a translation by the "Rabbi Chaleb," for example, but this attribution is notably missing from the 1950 Planet edition.[71] The many Hebrew and pseudo-Hebrew characters found in earlier editions of the Moses book had also dropped out.[72] And yet, prayers are

still offered in the 1950 edition to "You alone great Adonay, Eloim, Ariel, und Jehova." More strikingly, the one remaining Jewish pictographic symbol in the book, the Star of David, appears prominently, right on the cover. The one symbol most indelibly associated with Jews had endured.

Of course, a hexagram—a six-pointed star—has meanings other than the Star of David. It surfaces in Germany in many contexts: on the old doors of the Technical University in Munich; as a *Bierstern*, or "brewer's star," symbolizing the six ingredients used in beer making; even as Christmas decorations in 1980s-era West Berlin.[73] Scholars of ancient and medieval Christian magic have argued that Jewish idioms appearing in magic texts may sometimes have become so familiar, even indigenous, to their users, that they were no longer recognizable by those users as Jewish.[74] This familiarity may also have been true in modern magic books. There is a chapter in the Planet edition of *The Sixth and Seventh Books of Moses* called "the Kabbalistic circle," for example. By the twentieth century, Kabbalah had been part of the esoteric repertoire of non-Jewish European magic texts for centuries. References to it in the Planet edition of the Moses book seem to suggest arcane and mystical wisdom more than anything specifically Jewish.

Present-day scholars of magic—historians, anthropologists, and religion scholars—note that ritual scripts (a category that would include magic books) are sometimes augmented with elements from religious traditions their authors perceive as "exotic." Such elements can lend authority to magical practice by enhancing what British anthropologist Bronislaw Malinowski, in his famous work on the Trobriand Islanders, called its "coefficient of weirdness."[75] The vocabulary of Trobriand magic, he observed, was not just any vocabulary, not just any language. "A spell is believed to be a primeval text, which somehow came into being side-by-side with animals and plants, with winds and waves, with human disease . . . courage and . . . frailty." Why, then, would the idioms of magic "be as the words of common speech"?[76]

In short: both the potency and the efficacy of magical idioms depend on their being ancient, epic, legendary—and entirely distinct from what their users perceive as ordinary. This is perhaps one reason, among others, that Jewish symbols had so long been perceived in Christian and esoteric history as talismans.[77] Even with these caveats, though, it is hard to imagine that the six-pointed star did not retain a distinctive and potent charge after World War II, in light of its perverse and public abuse under Nazism.

• • •

None of this unsettling history surfaced when the case against Planet Publishers for publishing *The Sixth and Seventh Books of Moses* came to trial in Braunschweig.[78] Over three late November days in 1956, various experts took the stand to offer their testimony. The star witness for the prosecution was a professor of medicine, forensic pathologist Otto Prokop. Prokop—who, like Kruse, was a member of DEGESA—reviled magic books as road maps for mayhem and criminality. In court, he referenced a 1954 case in which three men in Westphalia had committed various crimes while using formulas from the Moses book to conjure the Devil.[79]

Prokop's opposite number was also a famous professor, not of medicine, but folklore. Originally from Silesia, Will-Erich Peuckert fled his home at war's end and since 1946 had held an appointment at the University of Göttingen. His main areas of research were magic and witchcraft, and he perceived the Moses book very differently from Prokop and Kruse. Peuckert saw it as a variety of *Hausväterliteratur*—a genre of books dating back to the sixteenth century containing agricultural knowledge and advice about household economics, animal husbandry, food preparation, and medical treatments.[80] In his view, the Moses book in essence represented a historical stage in the development of early modern German science. He had a point: the Planet edition did offer cures for burns, to stop bleeding, alleviate poisonous bites, and aid weak eyes.

Perhaps it is not surprising that the more disquieting history of the Moses book and "Jewish magic" failed to surface in the courtroom. Yet there was at least one direct connection to be made. The "Jew/Jewess" entry in *The Dictionary of German Superstition*, which ascribes magical powers to Jews, was written by none other than Peuckert himself, expert witness for Planet Publishers' defense.[81]

As it happens, Peuckert's discussion of Jews and magic was among the tamer aspects of that lengthy entry, which also offered this: "The Jew is an enemy of God"; "The Jew is hated by God, and the Jew's enemies were called upon in the Middle Ages, on God's orders, to exterminate him."[82] Citing a variety of scholarly literature with deep, learned footnotes, Peuckert presented this information, on the one hand, as "folklore" in a collection of "superstitions."[83] But he also wrote much of it in the present tense. Overall, his "Jew/Jewess" entry, like others in *The Dictionary of German Superstition*, lacks any scholarly "supranarrative." The information in it is often presented as though timeless, without any sense of authorial voice. This vagueness about time, the promiscuous mixing of historical perception with contemporaneity, makes it difficult to understand when Peuckert is talking about the historical past, when about old legends, and when about the beliefs some of his fellow citizens actively held in 1932.[84] The historical caveat that he offered—that God commanded his own to "exterminate" his enemies, the Jews, "in the Middle Ages"—can only be judged as extremely dissonant in light of subsequent events.

Despite this suspiciously worded entry, Peuckert was no particular friend of National Socialism, and the Nazis did not like him either. They labeled him politically unreliable and stripped him of his right to teach at a university (his *venia legendi*). They burned his book, *Folklore of the Proletariat*, which, quite in contrast to the discipline's mainstream tendency to romanticize the rural world, dealt instead with urban, working-class narrative traditions.[85] In short, Peuckert's "Jew, Jewess" entry, the stuff of nightmares though it is, was not the product of a scholar in any way especially attuned to racist Nazi doctrines— arguably, quite the contrary. As a scholar, Peuckert had a more historical bent than many of his colleagues, and could distinguish better than most between relics and contemporary German culture.[86]

As a discipline, though, the study of folklore in German-speaking lands had long been an intensely nationalist enterprise. Since the nineteenth century, it had focused on collecting: gathering up tales, legends, and songs, along with objects of material culture. In the early twentieth century, folklorists undertook massive surveys of the population in an effort to determine the distribution of particular customs, practices, and specific beliefs. All of this entailed a largely ahistorical attempt to see in present-day popular practices and oral lore some essential, enduring vestige of ancient Germanic traditions, beliefs, and customs. All of which, in turn, made folklore an especially ripe field of endeavor for the Nazis after 1933, though many folklorists' work aligned with ultra-nationalist identity politics well before the Nazis seized power.

The point here is that Nazi antisemitism emerged from and built on an existing German culture, which included Christian ideas about Jews being the enemy of God, about "Jewish magic" and mystical conspiracies. Such ideas had circulated for a very long time, and for scores of people were part of a deep, unreflected-on structure of thought, basic background knowledge of the world and how it works. As taboo as these associations were after 1945, they also outlasted the Third Reich in some form.

Kruse had railed consistently against folklore and fairy tales in his many letters to state officials and in his book. Despite the rebuff of such charges as exaggerated, he remained steadfast in his view that they transmitted pernicious ideas to schoolchildren. *The Dictionary of German Superstition*, with its loaded "Jew/Jewess" entry, shows up in the bibliography of *Are There Witches Among Us?* If anyone knew that the *The Sixth and Seventh Books of Moses* was regarded as a book of harmful magic and that Jews were accused of using it, Kruse did. But the former schoolteacher never seems to have raised this point in his campaign against the work. To have done so would have involved drawing direct parallels between the persecutions Germans had inflicted on Jews in the recent past and the present-day witch scare—which carried all the danger of any particularly potent social taboo.

At the same time, Kruse's knowledge of the subtexts, of the history lurking between the lines of a seemingly harmless pulp novelty like the Moses book, surely motivated him, because it allowed him to wage a surrogate battle in place of the one he could not wage. For him, *The Sixth and Seventh Books of Moses* was not just evidence of a generic lack of enlightenment among a gullible public, just as witch beliefs were not just "silly superstitions." That people wanted magical cures for syphilis was not the main issue. Kruse knew that vilifying beliefs can take many forms and lurk disguised in contexts that might seem otherwise innocuous. He had known so for decades, even if he no longer said so aloud, or at least not in so many words.

. . .

The court in Braunschweig sided with Kruse and Prokop, ruling against Planet. Publishers Ferdinand Masuch and Heinrich Schnell were fined nine thousand and one thousand marks respectively for fraud, dishonest business practices, and other charges. Remaining copies of their bestseller were confiscated.[87] Nearly a hundred different West German newspapers reported on the convictions.[88] Weeks later, a local newspaper in Grafschaft triumphantly announced that Dr. Heinz Rudolph, Lower Saxony's social policy minister, had "declared war" on "superstition and witch mania."[89] Things seemed to be going Kruse's way.

Within just a few months, however, Lower Saxony's investigation was suspended. What happened? The ministry acknowledged that there had been some terrible cases in which people suspected of being witches had been physically and mentally mistreated—and "not seldom driven to suicide." The number of cases, too, was "serious."[90] But making any further determinations had proved difficult. Each time officials came upon what looked like "concrete" instances of witch "superstition," a newspaper reported, they ran into "a wall of ice-cold silence."[91]

The same would ultimately prove true in Kruse's home state, Schleswig-Holstein. Late in 1957, Minister President Kai-Uwe von Hassel directed his interior minister to look into "taking action against so-called 'devil expellers' and 'witch banishers.'" But there, too, investigators found that the problem resisted scrutiny. "Hardly more than one percent of all such incidents come to the ears of the relevant agencies," officials estimated. The "preponderance of the superstitious" were afraid "that there might be something to" charges of witchcraft, and so "declined to make a report." State officials nonetheless made plans to issue an ordinance to help police "combat witch-doctor nonsense," and community arbitrators were asked to comb their records for local disputes related to witch scares.[92]

From one point of view, Kruse's activism had had a real impact. *The Sixth and Seventh Books of Moses* was off the shelves. State ministers, police, and health officials had been pursuaded that witch fears could have real, even deadly, consequences. Yet their investigations ultimately yielded little more than evidence of persecution's price. Not least out of a sense of self-preservation, local people refused the impertinent questions of curious outsiders concerning matters of internal, community concern.

• • •

Ultimately, even the Moses book case fell apart. In September 1957, publishers Masuch and Schnell appealed their case and were exonerated.[93] Though prosecutors made plans to try again, they would do so without their lead expert witness, Otto Prokop. Earlier that year, Prokop had taken up a prestigious appointment as director of forensic medicine at the famed Charité Hospital in East Berlin, where he went on to have an extraordinary career, training more than a generation of East German doctors and publishing dozens of books and articles on various topics to great acclaim.[94] This being the Cold War era, after taking that East German appointment, Prokop suddenly found that his invitations to give lectures in West Germany dried up. Adding insult to injury, Planet's defense lawyer impugned the pathologist's impartiality during the appeal hearings. Given the doctor's connections to communist East Germany, he could not possibly be objective, the lawyer said. And he went even further, insinuating that Prokop might have fascist sympathies, by claiming that DEGESA—the antisuperstition organization to which both the doctor and Kruse belonged—was the successor of a Nazi-era research institute.[95]

Kruse, who had been instrumental in bringing the Moses book case to trial in the first place, also found himself publicly maligned by the opposition—in his case, by the folklore professor, Will-Erich Peuckert. During his court appearance at the appeal hearings, Peuckert demanded to know how "a simple schoolteacher" who "didn't even know Latin" could possibly have the learning necessary to understand the historical significance of a text like *The Sixth and Seventh Books of Moses*. Peuckert suggested that Kruse's obsession with the subject was a bit odd: the retired teacher, he opined, had a "monomaniacal spirit."[96]

A few years later, Peuckert pursued Kruse even further, and in a much more public and pernicious way. In an essay he published on the Moses book controversy, the folklorist hinted—apparently as a way of explaining Kruse's driven nature—that Kruse's own mother had once been accused as a witch.[97] As both Peuckert and his nemesis knew better than almost anyone, these insinuations had the power to besmirch Kruse in a very particular way, since witchcraft was perceived to be passed generationally, in families. Peuckert had effectively hinted that Kruse himself might be a witch. After Peuckert's essay appeared, word spread. In November 1960, a writer who held a prominent position in Lower Saxony's cultural ministry confided in a memo that "the activities of Herr Kruse are motivated by regrettable experiences in his family circle. His mother was once denounced as a witch."[98]

Kruse had long maintained that intrigues within the state, the church, and academic circles prevented his message from getting through to a broader public. People in positions of power, he was sure, did not want to hear what he had to say about witch fears. And while Kruse's relentlessness and unmeasured tone no doubt wore down many a public figure over the years, it does seem that the obstacles he encountered may also have had an underlying political dimension, in a moment spiked with mistrust. He claimed, for instance, to have been "shut out" of the Bevensen Circle—a group focused on promoting local, Low-German, and Plattdeutsch literature—because he made the chair of the group "uncomfortable."[99] The minister president of Lower Saxony, Hinrich Kopf, as the circle's "patron," had granted the group's chair the power to exclude "irksome people," Kruse alleged.[100]

Kopf had been wanted by the Polish government for war crimes in the 1940s. Though a Social Democrat like Kruse, he had worked for the Nazi regime. During the occupation of Poland, he was tasked with expropriating Polish and Jewish property. Nonetheless, after the war he went on to have a distinguished career in politics. Eventually, Kruse was assured by letter that Kopf was not the circle's patron and had no authority "to shut out people annoying to him."[101]

The archives reveal no more than that about the incident and the nature of the conflict, if indeed there was one between Kruse and Kopf. But we can well imagine how old political grievances could affect relationships like those between a former Social Democrat turned war criminal and a former Social Democrat crusading to bring uncomfortable features of past and present to light. Official truces may have been declared and amnesties enacted, but old suspicions and enmities abided. Kruse thought he was being cast out for talking about witches, for making people "uncomfortable." He may well have been right.

DAWN OF THE NEW AGE

In late July 1957, Bruno Gröning stepped into a Munich courtroom to take part in what would turn out to be the final drama of his public life. It had been nearly eight years since he first rocketed to fame in the spring of 1949 amidst rumors of apocalypse. Back then, the press routinely referred to him as a Wunderdoktor, and high-ranking officials in Bavaria publicly effused about his apparently boundless ability to heal. Gröning had seemed to many to be a new messiah, an emissary of God, a healer who would bind wounds no one else seemed able to see, let alone mend. But in the years following his association with Otto and Renée Meckelburg, legal trouble dogged him. For several years he was pursued by police and prosecutors for violating the lay healer law. As a result, in the early 1950s he had largely withdrawn from public view. The giant crowds had dispersed. Though he continued to meet with groups of ardent disciples and cure-seekers, and still occasionally commanded tabloid headlines, by 1957 he had become a rather different figure—less a magic man or divine messenger than a New Age guru. He still talked about believing in God in order to be healthy and about avoiding evil, as he always had. But now he also talked about the pharmaceutical industry's dominance of medicine and the effects of environmental degradation on health.

It wasn't just Gröning who had changed over the intervening years. In fact, were one still in a mood to scan the heavens for signs by the end of the 1950s, one might find—quite in contrast to the moment in which Gröning emerged at the end of the '40s—that available signs presaged only better things to come.

The Federal Republic's firm incorporation into Western military and economic structures was, by then, assured. Germany's division into East and West, though much lamented, was becoming, like the Cold War itself, an accepted and seemingly permanent fact of life. The last German POWs—some of whom had been held in the Soviet Union for a decade or more—had by now returned home and were being reintegrated into society, effectively ending a war that, for many Germans, endured long after 1945. In 1954, West Germany had won the World Cup, after which the nation's citizens had celebrated, it was said, "being someone again." Economic good fortune smiled, if not on everyone, then on more people than in the past, and glossy magazines offered readers images of well-stocked refrigerators and other scenes from a good life of consumer plenty. Throughout the Cold War West, this was an era of dramatic cultural transformation: of Brando in *The Wild One* and Bardot in *And God Created Woman*. It was the era of Elvis Presley, Chuck Berry, and, in West Germany, the *Halbstarken*— youth rebels in leather and denim, rioting at rock and roll concerts.[1] Replacing an old, destroyed world burdened with memory with a shiny new and complacently forgetful one became its own type of redemption. From there "it was only a step," one historian writes, "to burgeoning pride in German competence and superiority."[2] In the face of so much good fortune, maybe people felt less need for cosmic solace, less fear of cosmic retribution. No wonder we associate the post-Nazi years more with economic miracles than religious ones.

This forgetting surely influenced public perception of the details of the Gröning trial unfolding in Munich's Palace of Justice that summer of 1957. As sordid as its details were, they must have felt like they belonged to a faraway time, almost to another era. The case revolved around a disturbing relationship that had developed during the early months of Gröning's fame. In autumn 1949, the healer had met Ruth K., a seventeen-year-old suffering from tuberculosis, and her father. Both had become almost impossibly devoted to Gröning. Right after meeting him, Ruth—with her father's blessing—dispensed with medical treatment. As she weakened and lay dying over the ensuing months, she never lost faith that Gröning would cure her, that he would "take away her illness." When she died, at the end of 1950, she weighed seventy pounds.

Six and a half years later, prosecutors charged Gröning with violating the lay healer ban and with negligent homicide. As the trial approached, the press showed little nostalgia for the wild Rosenheim days, when tens of thousands had assembled at the Trotter Farm to partake of soul medicine. Tabloids and newspapers reporting on the upcoming trial showed contrasting photographs. In some, dating back to 1949, mothers in kerchiefs and worn summer coats lie in open fields or hold their sick children aloft to receive the healer's cures. In others, we see a tanned, 1957-era Gröning, sometimes pictured alongside his new and fashionably dressed young French wife, Josette.[3] It's true that the headlines hadn't changed much in the intervening years: they still ranged—sometimes in one and the same paper—from "Gröning's Path to Becoming a Miracle Doctor" to "Gröning, Career of a Charlatan."[4] But those contrasting images of postwar distress and growing affluence tell a story about the distance a rapidly transforming Federal Republic wanted to put between its earliest, chaotic days of suffering and disarray and its much more prosperous, if conservative, present, one that aspired to keep the lid clamped down tight on disorderly scenes. Courtroom observers could be forgiven for imagining that maybe Herford and Rosenheim had been just a bad dream, an embarrassing episode from someone else's life.

· · ·

Police first learned of the circumstances surrounding Ruth K.'s death in 1951, from none other than Otto Meckelburg.[5] After his days managing Gröning's 1949–50 tour of the North Sea coast, Meckelburg had experienced some close shaves with the law. He was investigated for tax evasion, fraud, and other charges. Police dredged up his black-market past. In 1951, Gröning and Meckelburg were both pulled into court for violating the lay healer law. Meckelburg seems to have found it prudent to retain his correspondence with a number of high-profile public figures who had sought the help of, advocated for, or supported Gröning. He also kept a massive archive of tens of thousands of unanswered letters that sufferers had sent to Gröning, organized by type of ailment. Among the documents was a cache of letters from Ruth K.'s father. It seems unlikely that Meckelburg's motives for turning these documents over to police were entirely selfless, and more probable that doing so was related to what *Der Spiegel* called the "radical break" between the erstwhile partners.[6]

The archived letters from Ruth's father told a terrible story, narrating the teenage girl's slow but inexorable physical decline over several months and the agony that accompanied it. Ruth and her father had become steadfast followers of Gröning, unwavering in their certainty that he could cure anything, even tuberculosis. Bound by mutual devotion, father and daughter committed to a decision with a logic all its own: to follow Gröning, come what may. Once made, that decision had to be pursued to its conclusion. Ruth and her father came to believe that to break with Gröning would be somehow to break the spell of *faith*, meaning not only the enormous trust they had placed in him but the very stuff of redemption, even of life itself. At the same time, the letters also revealed Herr K.'s growing awareness, even as his daughter lay dying, that he may have made a grievous mistake by agreeing—against the wishes of his entire family—to allow his daughter to stop medical treatment.

Then again, who could blame them, considering what Ruth's treatment to that point had entailed, and what a diagnosis of tuberculosis could mean at that time? Ruth was born in 1932. From 1944 to 1947, she was treated in a sanatorium in the Taunus Mountains, near Frankfurt. Thereafter, she was released to the care of a local physician, Dr. Helene Volk, a senior medical officer in the small town of Säckingen, near the Swiss border, where the K. family lived.[7] Antibiotics were not yet widely available to treat tuberculosis, and Volk employed a form of treatment called collapse therapy.[8] A long needle would be inserted into the patient's thorax, between the ribs, under local anesthetic, partially collapsing the lung. This procedure was intended to allow the lung to rest and heal, and deprive TB bacteria of oxygen. Ruth endured these treatments every eight days, for a time, and every two to three weeks thereafter, a routine that went on for a year and a half all told.[9] In winter 1948, she began to cough up blood. Dr. Volk obtained a bed for her young patient at a Black Forest clinic, the Sanatorium Wehrawald, reputed to be the most up-to-date in all of Germany.[10] Among its treatment offerings was streptomycin, the first agent found effective to treat TB, and which Volk later said might have had a positive effect on Ruth's illness.[11]

But Ruth did not want to go to the clinic: her mother later testified that her daughter had been "terrified" of the possibility of being operated on. While Ruth was in the Taunus sanatorium, she had seen many girls just like her die after surgery.[12] What Ruth wanted, in the fall of 1949, was to meet Bruno Gröning. He was then in Bad Wiessee, roughly 450 kilometers from Säckingen. His fame—and the near-divine ability imputed to him—was at its peak. Ruth's father agreed to take her to see the healer. Renée Meckelburg, who later testified in court about meeting Ruth in Bad Wiessee, described how the pair had "talked together the whole day." Ruth told Renée that she "felt substantially better" after having met Gröning. Renée told Ruth in turn that she had been healed by him.[13]

A few months later, Otto Meckelburg wrote to Herr K.—on the freshly printed letterhead of the Association for Research and Promotion of the Gröning Healing Method—to share some "joyful news."

Ruth had been accepted as a patient in a soon-to-open Gröning clinic, where she would be treated free of charge.[14] Meckelburg's letter dated to a time—early February 1950—when he was convinced that Gröning clinics would be established imminently. Gröning had just made several appearances in Oldenburg, and the entourage was about to head back south, to Mittenwald.

Dr. Volk soon tried to follow up with her erstwhile patient, asking Ruth's father to bring his daughter in to be examined. Responding by letter, Herr K. appeared "obsessed with the unshakable belief," Volk later said, "that Gröning could make his daughter well." "Please, please do not perceive it as ungrateful," K. wrote to the doctor, but he would not bring Ruth in for an exam. He wanted "to avoid obstructing the Gröning healing methods or making them illusory." K. was not entirely without his doubts: the decision to withdraw from medical care, he told Volk, had been "terrible" to make, its consequences "unforeseeable." But he and Ruth were determined to stick to it. Later, in correspondence with the police investigating the case in late 1954, Volk had explained that she had not wanted "to shake the father's faith." In her view, once the family had refused treatment at the Black Forest clinic, "the young girl's fate was sealed."[15]

Ruth's illness progressed over the coming months. At home with her parents in Säckingen, she had daily fevers, a bad cough, sweats, and no appetite. Her father began writing to Otto Meckelburg frequently, pouring out his mounting anxiety over Ruth's condition in letter after letter. Despite her situation, his daughter "dismissed" the idea of being treated by anyone but Gröning, K. said. "Ruth's only desire," he told Meckelburg, "is to see Herr Gröning as soon as possible." He knew that this "might be Ruth's last wish." "Dear Herr Meckelburg," he pleaded,

> I beg you from the depths of my soul, tell Herr Gröning Ruth's wish as soon as possible and I beg you, come by car, we will pay. . . . Please don't waste a day, not an hour. . . . Please understand our suffering and how vast is our responsibility.

K.'s tone was one of supplication but also carried the mildest hint of accusation. After all, the "we" whose responsibility was so vast encompassed not just K. but Meckelburg and Gröning, too. In a concluding note, K. said that his daughter's coughing was now "so intense" that he was sometimes afraid she would "throw up her dinner."[16]

The following month, April, Ruth temporarily revived after reading "in the paper that Herr Gröning was in Constance," not too far from their home. She "laughed and joked," and was in good spirits about this news. K. continued to beg Meckelburg for a visit from Gröning, insisting that the healer had promised he would come. "Please tell Herr Gröning that Ruth believes still in the 'reunion' he so emphatically and definitively promised her at the last treatment session. Tell him please that Ruth still will not let a doctor come to her bedside. 'My doctor is Herr Gröning' is always the answer." But any meeting had to be soon, K. wrote. Ruth could not hold out much longer. "All of our relatives and friends are demanding that we call a doctor, but . . . we refuse." In his soul, Herr K. allowed, he felt a growing sense of "enormous responsibility." "Think what we have to answer for," he said darkly. Yet he was sure that, if only Meckelburg "could see Ruth, her belief, the way it can't be broken by anything," he would surely "wonder at it, and do anything, anything, to give her this one last wish."[17]

Around mid-May, Otto Meckelburg brought Gröning to Säckingen to visit; Renée Meckelburg joined them. This visit transported Herr K. to heights of rapture. "We are still deeply moved by your having come, and by your help," he wrote to Gröning afterward. "Since you left, our endless prayers of thanks reach up to heaven. . . . dear Herr Gröning, I clasp your hand unremittingly. In my world-upending joy, I wrote to the Minister President of Bavaria, 'Receive, German people, the greatest benefactor, and give him a license.' I don't know if it was right, I just had to open my heart."[18] K. also wrote Meckelburg a few days later. Ruth's condition, he said, had improved. He was now convinced, against considerable evidence to the contrary, that Ruth would recover fully and even begin to look for a career.[19]

The historical record contains little of Ruth's own voice, but she did write a few pages in a diary about her illness, including minute details of her physical condition.[20] These diary entries were written for Gröning to read. "Tuesday, May 30, 1950. A cold wave in the morning made itself felt today. . . . The activity in the lungs was not so strong. Today I could feel more in the kidneys. . . . Also my circulation was very brisk. My heart beat very heavily going up the stairs." The following day: "Wednesday, May 31, 1950. My head feels very muffled! I don't sense much today in my lungs. Just like yesterday, I feel something working in the center. My circulation is very brisk. . . . Around midday I had a temperature of 100.4 but then it sank back to 98.6." On Thursday, she reported that she "could not perceive anything special. The cold wave that comes at lunchtime was there. My circulation and pulse were very strong and fast." A few days after, Ruth was pleased to report, as a sign of an overall improvement in her health, that "finally . . . my period, which has been so very missed, has returned after a gap of eight weeks," and signed off with her customary "Warm greetings, Ruth." On Saturday, June 3, after "the cold wave," she felt a "very hot wave," which was "very strange" and made her eyes burn. Then she felt a particular warmth in her bronchia and windpipe.[21] Soon after, her father wrote to Otto to report that Ruth was "better," due, he thought, to an improvement in the air.[22]

There was a long gap in correspondence between June and October. By then, Gröning and the Meckelburgs had split, and Ruth's condition had changed for the worse. "Oh, dear Herr Gröning," K. wrote,

> please do not be angry with me, when I write as a father just a few lines to report about Ruth. It hurts me endlessly to see the child suffer, she endures it all so patiently, has surrendered herself completely to the Lord God, and trusts you unto death. Now the poor girl has wasted away to 76 pounds; she cannot go to the movies, or anywhere, anywhere else. Release the child from this terrible dry cough, which begins at 10 p.m. and goes on without ceasing

until 2 or 3 in the morning. Her urine, too, has a horrible color. I fear the worst. Have mercy on this great, pure, and good soul. If your schedule can reasonably allow it, please write a few lines. She hungers for some sign of your support.[23]

Not having heard from Gröning a week later, K. tried frantically to contact him through his Munich associate, the lay healer Eugen Enderlin. "Things are truly very bad with my daughter," K. wrote. "Herr Gröning knows this very well, how it is with her. I don't need to tell him what kind of suffering the poor child is now going through." K. continued, "My daughter has placed her faith so powerfully in our father above. . . . She trusts Herr Gröning unto death. She will not let a doctor near her. Herr Gröning cannot abandon the poor child." And he closed, "Herr Enderlin, please, please be so kind, if you cannot deliver this letter, could you please send me some word?"[24] Enderlin later told the court that Herr K.'s letters at this point were coming "every other day."[25]

By November 1, Ruth suffered from diarrhea and could not eat. She could no longer walk much. "And yet her courage does not slip," her father reported to Gröning. "Just today she repeated your own words . . . 'Miss Ruth, you can trust in Gröning completely, I will help you.'" And Ruth continued, her father said:

"Or do you believe that he could leave me in the lurch? No, no, I depend entirely on his word. In May he told me: I have come to teach you about what may come, because in the second phase you will have to suffer even more than before." She looked at you so victoriously, so full of faith in our heavenly father.

"This is how we speak to each other every evening when we sit together with our tinfoil balls," K. wrote to Gröning. Ruth just needed some sign, he said, "a fortifier." Or maybe her father did? He was constantly asked, he wrote, "who is your doctor, what does he say?" With some people the family kept mum about the truth—that Ruth had no doctor—to avoid opprobrium. If Gröning would please just write a few lines? "We are constantly shaken by the suffering of our child and we fear the worst. . . . Please, please send some word to help us understand."[26]

By early December, Ruth was almost motionless. "Herr Gröning cannot come but also writes not a single word," her father wrote to Enderlin.

> I know how life is around Herr Gröning, I know about the mercurial character, I know that he is constantly being distracted. Because I know this, I beseech you again and again, keep our child close to your heart, remember her. And if it is not too much to ask, if you could tell me as soon as the license to treat has been given. We read that Herr Gröning has been given trouble about that. And besides that bad people are really not making his life easy.[27]

Ruth had terrible pains in her lungs. "I pray daily that God will give Herr Gröning the strength to heal our child," K. wrote. "Herr Gröning may not abandon our child now. . . . It was just about one year ago that our daughter was supposed to go to the sanatorium . . . in the Black Forest. The best Swiss doctors are there. . . . Our daughter pleaded with us so earnestly to bring her instead to Herr Gröning."

They had done so, K. said, and Gröning had given his word. K. referred again to having "taken on the fateful responsibility" of not sending Ruth to the clinic. "You can imagine what a burden this is for me," he explained to Enderlin.

> We will lapse into insanity, if our daughter is denied help. . . . It would be horrible, abominable, and absolutely unthinkable if the child despairs from lack of a word from him. Dear Herr Enderlin, do everything, save our darling from a terrible end. Please greet Herr Gröning very warmly from us. He should please tell us if this phase will soon be over or if a bit more time will pass.[28]

Less than two weeks later, on December 30, 1950, Ruth died. K. sent one last letter.

> Very esteemed Herr Gröning, the end was ghastly, and the awakening horrifying. Commentary is superfluous. I blame you and yet do not. But I may remind you about Bad Wiessee, where you gave my child your word in my presence that she would be healed, and I remind you of your assurance on May 14, that her lungs would be all right. In her unbending belief the child called out to you for help until the last hour. You will have to make your excuses to God. In deepest sadness and bearing the massive burden of this error, yours, K.[29]

Gröning had not been an earthbound god who could heal even tuberculosis through mysterious energies and the indomitable power of faith. As K. learned the hard way, he was merely a man, and a moody, inconstant one at that. The power of Ruth's belief, which seemed so extraordinary to her father—so pious, the expression of a pure soul, a faith that could not be broken by anything—became a millstone around K.'s own neck, an inescapable and unbearable weight. He himself died only weeks later. The medical cause given was a liver ailment, though the press sometimes claimed—melodramatically, perhaps, but given the content of his letters, also plausibly—that the cause was a broken heart.[30]

. . .

As disturbing as Herr K.'s letters are, officials who received them from Otto Meckelburg in June 1951—when Meckelburg and Gröning were being tried for violating the lay healer law—seem not to have found in them sufficient cause to investigate beyond taking an initial statement from Gröning's then partner, Eugen Enderlin.[31] At the time, authorities were much less interested in the circumstances of Ruth's death than in whether Gröning's ongoing activities—meetings with cure-seekers for what he called "belief lectures"—violated the lay

healer regulations. The truth was that in the early 1950s, many officials remained quite conflicted about the matter. A man wishing to file
a complaint against him in 1951 for fraud was told by a senior public prosecutor in Munich that Gröning "irrefutably had a favorable
influence on sick people," which "in countless cases" had resulted in
"surprising cures."[32]

In 1952, Gröning was acquitted for the second time of violating the lay healer law, due to lack of evidence. The court noted how
ambiguous the law was and how difficult to define "healing" under it,
given "the anomaly of Gröning's particular therapy."[33] The law, which
had attempted to reserve to physicians the diagnosis and treatment
of suffering and illness, had always been a rough fit with Gröning's
work, which seemed to entail not just a technique or a philosophy of
diet or exercise, but something outside the law's grasp.

Doctors from the state health office visiting one of Gröning's belief
lectures in late 1952 told him that these sessions skated close to the
line legally, because people were "obviously not coming for the content of the lectures" but for a cure. Yet the doctors were also convinced that Gröning "seemed honestly to be trying to find a legal way
to carry out his activities," and were encouraged that he was even
thinking of applying for a lay practitioner license.[34] Police were often
more skeptical. They wondered, for example, why Gröning contin-
ually asked members of his lecture audiences how they felt. "That
alone shows that he is working on people or trying to. He acts as if
he were able to trigger some process inside people," county police in
Bavaria reported.[35] In the northern city of Hamelin, the site of the Pied
Piper folktale (an ironic location, given how often the press compared
Gröning's effect on people to that of the famous rat catcher), a state
health officer reported Gröning to authorities for treating the sick—
one of whom was the wife of a retired high-ranking city official.[36]
The general public remained no less divided than judicial, police, and
health authorities. In "the interest of science," a man named Michelson went in late 1953 to a Munich inn where Gröning was meeting
with cure-seekers, "to unmask him as a swindler . . . and discredit

his hocus-pocus." Those who had gathered to hear the healer speak protested to Michelson: Gröning was no con man, they said. Rather, "he had something divine in him, something that makes him like a Jesus."[37]

The belief lectures were Gröning's response to ongoing, if ambivalent, legal opposition. After his 1951 and 1952 trials, he settled into a low-key routine, meeting regularly with gatherings of thirty to fifty people.[38] A woman named Magdalena, who worked as a maid, attended one. "I only remember that he said he wanted to heal sick people," she later told investigators, "but the sick had to believe in him. Among other things, he also mentioned that we had to believe in our Lord God and . . . pray."[39] Lecturing was part of an overall strategy to avoid conflict with the law while still being able to "reach the sick," as Gröning often put it. His lawyer, a man named Reuss, had told him in no uncertain terms after his 1952 trial, "They are really out for you now," referring to Bavarian prosecutors, "and you must, as I have said again and again, limit yourself to your lecture work and not 'healing' and also do not use the term 'healing,' as you have continued to do. Because: if they get you for violating the law on lay healers, you will have to count on a serious penalty, one I won't be able to save you from. So: only lectures! No healings!"[40] Reuss concluded his letter by thanking his client for a coffee machine Gröning had sent him as a gift.

One tabloid succinctly captured Gröning's status in 1953 as one of "legal illegality."[41] Though he continued to brush up against the law's limits, he also tried to operate in a new way. He met new associates and came under new influences. A group of aristocrats, including members of the von Zeppelin family, founded an entity called the Bruno Gröning Laboratory, Inc., to produce "biological remedies," and sought for it (unsuccessfully, as it happened) the patronage of Theodor Heuss, West Germany's federal president.[42] Gröning's disciples published pamphlets about him, elaborating concepts and techniques in ways he himself had never really done. The earliest books about him, written in the heady Herford days, had focused on the biblical scenes he seemed to reenact. But *Bruno Gröning's Healing Current*, published in 1953, evangelized his abilities both as spiritual *and* "scientific-metaphysical" facts.[43]

Some of these changes in practice and rhetoric can probably be attributed to Egon Arthur Schmidt. The erstwhile Gröning manager and critic came back into the fold as the healer's "press consultant" in the mid-1950s and launched a media blitz to highlight the Wunderdoktor's new activities. Newspapers reported plans to bring knowledge of Gröning's methods of "healing through spiritual power" to all "circles of the people." An organization called the Gröning League was founded with the intention of establishing clinics, hospitals, and research centers "to study the healing powers of Bruno Gröning systematically."[44] Gröning even began to refer to himself as *Privatgelehrter*, which we might translate as "independent scholar," "adept," or perhaps "learned one."[45] He began describing cure-seekers as "listeners," to whom he gave balls fashioned from tinfoil the way "churches give their believers holy pictures, amulets," so they would "always remember my words."[46]

Belief lectures, spiritual self-help, critiques of pharma-fueled modern medicine, "legal illegality": these might have formed the outlines of a more "established" Gröning. At a certain moment, the healer appeared to be on his way to becoming something of an institution: less a media messiah, perhaps, than a sage of what we would now call alternative medicine. But in summer 1954, for reasons that the archives do not make clear, authorities shifted their attention from investigating Gröning's possible violations of the lay healer law to the case of Ruth K. and to negligent homicide.[47] Criminal police in Stuttgart interviewed Gröning for two days in early 1955, asking, "If someone comes to you with a bad case of TB, are there still chances for improvement?" In his typically gnomic and syntactically challenged style, the healer replied: "I give the person advice, in case he up to then has not paid much attention to his body, to do so and to catch up on what has been lost, but now properly and always being attentive to his body and not to think about his illness." Gröning also quoted

Paracelsus, a Renaissance-era physician and touchstone for natural healers of many stripes: "Every illness is curable, but not every human being is." And then Gröning said, "I am not against death. That's how I oriented the father." What Gröning seems to have meant was that he prepared K., in some sense, for his daughter's death.[48]

When police interviewed Gröning again the following year, he came armed with fresh powder. He cited the best-selling Norman Vincent Peale, whose *The Power of Positive Thinking* Gröning had read about and in which he found new support for his own ideas about the connection between belief and health. He quoted to police investigators from a book called *Lucifer's Grip on the Living*, by Dr. Erwin Gamber, which indicted purely rationalist thinking as the source of various evils: atomic weapons, genetic experimentation, chemical food additives, a massive overreliance on pharmaceuticals, and the fact that "large portions of the earth" would soon "become uninhabitable." Gröning told police that he wanted people to realize that "they had become blind to godly power." They needed to "relearn" it, to use spiritual power "to recover and maintain the divine order." He also praised folk medicine for knowing long before the advent of penicillin that laying moldy bread on a wound could be beneficial.[49]

What he left out of all of these comments were the elements of magic, and the battle between good and evil, that had always been— and indeed remained—a part of his repertoire. A woman who attended a belief lecture subsequently told police that good and evil had been Gröning's topic of discussion. She also remembered a man who had been there, who walked with the aid of two canes, and that Gröning had worked a charm on the canes.[50] Many of those who sought Gröning's cures—people suffering from conditions as different as migraines, a brain tumor, or a broken rib that would not heal—said Gröning had returned them to health through his lectures or by bringing them back to God.[51] The truth was that no matter what Gröning said about his treatments, for many of his followers it remained true that he himself was the medicine. His words were always secondary to simply being in his curative presence. It was true that many seeking healing from Gröning said that his teachings made them well, but others said more ambiguous things: that they got better after a visit from him, or having coffee with him. Whether Gröning or his disciples presented him as a New Age shaman or humble preacher, people still mobbed him in public, eager to touch him or to get a tinfoil ball straight from his hands.

. . .

The Cold War era saw a renaissance in the scientific study of parapsychology—clairvoyance, ESP, second sight, and parakinesis, among other phenomena. By the latter half of the 1950s, the field was being rapidly institutionalized in West Germany, as in other parts of Europe and the United States. Freiburg psychology professor Hans Bender, already famous in the Third Reich, was emerging as one of Western Europe's leading figures in the field.[52] Dr. Inge Strauch, one of Bender's colleagues, took a particular scientific interest in spiritual healing and conducted experiments with Gröning's former disciple and compatriot Kurt Trampler—who had since become a well-known healer in his own right—at Bender's parapsychology research center, the Institut für Grenzgebiete der Psychologie und Psychohygiene (IGPP), the Institute for Frontier Areas of Psychology and Mental Health.

Strauch attributed Trampler's success as a healer to the "intensive affective field" in which his treatments unfolded, in which a patient's will to believe focused on "the 'numinous' power of the healer" in a "reciprocal process."[53] Arthur Jores, a Hamburg physician, came to a similar conclusion about miracle healers. In a 1955 article, "Magic and Sorcery in Modern Medicine," published in the weekly newsletter of the German Society for Internal Medicine, Jores described the intangible interaction between doctor and patient as a "magical . . . relationship" that helped "produce a healing effect." It was that effect, he continued, that enabled the "great medicine men of our time"—the Grönings and Tramplers—to "drift through the country . . . finding throngs of followers from every stratum of our population" despite their having "no training in anatomy or physiology." Those seeking treatments simply "knew" that lay healers possessed "'powers' that university-trained doctors don't have."[54]

These explanations sounded new, but they weren't, not really. Both Jores's and Strauch's views fundamentally rehashed those of another German physician, Erwin Liek, an advocate in the 1920s and '30s of holism.[55] Liek had rejected a purely mechanistic view of human bodies that reduced them to their biological processes. Decades before Jores and Strauch, he wrote about the ancient connection between physician and priest and its healing power, and about doctors who could call forth astonishing cures through the sheer force of their personalities.[56] What *had* changed since Liek's time related to his unapologetically religious view of nature, life, and health. Parapsychology researchers of the 1950s glossed the abilities of a Trampler or a Gröning in the language of psychology and science, rather than the language of the soul.

In that sense, Gröning's work was becoming secularized by the late 1950s, and thus more mainstream in a country in which large numbers of people were shedding their religion. Moreover, he was no longer the extraordinary novelty he had seemed in 1949. He now shared the field of spiritual healing with many other household names at home and abroad: in West Germany, Trampler and Pietro Tranti; in France, Yves Albre and Lucien Rivet; in Great Britain, Harry Edwards; in the Netherlands, Greet Hofmans.[57] When the press described the Ruth K. case as "one of the strangest of our time," they revealed, perhaps, not just how quickly the memory of Herford and Rosenheim had faded, but also how much the kind of devotion Ruth and her father demonstrated toward Gröning had come to appear alien, even dangerous. Faith of that intensity seemed out of step with a society in transition, a society more inclined to want its beliefs validated, its miracles vetted, its holy men scrutinized.

. . .

Gröning's celebrity may no longer have had quite the frenetic, world-upending quality in 1957 that it did in 1949, but huge crowds nonetheless turned up at Munich's Palace of Justice hours before the proceedings began that July. As Gröning stood and smiled and passed out tinfoil balls to "throngs of spectators pressing in," crowds surged forward to touch him and "practically ripped [them] from his hands."[58] *Revue*, the magazine that had contributed so substantially to Gröning's early notoriety, told readers that the healer's popularity was undiminished: he still received some three hundred letters per day.[59] The *Bild* tabloid described a war veteran and a blind man clamoring around Groning for cures during a break in the proceedings, while "excited women fell all over themselves to be allowed to kiss his hand." The healer's hair—a "womanish lion's mane," per *Bild*—drew particular attention.[60] It gave Gröning the appearance of a "kohlrabi apostle," one journalist observed, invoking a term once used to describe an earlier generation of lay religious figures in Germany. Some of those, like the itinerant preacher gusaf nagel (who preferred to lowercase his name), and the painter, pacifist, and vegetarianism-and-free-love proponent Karl Wilhelm Diefenbach, had grown their hair long in the style of biblical prophets.[61]

German criminal court cases are largely conducted by a tribunal of judges; some are professional, others politically appointed lay people. Professional judges call witnesses forward in turn. The first witness called that day was Gröning himself, who offered a statement in response to the charges against him. He began with details of his biography—his family, schooling, and work history, before and after the war—and then circled in general ways around the question of what he did and how it worked, whether he tried to *cure* illness or simply hoped to impart some spiritual or philosophical principles about health.

Under the harsh spotlight of the courtroom, Gröning the guru seemed eager to press Gröning the magician back into the shadows of 1949. There was nothing especially salubrious about *him*, he stressed. He did not touch people and did not tell anyone he could cure them. It was true that he gave people tinfoil balls, but only as keepsakes, mementos. Sometimes he gave them out because the audience expected them and "was sad when they didn't get any." When

people asked for a cure, he told them, "It's not that I heal, but 'it' can lead to healing"—referring to the *Heilstrom*, the healing current. Yet Gröning did correct the posture of audience members (to help energies flow better), and asked those to whom he gave tinfoil balls what they sensed. "I told my listeners that a human being can heal himself," Gröning said, but each "person had to pay attention to *his* body, and not mine." It was true, he said, that he talked about sickness sometimes, because he wanted people to think about "why the body is ill." He admitted that he knew that people saw him as "a transmitter of supernatural powers."[62]

Gröning recalled meeting Ruth and her father. "K. told me that his daughter had been given up on by doctors and he could not even think of handing her back to them as a guinea pig." Ruth, too, had said "she could not think of going back to a doctor." Gröning claimed he had not known what was wrong with her. After hearing him speak to a group in Bad Wiessee, he recalled, "she said that she felt very well," and "believed that she was cured." Upon learning that Ruth was supposed to leave the next morning for "a sanatorium or hospital," Gröning said he asked, "then what are you doing here?"[63] Yet he did not want to shake her faith in the possibility of getting well again, so he encouraged her to seek medical treatment, and told her father to get his daughter an X-ray.[64] He claimed never to have seen the letters Herr K. wrote, though he did recall Otto Meckelburg telling him later that both father and daughter were "writing their fingers down to the bone" pleading for him to visit. When a visit was finally arranged and he and Otto arrived at the K. family home in Säckingen, Gröning said that Otto Meckelburg, not he, told K., "Now Gröning is here to take away the rest of your daughter Ruth's illness!"[65]

A number of other witnesses now offered their testimony. Enderlin, the Munich healer with whom Gröning had worked, said he had received desperate letters from Herr K. every other day. He said he had asked Gröning to go to Säckingen to see Ruth. In what must have been a dramatic moment in the courtroom, the prosecutor asked for some of K.'s letters to be read aloud. Against Gröning's assertion that he had not received any letters, Enderlin said he "had given some . . . to the accused personally."[66]

The testimony of even the friendliest of witnesses pitted Gröning as spiritual sage against Gröning the Wunderdoktor. A woman whose asthma Gröning had helped explained that in her view, the tinfoil balls he handed out during his belief lectures were *angesprochen*— that is, laden with magical power. She said people went to see Gröning "because they knew that a healing power streamed out of him." Other witnesses said Gröning had told them that the "process of healing" was a "matter of belief," and that one had to believe to be healthy. Yet others recalled feeling "a tickle in their hands and feet" after talking to him.[67]

The next day, Ruth's sixty-five-year-old mother, wearing blue sunglasses on the witness stand, described a bitter divide in her family between her husband and daughter—the ones committed to Gröning—and the rest of them, who openly blamed Herr K. for Ruth's refusing medical treatment. Frau K. contradicted Gröning's statement about who said the healer had come "to take away the rest of" Ruth's illness. Gröning said that himself, she claimed. She also told the court that her husband said Gröning had forbidden Ruth to be X-rayed, though she conceded that she had never herself heard Gröning say that Ruth was not allowed to go to a doctor.[68]

Witness seventeen was Otto Meckelburg. The trial transcript describes him as a businessman, and indeed he seems to have remained a Wunderdoktor manager after his breakup with Gröning. In 1954, *Der Spiegel* had reported that he was handling the career of Pietro Tranti, who made a splash in the early '50s, the first miracle healer of national (and international) reputation to emerge in Gröning's wake. *Der Spiegel*'s story said that in 1952, Meckelburg had claimed to be in talks with the Argentine ambassador in Bonn and other officials to arrange for Tranti to visit a dying Eva Peron.[69] Now, on the stand in Munich, Meckelburg had relatively little to say, especially considering how central he had been to the case being presented in court. He claimed that Herr K. told him that Gröning "promised he would heal his daughter," and that the "accused confirmed to me that he would cure her." He and Gröning had talked about the case and the letters many times, Meckelburg said. Renée Meckelburg also testified, saying she, too, had spoken with Gröning about Ruth. After their first meeting in Bad Wiessee, Ruth told Renée that Gröning said: "you are healthy, go and get X-rayed." The X-ray, Renée's testimony seemed to suggest, was intended to confirm that Ruth was cured.[70]

After the witnesses had all spoken, the state's attorney, Helmut Fey, asked for a one-year jail sentence for Gröning on the combined charges of negligent homicide and violating the lay healer law. Fey also asked the court to confiscate Gröning's tinfoil sheets and balls.[71]

The court did confiscate the tinfoil.[72] Gröning was found guilty of violating the lay healer law and sentenced to a fine of two thousand marks or a three-month stay in jail. But he was cleared of the more serious charge of negligent homicide. In its decision, the court noted that when he met Ruth, in 1949, Bavarian authorities had not yet banned Gröning from treating people. The court was also sympathetic to Ruth's father's plight: his daughter had been "given up on" by doctors and he no longer wanted her treated as a "guinea pig." No one had refuted this statement, the court said, and "after all," Herr K. "must have had a reason for turning to the accused."[73]

The past slipped quietly into view with this utterance, rather like a ghost no one wanted to acknowledge. No one mentioned specifically what role tuberculosis may have played in Ruth's actions. It was and is a terrible disease under any circumstances. But if it was not a sign of sin in the moral framework of folk medicine, it nonetheless had been fearsomely stigmatized in the Third Reich. Individuals with infectious diseases—like TB—had been forbidden to marry under 1933's Law for the Protection of the Hereditary Health of the German People. TB patients' rations and care were sharply curtailed (and cut altogether if they were Jews). The state planned to house TB patients involuntarily in asylums until this proved impracticable.[74] People avoided being screened for the disease at all.[75] How long these uneasy memories circulated and to what effect, we can only imagine.

In her young life, Ruth had seen girls like her die under treatment, and she herself endured months of agonizing therapies. Whether or not K. had lost faith in the medical treatment Ruth received, "his daughter had obviously" done so, the judges concluded. Nor had anyone proved that Gröning actually told the K. family to stop Ruth's medical treatment. Her father had refused to take Ruth to the doctor even when the rest of his family insisted on it, and so bore some responsibility. Lastly, it was not clear to the court why "precisely he"—Gröning— should have done differently, "with his educational level." The suggestion, it seems, was that Gröning had been ill-prepared to resist the phenomenon in which he, like his disciples and cure-seekers, had been swept up. At the time he met Ruth, the court noted, "the accused was publicly praised as a Wunderdoktor."[76]

. . .

Before Gröning's trial began, during the process of interviewing various witnesses, the court solicited the expert opinion of doctors from the University of Freiburg's Psychiatric and Nerve Clinic, who were asked to assess the healer's legal responsibility. Dr. Richard Jung, professor of clinical neurophysiology and psychiatry, invited Gröning to a fourteen-day stay at the clinic in February 1957.[77] Jung's report suggests that his conversations with Gröning focused a lot on themes of belief and trust. The healer told Jung that he knew the danger of "blind faith" where the most serious illnesses were concerned. But people who came to him—and this was certainly the case with Ruth K.—had often lost their faith in doctors. In the early days of his work, Gröning said, he had been oriented toward sickness, but now he worried about bringing order to the soul. He always relied on his moods and trusted his feelings. He could even tell when his secretary, a floor below him, was upset. His success, he said, came from his ability to sense other people's "inner disharmony."[78]

"People had always drawn him in, really drawn him," Jung reported Gröning explaining. If he followed his moods, he "could really do something." He remembered such a time, in Rosenheim. "Speaking to the masses, he felt so at ease and became so light that he had jumped down from the balcony into the crowd." As he became light, so did they. They "lost their afflictions." It was a feeling of "community and happiness," he said—one that could never be as strong "in conversation with an individual as in a greater circle." What drew Gröning to people was a feeling of "becoming 'light' and 'pumped up' together."[79]

Psychiatrist Alexander Mitscherlich, who had been asked by the court to assess Gröning during the healer's 1951 trial, had found the healer's intelligence wanting, to say nothing of his moral character. But Jung judged Gröning's intellect to be "easily above average." He did agree with his colleague that Gröning had an "elevated need for recognition and feelings of community." While this quality made him highly suggestible, according to Jung, it also was the source of the effect he had on people.[80]

Maybe we'll never know exactly what went on in the summer of 1949 between Bruno Gröning on that Rosenheim balcony and the people below. Maybe we'll never be able to explain fully how soul medicine worked, or the cures in Herford, or the *Heilstrom*, or the tinfoil balls. But it seems that Gröning, at least, had been a different person then, and maybe the crowds below with all their pent-up fervor had been, too. Where Mitscherlich and others saw "unenlightened" people easily led by would-be dictators, sucked in by their emotions and blinded by a lack of insight, Gröning remembered spiritual unity, wholeness, a sense of being "pumped up": a state in which people lost their afflictions, whether of mind, body, or soul. Under National Socialism, Germans had intensely prized an "elevated need for feelings of community." Only eight years later, memories of great throngs of people standing together in a Rosenheim field, singing religious songs, awaiting some final unveiling, and hoping for salvation seemed alien, distasteful.

We probably can't know, either, what exactly happened to Ruth K. under Dr. Volk's care, or before, in the Taunus clinic. We can't tell what had made meeting Gröning so urgent for her, or what might have happened had he never entered the picture.

Gröning's August 1957 acquittal of the charge of negligent homicide was annulled on appeal just a few months later. "To the court it appears out of the question," the documents read, that the healer had not known "that Ruth K. suffered from TB." The court was also convinced, based on evidence in Herr K.'s letters, that Gröning had "promised to make the girl well." Having taken over her care "in connection with promising her a cure" made him the cause of her death, because that had prompted father and daughter to stop medical treatment and to cancel Ruth's stay in the Black Forest clinic. Gröning "knew of their unshakeable belief" and "blind zeal," making what happened to Ruth also foreseeable. In January 1958, he was sentenced to eight months in jail and a fine of five thousand marks. During sentencing, the court named as a mitigating factor Ruth's father's responsibility and also suggested that Dr. Volk had had legal options she had not used to compel Ruth to resume treatment. Still, the court condemned what it called Gröning's "indifference" to the young woman's fate.[81]

As members of the public, in turn, took up their pens to condemn the court, more unacknowledged ghosts crowded in. August Unger, the former Nazi mayor of Plaidt, who called himself "Adolf II" and led the far-right "Party of Good Germans," addressed himself to the "great punisher of the regional court." "With regret I read today that Gröning has been the subject of yet another trial. I find this treatment outrageous in our civilized times." With no sense of irony, he compared the trials of Bruno Gröning to "the age of witch burning." A postcard sent to the court denounced the whole affair as "miserable." One woman's letter, addressed to "the highest state authorities of the German Reich," condemned the "high court in Munich," which had "unwittingly *rejected God* for the entire German people." Gröning had saved her from cancer, the woman wrote, and she compared the court's decision to "the crucifixion of our Lord Jesus Christ 2,000 years ago . . . Herr Bruno Gröning is the good Son of God." A man named Zimmermann wrote to say how "delighted" he would be just "to spend a few weeks" around Gröning. "That would surely alleviate my suffering and give me new will to live." A woman from Hamburg, meanwhile, lectured the court that "a sick person has the RIGHT to believe in her own healing." Gröning had shown a greater sense of responsibility than a doctor might have, she insisted: he had refused to take Ruth's "hope away by coldly explaining the truth of her illness." The healer, at least, had given her faith.[82]

In March 1958, a state's attorney in Munich filed papers asking that a harsher sentence be imposed against Bruno Gröning. It was hard to imagine that the healer would lead a law-abiding life, the state's attorney wrote: he would almost certainly continue his healing work, "if in a disguised form."[83] But before another round could commence in the case, the whole affair abruptly ended, rather more quietly than it had begun back in the summer of 1949. A short, indirectly worded, bureaucratic notice, dated February 21, 1959, alerted concerned parties that the "proceedings are concluded by the death of the accused."[84] Bruno Gröning was gone, dead of stomach cancer at age fifty-two. The healer's death was not just his own end; it was the end of an era. It was a metaphor, too. One of the most prominent manifestations of the postwar era—of the agony of defeat, of social turmoil and spiritual sickness—was gone.

It had been almost exactly ten years since the healer made his national debut in Herford. *Der Spiegel*'s obituary for Gröning noted that Dieter Hülsmann, the boy whose miraculous first steps after a winter in bed had led tens of thousands of pilgrims to that Westphalian town, had died himself a few years earlier, at age sixteen. He lay buried in Herford, the paper said, in an untended grave.[85] To the German reader, the meaning of this would have been immediately clear: in a country that took the tending of graves seriously, Dieter's neglected patch of earth telegraphed his abandonment. The world, in its way, had moved on.

CONCLUSION

Fears of evil did not take their leave with Bruno Gröning, at least not entirely. A cache of newspaper clippings in a Berlin church archive attests that witchcraft accusations continued sporadically to surface into the mid-'60s. In 1962, for example, in Bavarian Mailach, a twenty-five-year-old auto mechanic admitted to burning down the home of a woman in her sixties who he claimed was a witch. Locals refused to clear the area for fear of coming into contact with what was left of her possessions.[1]

But the wave of accusations did appear, by the sixties, distinctly retrospective to many observers. In February 1961, the publishers of *The Sixth and Seventh Books of Moses* had gone back to court once again, but were convicted only of dishonest advertising. That same year, the interior minister of Schleswig-Holstein wrote a report on the state's investigation of witch fears. The number of "witch cases" that could be "established" had been so few, he said, that "intervention with repressive measures" seemed "unnecessary." Other states in the republic had already dropped the matter. The minister's view was that "superstition cannot be eliminated with prohibitive norms" but only through "public enlightenment." For instance, apothecaries had agreed to sell preparations used in magical recipes, like "devil's dung," only "under ordinary German names," presumably to strip them of any mystical residue.[2]

A June 1961 memo in the archives announcing the conclusion of Schleswig-Holstein's witch investigation reads like a coda to a decade of careful omissions and sealed-off histories: "The whole matter from here on out should be regarded as finished."[3] People sensed that the accusations belonged not just to the past, but more specifically to the postwar past. "There are no more stories in the newspapers about witches," folklorist Leopold Schmidt wrote in 1965, or about "the Catholic Church's war against the desperate pilgrims of Herolds-bach."[4] "Is the Witch Craze Over and Done With?" asked the *Frank-furter Rundschau* the same year. The social minister of Lower Saxony, Heinz Rudolph, who had "declared war" on superstition just a few years earlier, told reporters that "effectively in the last five years we have not heard of a single case." "We don't know ourselves what happened," Rudolph said.[5]

Some posited that perhaps the change had something to do with the advent of television. Others pointed to space travel, riffing on Hamlet's line to Horatio: perhaps it had cleared away "once and for all a lot of peculiar ideas about things that go on between heaven and earth."[6] What seems more likely than the idea that new technology could simply banish popular fears of evil at a stroke is that the actual roots of the 1950s witchcraft scare—latent recriminations, social mistrust, and spiritual insecurity—had themselves subsided, leached gradually away. With fears of retribution went fears of witches and other shadowy conspirators.

As for Gröning, he continued, in death as in life, to be tabloid fodder. In 1959, a scandal sheet called *7 Days* bruited the accusation that he had not died of cancer. Rather, it was said, his wife had conspired to kill him by forcing him to submit to an unnecessary operation to remove his goiter. A different theory held that he had died because he had so often requested that his patients "give him their ill-nesses." Having accumulated in his body, these finally took their toll.[7] Gröning's ashes were buried in Dillenburg, next to his younger son, Günter. People kept up a steady pilgrimage there, leaving wreaths. A cemetery official told the *Bild* tabloid in 1960 that "hardly a day" went by that someone did not inquire about it. A local businessman worried that the site would soon displace Dillenburg's "tourist attrac-tion number one"—the town was, after all, the birthplace of William of Orange.[8] But by the mid-1960s, the Gröning phenomenon, too, appeared merely backward looking. A series in the tabloid *New Illus-trated* proclaimed him "the best-known German of the postwar era," "more famous than Adenauer and Erhard."[9]

• • •

The war had left behind death and material damage of unthinkable proportions. But the moral questions it generated were so vast and stupefying that even today, long after the rubble has been cleared, and mortar has filled in the holes left in building facades by bullets and shrapnel, and the last soldiers who fought are dying of old age, these questions—about the furthest extremities of human behavior, about how mass murder can be countenanced and undertaken—remain only partially answered at best.

The past refuses to be denied. History has ways of making itself felt no matter how sharply rebuffed, how studiously disavowed. In the United States, for example, since the eighteenth century, there have been persistent cultural references and tales told about haunted Indian burial grounds. These tales hide, as one writer puts it, "a cer-tain anxiety about the land on which Americans—specifically white, middle-class Americans—live. Embedded deep in the idea of home ownership . . . is the idea that we don't, in fact, own the land."[10] Tales of hauntings express an otherwise unspoken and sublimated terror at the center of white American life: that vengeful ghosts will come back and reclaim what's theirs. Similarly, revenants lingered at the center of German social life after the Holocaust and after Nazism.

The haunting of postwar West German society took two princi-
pal forms. One was vertical: individuals who felt afflicted, guilty, or
damned looked up to a savior, who just happened to show up in
the moment of their direst need. Significantly, Bruno Gröning had
his greatest successes treating chronic illnesses, various ailments
that doctors said did not exist, and mysterious afflictions they had
given up trying to remedy. What were these ailments, many of which
resolved themselves so quickly in interactions with Gröning, or in the
crowds that gathered at his feet, in the dark, under the spotlights?
Maybe a better question might be: what were these ailments *symptoms* of, exactly? Some doctors after the war seemed to have an idea.
They spoke of the connections between guilt and illness, and sickness
that came from sin, and healing that required atonement, expiation.
To be "sick," Gröning had said, was to be inhabited by evil. But what
was evil's source? In some ways, Gröning suggested that turning away
from God permitted evil and sickness. Yet the Wunderdoktor's talk of
evil may also have hinted at the realization that everything had gone
wrong, that so many terrible things had been done, and that those terrible things had often gone unpunished. Everyone has a *Schweinhund*
in him, Gröning said.

The other form of haunting was more horizontal: the witch scare,
which spread unease over whole communities in the 1950s, was a
neighbor-to-neighbor phenomenon. A lot was packed into that episode. The countryside in Schleswig-Holstein, the state that seems
to have played host to more witch trials than any other, had been
upended by change: millions of refugees from Germany's former east
and other eastern European German communities were resettled
there, which caused friction. At the same time, there are clear signs
that many of the troubles might have been stirred up by unresolved
grievances, fears of exposure, and suppressed hostilities related to the
Nazi era and to denazification. In a part of the country that had such
a large percentage of former Nazi Party members, denazification in
small communities kicked up a great deal of anxiety. No one knew

who might have said what to whom. Accusing a neighbor of being a witch allowed for various hatreds and anxieties to be aired while also being concealed, mislabeled, suppressed.

• • •

This book has focused on the past, and the first, extremely difficult years in the Federal Republic following Germany's defeat in World War II. But the history of postwar witch scares and mystical healings also raises broader questions, many of them no less relevant today than in the 1950s. One is the question of how knowledge, authority, trust, and morality intertwine in society. It's important to understand better what social conditions give credence to ideas or, conversely, jeopardize the world's knowability and knowledge's believability. If society comprises a set of commonly held ideas about how the world works, what happens when the conditions that make consensus possible no longer obtain? Can society continue, or will it fracture and fall apart?

West German society, as we know, did not fall apart. West Germans built a successful democracy and economy. Within the parameters of the Cold War, peace endured. But it is that "success story" that really requires the hardest thinking. For what does it mean, for all of us, if a nation can turn so quickly from building Auschwitz to constructing an affluent and neon-lit world? What remains unsaid, what is pushed out of sight to achieve and grimly maintain a sense of reality, let alone "normalcy," after genocide and moral collapse? And what kind of normalcy is that, exactly? "Realist" historical answers to questions of such awesome significance are bound to have limitations, to say the least. Details of political party foundings, unemployment statistics and trade agreements, federal family policy: these might hide as much as they reveal. They might create an aura of order and coherence that is entirely out of sync with the way most people actually lived and experienced their lives.[11]

Sometimes, we just have to listen for what the ghosts have to tell.

Because in a haunted society, sociologist Avery F. Gordon writes, "the ghost always carries the message," but "not in the form of an academic treatise, or the clinical case study, or the polemical broadside, or the mind-numbing factual report."[12] Some questions, by their very nature, require a sensitivity to other realities.

NOTES

INTRODUCTION

1. Frau N.'s story is one of several case studies in Inge Schöck, *Hexen-glaube in der Gegenwart: Empirische Untersuchungen in Südwest-deutschland* (Tübingen: Tübinger Vereinigung für Volkskunde, 1978), 177–90.
2. Herbert Schäfer, *Der Okkulttäter: Hexenbanner—Magischer Heiler—Erdentstrahler* (Hamburg: Vlg. f. kriminalistische Fachliteratur, 1959), 36.
3. Carlo Caduff, *The Pandemic Perhaps: Dramatic Events in a Public Culture of Danger* (Berkeley: University of California Press, 2015), 7–8.
4. Ulrich Beck, "The Anthropological Shock: Chernobyl and the Contours of the Risk Society," *Berkeley Journal of Sociology* 32 (1987): 153–65.
5. Jeffrey K. Olick, *In the House of the Hangman: The Agonies of German Defeat* (Chicago: University of Chicago Press, 2005), 58–64.
6. "The mass production of corpses" is Hannah Arendt's phrase. See "The Concentration Camps," *Partisan Review* 15 (1948): 745.
7. Robert Jay Lifton, "On Death and Death Symbolism: The Hiroshima Disaster," *The American Scholar* 34:2 (Spring 1965): 259.
8. Karl Jaspers, "Is Science Evil? Answering the Attack on Modern Knowledge and Technology," *Commentary*, March 1, 1950.

9. Richard Bessel, *Germany 1945: From War to Peace* (New York: Harper-Collins, 2009), 178.

10. Clemens Escher, *"Deutschland, Deutschland, Du mein Alles!" Die Deutschen auf der Suche nach einer neuen Hymne, 1949–1952* (Leiden: Schöningh, 2017), 27–28; Peter Limbach, "Trizonesien-Lied sorgte 1949 für Aufregung," *Kölner Stadt Anzeiger*, November 5, 2004. Accessed at https://www.ksta.de/trizonesien-lied-sorgte-1949-fuer-aufregung-14563906, April 3, 2018.

11. Olick, *In the House of the Hangman*, 65–94.

12. R. M. Douglas, *Orderly and Humane: The Expulsion of the Germans After the Second World War* (New Haven: Yale University Press, 2012), 1.

13. Will-Erich Peuckert, *Hochwies: Sagen, Schwänke, und Märchen* (Göttingen: Schwartz, 1959), vii.

14. Thomas A. Kohut, *A German Generation: An Experiential History of the Twentieth Century* (New Haven: Yale University Press, 2012), 182.

15. "Bericht aus Akten der Geschäftsführenden Reichsregierung Dönitz von Ende März 1945," in Heinz Boberach, ed., *Meldungen aus dem Reich, 1938–1945*, Band 17 (Herrsching: Manfred Pawlak, 1984), 6738.

16. Michael Geyer, "There Is a Land Where Everything Is Pure: Its Name Is Death: Some Observations on Catastrophic Nationalism," in Greg Eghigian and Matthew Paul Berg, eds., *Sacrifice and National Belonging in Twentieth-Century Germany* (College Station, TX: Texas A&M University Press, 2002), 125; Sven Keller, *Volksgemeinschaft am Ende: Gesellschaft und Gewalt, 1944–45* (Munich: Oldenbourg Vlg., 2013); Michael Patrick McConnell, "Home to the Reich: The Nazi Occupation of Europe's Influence on Life Inside Germany, 1941–1945" (PhD dissertation, University of Tennessee, Knoxville, 2015).

17. Thomas Brodie, "German Society at War, 1939–45," *Contemporary European History* 27:3 (2018): 505.

18. H. Kretz, "Folgen der Sterilisation: Zur Frage der Entschädigung Zwangssterilisierter nach dem Bundesentschädigungsgesetz," *Medizinische Klinik: Die Wochenschrift f. Klinik u. Praxis*, 62. Jhg., II. Halbjahr 1967, 1301.

19. Franziska Becker, *Gewalt und Gedächtnis: Erinnerungen an die nationalsozialistische Verfolgung einer jüdischen Landgemeinde* (Göttingen: Schmerse, 1994); Frank Bajohr, *"Arisierung" in Hamburg: Die Verdrängung der jüdischen Unternehmer, 1933–1945* (Hamburg: Christians, 1997), 331–38.

20. Neil Gregor, "A *Schicksalsgemeinschaft*? Allied Bombing, Civilian Morale, and Social Dissolution in Nuremberg, 1942–45," *The Historical Journal*

43:4 (2000); and *Haunted City: Nuremberg and the Nazi Past* (New Haven: Yale University Press, 2008).

21. Robert Gellately, *Backing Hitler: Consent and Coercion in Nazi Germany* (Oxford, UK: Oxford University Press, 2001).

22. Alexander Mitscherlich and Fred Mielke, *Doctors of Infamy: The Story of the Nazi Medical Crimes* (New York: Henry Schuman, 1949), 151.

23. Leo P. Crespi, "The Influence of Military Government Sponsorship in German Opinion Polling," *International Journal of Opinion and Attitude Research* 4:2 (Summer 1950): 175.

24. Steven Shapin, *A Social History of Truth: Civility and Science in Seventeenth-Century England* (Chicago: University of Chicago Press, 1994), 8–41; Mary Douglas, *Rules and Meanings* (Harmondsworth: Penguin, 1973).

25. Peter Geschiere, *Witchcraft, Intimacy, and Trust: Africa in Comparison* (Chicago: University of Chicago Press, 2013), 32–33.

26. Alice Weinreb, *Modern Hungers: Food and Power in Twentieth-Century Germany* (New York: Oxford University Press, 2017), 99.

27. See, for example, Staatsarchiv München (hereafter: StAM) Staatsanwaltschaften 3178/1, document prepared for the Auslands Strafregister Berlin requesting "unbeschränkt [*sic*] Auskunft über Bruno Gröning," describes Danzig as belonging to the *Land* "Ostpreussen," which has been crossed out in pink pencil with "Polen" written over it.

28. Hannah Arendt, "The Aftermath of Nazi Rule: Report from Germany," *Commentary* 10 (October 1950): 344.

29. W. G. Sebald, *On the Natural History of Destruction*, trans. Anthea Bell (New York: Modern Library, 2004), 10.

30. Hans Jonas, *Memoirs*, ed. Christian Wiese, trans. Krishna Winston (Waltham, MA: Brandeis University Press, 2008), 135.

31. Hans Erich Nossack, *The End: Hamburg 1943*, trans. Joel Agee (Chicago: University of Chicago Press, 2004), 22.

32. Heinrich Böll, *Und sagte kein einziges Wort* (Munich: DTV, 2004).

33. As Frank Biess and Astrid Eckert underscore in "Introduction: Why Do We Need New Narratives for the History of the Federal Republic?" *Central European History* 52:1 (2019): 4. Histories of the FRG in this vein include: Axel Schildt, *Ankunft im Westen: Ein Essay zur Erfolgsgeschichte der Bundesrepublik* (Frankfurt: Fischer, 1999); Hans-Ulrich Wehler, *Deutsche Gesellschaftsgeschichte*, vol. 5: *Bundesrepublik und DDR 1949–1990* (Munich: C. H. Beck, 2008); Edgar Wolfrum, *Die geglückte Demokratie: Geschichte der Bundesrepublik von ihren Anfängen bis zur Gegenwart* (Stuttgart: Kletta-Cotta Vlg., 2006).

34. Konrad H. Jarausch, *Broken Lives: How Ordinary Germans Experienced the 20th Century* (Princeton: Princeton University Press, 2015), 264.

35. Philipp Felsch and Frank Witzel, *BRD Noir* (Berlin: Matthew & Seitz, 2016).

36. During the Cold War, West German history was shaped by a handful of inter-related paradigms—modernization, democratization, Americanization—whose foundations lay in the disciplines of economics and political science. More recently, cultural historians—of memory, emotions, gender, sexuality, race, war, and the family, among others—have contributed to a multidimensional image of postwar life and society. Books that, like this one, deal chiefly with the earliest postwar years would include, among others: Anna Parkinson, *An Emotional State: The Politics of Emotion in Postwar West German Culture* (Ann Arbor: University of Michigan Press, 2015); Werner Sollors, *The Temptation of Despair: Tales of the 1940s* (Cambridge: Harvard University Press, 2014); Jennifer Evans, *Life Among the Ruins: Cityscape and Sexuality in Cold War Berlin* (Basingstoke: Palgrave, 2011); Svenja Goltermann, *Die Gesellschaft der Überlebenden: Deutsche Kriegsheimkehrer und ihre Gewalter-fahrungen im Zweiten Weltkrieg* (Stuttgart: Deutsche Verlagsanstalt, 2009); Frank Biess, *Homecomings: Returning POWs and the Lega-cies of Defeat in Postwar Germany* (Princeton: Princeton University Press, 2006); Heidi Fehrenbach, *Race After Hitler: Black Occupation Children in Postwar Germany and America* (Princeton: Princeton University Press, 2005); Jörg Echternkamp, *Nach dem Krieg: Alltagsnot, Neuorientierung und die Last der Vergangenheit, 1945–1949* (Zurich: Pendo Verlag, 2003); and Hanna Schissler, *The Miracle Years: A Cul-tural History of West Germany, 1949–1968* (Princeton: Princeton University Press, 2001).

37. Alan Frank Keele, *The Apocalyptic Vision: A Thematic Exploration of Postwar German Literature* (Potomac, MD: Studia Humanitas, 1983), ix–x, 30–33.

38. Arendt, "Aftermath," 342.

39. Hermann Lübbe, *Vom Parteigenossen zum Bundesbürger: Über beschwie-gene und historisierte Vergangenheiten* (Munich: Fink Vlg., 2007), 20–22.

40. Axel Schildt, "Der Umgang mit der NS-Vergangenheit in der Öffentlich-keit der Nachkriegszeit," in Wilfried Loth and Bernd-A. Rusinek, eds., *Ver-wandlungspolitik: NS-Eliten in der westdeutschen Nachkriegsgesellschaft* (Frankfurt: Campus Vlg., 1998), 22.

41. Philipp Gassert, "Zwischen 'Beschweigen' und 'Bewältigen': Die Ausein-andersetzung mit dem Nationalsozialismus in der Ära Adenauer," in

Michael Hochgeschwender, ed., *Epoche im Widerspruch: Ideelle und kulturelle Umbrüche der Adenauerzeit* (Bonn: Bouvier, 2011), 186; Benjamin Möckel, *Erfahrungsbruch und Generationsbehauptung: Die 'Kriegsjugendgeneration' in den beiden deutschen Nachkriegsgesellschaften* (Göttingen: Wallstein, 2014), 226–34.

42. Till van Rahden, "Fatherhood, Rechristianization, and the Quest for Democracy in Postwar West Germany," in Dirk Schumann, ed., *Raising Citizens in the 'Century of the Child': The United States and German Central Europe in Comparative Perspective* (New York: Berghahn Books, 2010).

43. Eric Kurlander, *Hitler's Monsters: A Supernatural History of the Third Reich* (New Haven: Yale University Press, 2017); Jason Ā. Josephson-Storm, *The Myth of Disenchantment: Magic, Modernity, and the Birth of the Human Sciences* (Chicago: University of Chicago Press, 2017); Anna Lux and Sylvia Paletschek, eds., *Okkultismus im Gehäuse: Institutionalisierungen der Parapsychologie im 20. Jahrhundert im internationalen Vergleich* (Berlin: De Gruyter, 2016); Monica Black and Eric Kurlander, eds., *Revisiting the 'Nazi Occult': Histories, Realities, Legacies* (Rochester, NY: Camden House, 2015); Heather Wolffram, *The Stepchildren of Science: Psychical Research and Parapsychology in Germany, c. 1870–1939* (Amsterdam: Rodopi, 2009); Corinna Treitel, *A Science for the Soul: Occultism and the Genesis of the German Modern* (Baltimore: Johns Hopkins University Press, 2004); Ulrich Linse, *Geisterseher und Wunderwirker: Heilssuche im Industriezeitalter* (Frankfurt a.M.: Fischer, 1996).

44. The dominance of German religious history by church history, theology, and the social-historical "milieu model" has left the field relatively untouched by concerns about religious subjectivity, experience, symbolic practice, and systems of meaning. A good, brief introduction to these issues is Claudius Kienzle, *Mentalitätsprägung im gesellschaftlichen Wandel: Evangelische Pfarrer in einer württembergischen Wachstumsregion der frühen Bundesrepublik* (Stuttgart: Kohlhammer, 2012), 11–19. One intention of the present book is to contribute to a new cultural history of religion in Germany, along similar lines to those presented in Robert A. Orsi, *Between Heaven and Earth: The Religious Worlds People Make and the Scholars Who Study Them* (Princeton: Princeton University Press, 2005).

1. READING SIGNS

1. Wolfgang Behringer, *Witches and Witch-Hunts: A Global History* (Cambridge: Polity Press, 2004), 123; Jürgen Scheffler, "Lemgo, das Hexennest:

Folkloristik, NS-Vermarktung und lokale Geschichtsdarstellung," *Jahrbuch f. Volkskunde,* Neue Folge 12 (1989): 114.

2. Ursula Bender-Wittmann, "Hexenprozesse in Lemgo, 1628–1637: Eine sozialgeschichtliche Analyse," in *Der Weserraum zwischen 1500 und 1650: Gesellschaft, Wirtschaft und Kultur in der Frühen Neuzeit* (Marburg: Jonas Vlg., 1992), 239.

3. Cited in Scheffler, "Lemgo, das Hexennest," 115.

4. Scheffler, "Lemgo, das Hexennest," 123–25.

5. Scheffler, "Lemgo, das Hexennest," 125, 128.

6. Otto Dov Kulka and Eberhard Jäckel, eds., *Die Juden in den geheimen NS-Stimmungsberichten, 1933–1945* (Düsseldorf: Droste Vlg., 2004), 321–22.

7. Moritz Rülf, "Die Geschichte der Juden in Lippe," 17, and Jürgen Scheffler, "Zwischen ständischer Ausschließung und bürgerlicher Integration: Juden in Lemgo im 19. Jahrhundert," 31, 40: both essays appear in Vlg. f. Regionalgeschichte, ed., *Juden in Lemgo und Lippe: Kleinstadtleben zwischen Emanzipation und Deportation,* Forum Lemgo, Heft 3 (Bielefeld: Vlg. f. Regionalgeschichte, 1988).

8. Hanne Pohlmann, *Judenverfolgung und NS-Alltag in Lemgo: Fallstudien zur Stadtgeschichte* (Bielefeld: Vlg. f. Regionalgeschichte, 2011), 34; Kulka and Jäckel, *Die Juden in den geheimen NS-Stimmungsberichten,* 503, SD-Außenstelle Detmold, July 31, 1942.

9. Kulka and Jäckel, *Die Juden in den geheimen NS-Stimmungsberichten,* 503, SD-Außenstelle Detmold, July 31, 1942. Cited in Nicholas Stargardt, *The German War: A Nation Under Arms, 1939–1945* (New York: Basic Books, 2015), 249–50.

10. Stargardt, *The German War,* 6.

11. Stargardt, *The German War,* 385.

12. Stargardt, *The German War,* 3–6, 375–81; Frank Bajohr and Dieter Pohl, *Der Holocaust als offenes Geheimnis: Die Deutschen, die NS-Führung und die Alliierten* (Munich: C. H. Beck, 2006), 65–76; Alon Confino, *A World Without Jews: The Nazi Imagination from Persecution to Genocide* (New Haven: Yale University Press, 2014), 221–22; Dietmar Süss, *Death from the Skies: How the British and Germans Survived Bombing in World War II,* trans. Lesley Sharpe and Jeremy Noakes (Oxford, UK: Oxford University Press, 2014), 250–63. Süss argues that among religious Germans, bombings could also provoke other responses, including the idea that the experience of violence could "purify." For a discussion of more temporal manifestations of "revenge anxiety" see Frank Biess, *Republik der Angst: Eine andere Geschichte der Bundesrepublik* (Reinbek bei Hamburg: Rowohlt, 2019), chapter 1.

13. Bruno Grabinski, "Kriegsprophezeiungen," *Neues Tageblatt*, October 15, 1946, 3. Clipping in Hauptstaatsarchiv Hannover (hereafter: HH), ZGS 2.1. The prophecies Goebbels had sent out through the mail seem to have been those of Anton Johansson, a Swedish ice fisherman and clairvoyant whose predictions were published in German in 1953 as the antisemitic and anticommunist tract *Merkwürdige Gesichte: Die Zukunft der Völker* (Stockholm: Sverigefondens Förlag, 1953).

14. Alfred Dieck, "Der Weltuntergang am 17. März 1949 in Südhannover," *Neues Archiv für Niedersachsen*, Bd. 4 (1950): 704–20; here, 705.

15. Fred Ritzel, " 'Was ist aus uns geworden?—Ein Häufchen Sand am Meer': Emotions of Post-war Germany as Extracted from Examples of Popular Music," *Popular Music* 17:3 (1998): 293–309; here, 294.

16. Archives of the Institut für Volkskunde der Deutschen des östlichen Europa (formerly the Johannes-Künzig-Institut für ostdeutsche Volkskunde), Sammlung Karasek, Neue Sagenbildung (hereafter: JKI/SK/NS) 04/01-2.

17. JKI/SK/NS, 04/03-109.

18. JKI/SK/NS, 04/01-49.

19. JKI/SK/NS, 04/01-01.

20. Elisabeth Reinke, "Die Zerstörung der Stadt Friesoythe und das 'Zweite Gesicht,'" *Oldenburgische Volkszeitung*, July 8, 1950. Clipping in HH, VVP 17, Nr. 3502.

21. Bessel, *Germany 1945*, 12.

22. Rüdiger Overmans, *Deutsche militärische Verluste im Zweiten Weltkrieg* (Munich: Oldenbourg, 1999), 319.

23. Bessel, *Germany 1945*, 11.

24. Richard Bessel, *Nazism and War* (New York: Modern Library, 2006), 179, citing Dietrich Eichholtz, *Geschichte der deutschen Kriegswirtschaft 1939–1945, Band III: 1943–1945* (Berlin: Akademie-Vlg., 1996), 632–34.

25. Süss, *Death from the Skies*, 105, 451.

26. All quotes in this paragraph: "Bericht aus Akten der Geschäftsführenden Reichsregierung Dönitz von Ende März 1945," in Heinz Boberach, ed., *Meldungen aus dem Reich, 1938–1945*, Band 17 (Herrsching: Manfred Pawlak, 1984), 6735, 6737.

27. Boberach, *Meldungen*, "Bericht," 6738, 6735.

28. Nossack, *The End*, 1–2.

29. The expression "societies of the uprooted" comes from Bessel, *Germany 1945*.

30. Keith Lowe, *Savage Continent: Europe in the Aftermath of World War II* (New York: St. Martin's Press, 2012), chapter 9.

31. J. Glenn Gray, *The Warriors: Reflections of Men in Battle* (New York: Harper & Row, 1959), 220.

32. *Foreign Relations of the United States: Diplomatic Papers: The Conferences at Malta and Yalta 1945* (Washington: US Government Printing Office, 1955), 970–71.

33. John H. Herz, "The Fiasco of Denazification in Germany," *Political Science Quarterly* 63:4 (Dec. 1948): 570.

34. Alice Weinreb, *Modern Hungers: Food and Power in Twentieth-Century Germany* (New York: Oxford University Press, 2017), 96.

35. "Morally unclean": Steven M. Schroeder, *To Forget It All and Begin Anew: Reconciliation in Occupied Germany* (Toronto: University of Toronto Press, 2013), 17.

36. Ulrike Weckel, *Beschämende Bilder: Deutsche Reaktionen auf alliierte Dokumentarfilme über befreite Konzentrationslager* (Stuttgart: Franz Steiner, 2012).

37. Parkinson, *An Emotional State*, 2.

38. Norbert Frei, *Adenauer's Germany and the Nazi Past: The Politics of Amnesty and Integration*, trans. Joel Golb (New York: Columbia University Press, 2002), xiii.

39. Jessica Reinisch, *The Perils of Peace: The Public Health Crisis in Occupied Germany* (Oxford, UK: Oxford University Press, 2013), 163.

40. Olick, *Hangman*, 124–25.

41. Herz, "Fiasco," 572.

42. Alexandra F. Levy, "Promoting Democracy and Denazification: American Policymaking and German Public Opinion," *Diplomacy & Statecraft* 26:4 (2015): 614–35.

43. Perry Biddiscombe, *The Denazification of Germany: A History, 1945–1950* (Stroud: Tempus, 2007), 191.

44. Atina Grossmann, *Jews, Germans, and Allies: Close Encounters in Occupied Germany* (Princeton: Princeton University Press, 2007), 37–39.

45. Werner Bergmann, "Die Reaktion auf den Holocaust in Westdeutschland von 1945 bis 1989," *Geschichte in Wissenschaft und Unterricht* 43 (1992): 331–32; Donald Bloxham, *Genocide on Trial: War Crimes Trials and the Formation of Holocaust History and Memory* (Oxford, UK: Oxford University Press, 2001), 138–39.

46. Weckel, *Beschämende Bilder*, 283–84.

47. Olick, *Hangman*, 180–86. See also Aleida Assmann and Ute Frevert, *Geschichtsvergessenheit: Vom Umgang mit deutschen Vergangenheiten nach 1945* (Stuttgart: Deutsche Verlagsanstalt, 1999).

48. Ralf Dahrendorf, *Society and Democracy in Germany* (Garden City, NY: Doubleday, 1967), 288–89. See also A. Dirk Moses, *German Intellectuals*

and the Nazi Past (New York: Cambridge University Press, 2007), especially 19–27; and Olick, *Hangman*, 198, and, more broadly, chapter 9.

49. Helmut Dubiel, *Niemand ist frei von der Geschichte: Die nationalsozialistische Herrschaft in den Debatten des Deutschen Bundestages* (Munich: Carl Hanser, 1999), 71; Olick, *Hangman*, 183.

50. Stephen Brockmann, *German Literary Culture at the Zero Hour* (Rochester, NY: Camden House, 2004), 29; see also Norbert Frei, "Von deutscher Erfindungskraft oder: Die Kollektivschuldthese in der Nachkriegszeit," *Rechtshistorisches Journal* 16 (1997): 621–34.

51. Moses, *German Intellectuals*, 19–27.

52. Jan-Werner Müller, *Another Country: German Intellectuals, Unification, and National Identity* (New Haven: Yale University Press, 2000), 31. See also Olick, *Hangman*, chapter 12.

53. Thomas Kühne, *Belonging and Genocide: Hitler's Community, 1918–1945* (New Haven: Yale University Press, 2010), 161.

54. Bessel, *Germany 1945*, 167.

55. Andreas Kossert, *Kalte Heimat: Die Geschichte der Deutschen Vertriebenen nach 1945* (Munich: Siedler Vlg., 2008), 71–86; Rainer Schulze, "Growing Discontent: Relations Between Native and Refugee Populations in a Rural District in Western Germany After the Second World War," in Robert G. Moeller, ed., *West Germany Under Construction: Politics, Society, and Culture in the Adenauer Era* (Ann Arbor: University of Michigan Press, 1997).

56. Andreas Kossert, quoted in Neil MacGregor, *Germany: Memories of a Nation* (New York: Vintage, 2004), 483.

57. Two million is the number most often cited as an estimate of rapes Allied soldiers committed against German women. However, Miriam Gebhardt in *Crimes Unspoken: The Rape of German Women at the End of the Second World War*, trans. Nick Somers (Cambridge: Polity Press, 2017), offers the figure 860,000. This more conservative (though nonetheless shocking) figure is based on West German statistics concerning "occupation children" fathered by Allied soldiers; Gebhardt's analysis also extends temporally beyond the immediate period of conquest.

58. Elizabeth D. Heineman, *What Difference Does a Husband Make? Women and Marital Status in Nazi and Postwar Germany* (Berkeley: University of California Press, 1999), 108–36.

59. Goltermann, *Die Gesellschaft der Überlebenden*, 56.

60. Frei, *Adenauer's Germany*, 6–8.

61. Frei, *Adenauer's Germany*, 6.

62. Frei, *Adenauer's Germany*, 13–14, 23–24.

63. Frei, *Adenauer's Germany*, 305–6, 310–12, quote on 14.

64. "Die kleine Amnestie," *Christ und Welt*, Nr. 2, Jhg. III, January 12, 1950, 2. Cited in Frei, *Adenauer's Germany*, 19–20.

65. Norbert Sahrhage, *Diktatur und Demokratie in einer protestantischen Region: Stadt und Landkreis Herford 1929 bis 1953* (Bielefeld: Vlg. f. Regionalgeschichte, 2005), 456–58.

66. StAM Pol. Dir. 11298, Abschrift vom Abschrift, Urteil . . . wegen Hellseherei . . . gegen Irlmaier, Alois, May 19, 1947; C. Adlmaier, *Blick in die Zukunft* (Traunstein/Obb.: Chiemgau Druck, 1950), 35; "Er sah, was er sagte," *Der Spiegel* 39, September 25, 1948, 27.

67. StAM, Pol. Dir. 11301, Kriminaluntersuchungsabteilung, betr.: Experimentalabend Léon Hardt, March 31, 1947.

68. A. E., "Die Gesundbeter sind wieder da," *Der Ruf*, September 15, 1947. Source cited in Jennifer M. Kapczynski, *The German Patient: Crisis and Recovery in Postwar Culture* (Ann Arbor: University of Michigan Press, 2008), 69–70.

69. "Big bang": Ulrich Herbert, *Geschichte Deutschlands im 20. Jahrhundert* (2014), 598.

70. Dieck, "Weltuntergang," 714–16, 718.

71. Wijnand A. B. van der Sanden and Sabine Eisenbeiss, "Imaginary People: Alfred Dieck and the Bog Bodies of Northwest Europe," *Archäologisches Korrespondenzblatt* 36 (2006): 112; Hermann Behrens and Elke Heege, "Nachruf auf Alfred Dieck, 4.4.1906—7.1.1989," *Die Kunde* 40 (1989).

72. Dieck, "Weltuntergang," 706.

73. Claus Jacobi, "The New German Press," *Foreign Affairs* (January 1954): 324.

74. Dieck, "Weltuntergang," 707.

75. Siegfried Sommer, "Weltuntergang verschoben," *Süddeutsche Zeitung*, Nr. 33, March 19, 1949. Cited in Dieck, "Weltuntergang," 716.

76. Dieck, "Weltuntergang," 704.

77. Dieck, "Weltuntergang," 706.

78. Dieck, "Weltuntergang," 708, 713–14.

79. Adlmaier, *Blick in die Zukunft*, 38–39.

80. Elaine Pagels, *Revelations: Visions, Prophecy, and Politics in the Book of Revelation* (New York: Penguin, 2012).

81. Bundesarchiv Koblenz (hereafter: BAK), ZSG 132/2685, "Gedanken vor dem Einschlafen: Antworten auf eine Umfrage" (n.d., presumably 1949 or 1950). Quotes on pp. 2 and 16.

82. Kommunalarchiv Herford/Stadtarchiv Herford (hereafter: KAH), S 10/270, "Wunderheiler" Bruno Gröning (Akten des Hauptamtes, 1949–1950), 161. Letter from Kassel, June 29, 1949.

83. Elisabeth Noelle and Erich Peter Neumann, eds., *Jahrbuch der öffentlichen*

Meinung, 1947–1955 (Allensbach am Bodensee: Vlg. für Demoskopie, 1956), 114–15.

84. Dieck, "Der Weltuntergang," 707.

2. A STRANGER IN TOWN

1. UFOs: Greg Eghigian, "A Transatlantic Buzz: Flying Saucers, Extraterrestrials, and America in Postwar Germany," *Journal of Transatlantic Studies* 12:3 (2014): 282–303. Snow in LA: http://www.lamag.com/citythink/citydig-a-snowstorm-in-los-angeles-its-happened/, accessed September 19, 2019. On the twentieth century's capacity for creating new worlds of wonder, see Alexander C. T. Geppert and Till Kössler, eds. *Wunder: Poetik und Politik des Staunens im 20. Jahrhundert* (Berlin: Suhrkamp, 2011).

2. "Sogar Grönings Badewasser wird noch verlangt," *Fränkische Presse* (Bayreuth), March 21, 1950. Clipping in StAM, Staatsanwaltschaften 3178/5. Raise the dead: Egon-Arthur Schmidt, *Die Wunderheilungen des Bruno Gröning* (Berlin: Falken Vlg. Erich Sicker, 1949), 11–12.

3. The most comprehensive historical work on Bruno Gröning from an archival standpoint until now has been Florian Mildenberger's article-length study, "Heilstrom durch den Kropf: Leben, Werk und Nachwirkung des Wunderheilers Bruno Gröning (1906–1959)," *Zeitschrift für Wissenschaftsgeschichte*, 92:1 (2008): 353–64. Gustav: StAM, Staatsanwaltschaften 3178/1, 129, Vernehmungsniederschrift, June 17, 1950; Bernhard: StAM, Staatsanwaltschaften 3178/1, Aub an Geschäftsstelle des Schöffengerichts München-Land, June 13, 1951.

4. "Mich sendet Gott," *Stern*, No. 22 (n.d., ca. mid-May, 1949). Clipping in Institut f. Grenzgebiete der Psychologie und Psychohygiene (hereafter: IGPP), Busam Sammlung, PA 259.

5. Schmidt, *Wunderheilungen*, 85–86.

6. StAM, Staatsanwaltschaften 3178/2, p. 363, Vernehmungsniederschrift, Helmut Hülsmann, July 20, 1950.

7. Schmidt, *Wunderheilungen*, 85–86.

8. StAM, Staatsanwaltschaften 3178/2, p. 363, Vernehmungsniederschrift, Helmut Hülsmann, July 20, 1950.

9. Schmidt, *Wunderheilungen*, 86, says March 15. Gröning later said it was March 14: StAM, Staatsanwaltschaften 3178a/2, p. 290. Psychiatrische und Nervenklinik . . . der Universität Freiburg, an dem Schöffengericht München-Land February 9, 1957.

10. "Es zogen drei Jungfrauen durch den Wald," *Allgemeine Zeitung*, January 5, 1950. Clipping in HH, VVP 17, Nr. 3558.

11. Rainer Pape, *Das alte Herford: Bilder aus vier Jahrhunderten* (Herford: Maximilian Vlg., 1971), 104.

12. Haggard: Rp., "Der Wundertäter von Herford," *Badisches Tagblatt*, Nr. 72, June 23, 1949, clipping in IGPP, E 123/100. Nicotine-stained fingers: "Großverdiener um Gröning," *Wort und Bild*, 4 Jhg., Nr. 39, September 25, 1949. Clipping in IGPP, Busam Sammlung, PA 172.

13. Cigar: StAM, Staatsanwaltschaften 3178/3, Renée Meckelburg, "Tatsachenbericht," 485.

14. Jobst Klinkmüller, "Bruno Gröning in Frankfurt," *Frankfurter Neue Presse*, n.d. (presumably September 19, 1949). Clipping in IGPP/20/16, Busam Fotosammlung I, PA 001.

15. "Umgekehrt": "Bruno Gröning behandelt die seit 13 Jahren leidende Frau," *Revue*, Nr. 28, August 21, 1949, 10. Clipping in IGPP, Busam Sammlung.

16. KAH, E348/10, "Manuskript für Druck und Verlag," 8.

17. StAM, Staatsanwaltschaften 3178/2, p. 359, Vernehmungsniederschrift, Anneliese Hülsmann, July 20, 1950; Schmidt, *Wunderheilungen*, 85–86.

18. StAM, Staatsanwaltschaften 3178/2, p. 363, Vernehmungsniederschrift, Helmut Hülsmann, July 20, 1950.

19. StAM, Staatsanwaltschaften 3178/2, p. 359, Vernehmungsniederschrift, Anneliese Hülsmann, July 20, 1950.

20. "Dieter Hülsmann blieb gelähmt," *Freie Presse*, July 13, 1950. Clipping in KAH, S Slg. E/E 60.

21. Bruno Gröning, *Hilfe und Heilung: Ein Wegweiser* (Berlin: Einhorn Presse, 1991), 6; Danziger Verkehrs-Zentrale, ed., *Führer durch die Freistadt Danzig* (Danzig: Danziger Verkehrs-Zentrale, 1920), 54, 56; "Das Leben Bruno Gröning," *Revue*, Nr. 30, September 4, 1949, 11, clipping in IGPP Busam Sammlung.

22. Deutsche Dienststelle f. die Benachrichtigung der nächsten Angehörigen der ehemaligen deutschen Wehrmacht (WASt), per letter, December 16, 2014. Gröning's own account of his military service, which differs in certain details from the Wehrmacht records, is located in StAM, Staatsanwaltschaften 3178a/2, pp. 287–88, Psychiatrische und Nervenklinik . . . der Universität Freiburg, an dem Schöffengericht München-Land, February 9, 1957.

23. StAM, Staatsanwaltschaften 3178a/2, p. 289, Psychiatrische und Nervenklinik . . . der Universität Freiburg, an dem Schöffengericht München-Land, February 9, 1957.

24. StAM, Staatsanwaltschaften 3178/2, p. 395, Vernehmungsniederschrift, Bruno Gröning, November 27, 1950.

25. Anne-Kathrin Stroppe, "Die NSDAP-Mitglieder aus Danzig-Westpreußen und dem Saargebiet," in Jürgen W. Falter, ed., *Junge Kämpfer, alte*

Opportunisten: Die Mitglieder der NSDAP 1919–1945 (Frankfurt: Campus, 2016), 337–39; Peter Oliver Loew, *Danzig: Biographie einer Stadt* (Munich: C. H. Beck, 2011), 204; Dieter Schenk, *Hitlers Mann in Danzig: Albert Forster und die NS-Verbrechen in Danzig-Westpreußen* (Bonn: Dietz, 2000), 125–43.

26. BA-Berlin, PK (formerly Berlin Document Center), Sig. DO 182, file numbers 1656, 1670, 1748.

27. Peter Fritzsche, *Life and Death in the Third Reich* (Cambridge: Belknap Press of Harvard, 2008), 76.

28. Winson Chu, *The German Minority in Interwar Poland* (Cambridge, UK: Cambridge University Press, 2012).

29. J. F. C. Harrison, *The Second Coming: Popular Millenarianism, 1780–1850* (London: Routledge & Kegan Paul, 1979), 11–12.

3. THE MIRACLE OF HERFORD

1. "Der Wundertäter von Herford," *Badisches Tagblatt*, Nr. 72, June 23, 1949. Clipping in IGPP, Bestand E 123, Nr. 100.

2. Meister had briefly been mayor of Tahra, from 1932 to 1933. His tenure as Herford town manager began in 1947. Sahrhage, *Diktatur und Demokratie*, 407.

3. Sahrhage, *Diktatur und Demokratie*, 568–75.

4. Reinisch, *Perils of Peace*, chapter 5, quote on 179.

5. Carol Poore, *Disability in Twentieth-Century German Culture* (Ann Arbor: University of Michigan Press, 2007), 170–71.

6. A. P. Meiklejohn, "Condition of Children in Western Germany," *The Lancet*, October 16, 1948, 620–21, 623.

7. Wolfgang Uwe Eckart, *Medizin in der NS-Diktatur: Ideologie, Praxis, Folgen* (Vienna: Böhlau, 2012), 353.

8. Michael Oldemeier, "Das Wachstum der Stadt Herford im 19. und 20. Jahrhundert," in Theodor Helmert-Corvey and Thomas Schuler, eds., *1200 Jahre Herford: Spuren der Geschichte* (Herford: Maximilian Vlg., 1989), 127–30. The population of Herford in 1945 ("not including military personnel"), was 46,753; in 1946: 43,882; 1948: 47,189; 1950: 49,309. Rainer Pape, *Sancta Herfordia: Geschichte Herfords von den Anfängen bis zur Gegenwart* (Herford: Bussesche Verlagshandlung, 1979), 353.

9. Sahrhage, *Diktatur und Demokratie*, 499; Bettina Blum, "My Home, Your Castle: British Requisitioning of German Homes in Westphalia," in Camilo Erlichman and Christopher Knowles, eds., *Transforming Occupation in the Western Zones of Germany* (London: Bloomsbury, 2018), 116.

10. KAH, S 32/7, Medizinalpolizei/Heilkunde, 1945–54. An den Herrn Regierungspräsident . . . von dem Oberstadtdirektor Herford, June 16, 1949.

11. *Revue*, Nr. 27, August 14, 1949, p. 10. Clipping in IGPP, Busam Sammlung; KAH, S 32/7, Medizinalpolizei/Heilkunde, 1945–54, report from Superintendent des Kirchenkreises Herford, May 1949.

12. KAH, S 32/7 Medizinalpolizei/Heilkunde, 1945–54. An Herrn Bruno Gröning von Oberstadtdirektor, May 3, 1949 and, on the back, "Bericht," dated May 4, 1949.

13. KAH, S 32/7 Medizinalpolizei/Heilkunde, 1945–54. Leaflet, dated May 28, 1949.

14. KAH, S 10/270, "Wunderheiler" Bruno Gröning (Akten des Hauptamtes, 1949–1950), p. 22. Letter from Löhne, May 19, 1949.

15. "Gröning-Anhänger demonstrieren vor dem Rathaus," *Westfalen-Zeitung*, June 9, 1949. Clipping in KAH, S Slg. E/E60.

16. KAH, S10/270, "Wunderheiler" Bruno Gröning, p. 108, letter from Brake/Lippe, June 13, 1949.

17. Thomas Faltin, *Heil und Heilung: Geschichte der Laienheilkundigen und Struktur antimodernistischer Weltanschauungen in Kaiserreich und Weimarer Republik am Beispiel von Eugen Wenz (1856–1945)* (Stuttgart: Steiner, 2000), 224–34.

18. Bundesarchiv Berlin (hereafter: BAB), R 86/1492/231. Clippings from *Braker Zeitung*, 29. Jahrgang, August 12, 14, and 16, 1907.

19. Faltin, *Heil und Heilung*, 242.

20. Robert N. Proctor, *Racial Hygiene: Medicine Under the Nazis* (Cambridge and London: Harvard University Press, 1988), 227–28; Faltin, *Heil und Heilung*, 231.

21. Walter Wuttke-Groneberg, "Heilpraktiker im Nationalsozialismus," in *Nachtschatten im weissen Land: Betrachtungen zu alten und neuen Heilsystemen*, Manfred Brinkmann and Michael Franz, eds. (Berlin: Verlagsgesellschaft Gesundheit, 1981), 127, 136–38; Corinna Treitel, *Eating Nature in Modern Germany: Food, Agriculture and Environment, c. 1870 to 2000* (Cambridge: Cambridge University Press, 2017), 332; Kurlander, *Hitler's Monsters*, 247. Though an official, state-sanctioned program aimed at "synthesizing" biomedicine and natural healing methods emerged in the Third Reich, this trend actually began years before, at the turn of the century, when doctors began institutionalizing natural therapies and chairs were established (at the Friedrich Wilhelm University in Berlin, for example) for light therapy and massage. Petra Werner, "Zu den Auseinandersetzung um die Institutionalisierung von Naturheilkunde und Homöopathie an der Friedrich-Wilhelms-Universität zu Berlin zwischen

1919 und 1933," in *Medizin, Gesellschaft und Geschichte* 12 (1993): 205; Avi Sharma, "Medicine from the Margins? *Naturheilkunde* from Medical Heterodoxy to the University of Berlin, 1889–1920," *Social History of Medicine* 24:2 (2011).

22. Robert Jütte, *Geschichte der alternativen Medizin: Von der Volksmedizin zu den unkonventionellen Therapien von heute* (Munich: C. H. Beck, 1996), 53.

23. Anne Harrington, *The Cure Within: A History of Mind-Body Medicine* (New York: Norton, 2008), 87.

24. There had been prior attempts to end *Kurierfreiheit*, as documents in BAB, R 86/1492/231 and BAB, NS 22/445 demonstrate. Decisive, according to Wuttke-Groneberg, "Heilpraktiker im Nationalsozialismus," 134, was the Anschluß with Austria. Austria had no "freedom to cure" and so Germany's had to be scrapped for the empire's laws to be unified.

25. Wuttke-Groneberg, "Heilpraktiker," 143; Florian Mildenberger, *Medikale Subkulturen in der Bundesrepublik Deutschland und ihre Gegner (1950–1990)* (Stuttgart: Franz Steiner, 2011), 14, n. 20, on political vetting of lay healers.

26. KAH, S 10/270, "Wunderheiler" Bruno Gröning (Akten des Hauptamtes, 1949–1950), p. 20. Letter from Lüdenscheid, May 18, 1949.

27. KAH, S 10/270, "Wunderheiler" Bruno Gröning (Akten des Hauptamtes, 1949–1950), p. 17. Letter from Castrop-Rauxel, May 16, 1949.

28. KAH, S 10/270, "Wunderheiler" Bruno Gröning (Akten des Hauptamtes, 1949–1950), 6. Letter from Bottrop, May 15, 1949.

29. KAH, S 32/7 Medizinalpolizei/Heilkunde, 1945–54. Letter to Bruno Gröning from Oberstadtdirektor, June 7, 1949; StAM, Polizeidirektion 15558, lfd. Nr. 90, September 12, 1950.

30. Kristian Buchna, *Ein klerikales Jahrzehnt? Kirche, Konfession und Politik in der Bundesrepublik der 1950er Jahre* (Baden-Baden: Nomos, 2014), 232–76.

31. KAH, S 32/7, Medizinalpolizei/Heilkunde, 1945–54. Report from Superintendent des Kirchenkreises Herford (Pastor Kunst), May 1949.

32. KAH, S 32/7, Medizinalpolizei/Heilkunde, 1945–54. Report from Superintendent des Kirchenkreises Herford (Pastor Kunst), May 1949.

33. "Grönings Grenzen: 'Geheilte' werden wieder krank," *Freie Presse*, Nr. 66, Pfingsten 1949 (either June 5 or 6). Clipping in KAH, S Slg. E/E60.

34. Schmidt, *Die Wunderheilungen*, 50.

35. KAH, S 32/7, Medizinalpolizei/Heilkunde, 1945–54. Report from Superintendent des Kirchenkreises Herford (Pastor Kunst), May 1949.

36. "Ein 'neuer Messias,'" *Die Welt* (Hamburg), Nr. 53, May 7, 1949. Clipping in Hamburgisches Welt-Wirtschafts-Archiv.

37. Johannes Dillinger, *"Evil People"*: *A Comparative Study of Witch Hunts in Swabian Austria and the Electorate of Trier*, trans. Laura Stokes (Charlottesville: University of Virginia Press, 2009), 96.

38. Wolfgang Behringer, *Witchcraft Persecutions in Bavaria: Popular Magic, Religious Zealotry and Reason of State in Early Modern Germany* (Cambridge: Cambridge University Press, 1997), 353.

39. Behringer, *Witches and Witch-Hunts*, 2; Ronald Hutton, "Anthropological and Historical Approaches to Witchcraft: Potential for a New Collaboration?" *The Historical Journal* 47:2 (June, 2004): 421–23.

40. E. E. Evans-Pritchard, *Witchcraft, Oracles, and Magic Among the Azande* (Oxford, UK: Clarendon Press, 1976), quotes on 18, 24.

41. Byron J. Good et al., eds. *A Reader in Medical Anthropology: Theoretical Trajectories, Emergent Realities* (Malden, MA: Wiley-Blackwell, 2010), 10.

42. Gustav Jungbauer, *Deutsche Volksmedizin: Ein Grundriß* (Berlin: Walter de Gruyter, 1934); first comprehensive: Jutta Dornheim, *Kranksein im dörflichen Alltag: Soziokulturelle Aspekte des Umgangs mit Krebs* (Tübingen: Tübinger Vereinigung für Volkskunde, 1983), 11, n. 2.

43. Jungbauer, *Deutsche Volksmedizin*, 1–2, 5, 22, 43.

44. Jungbauer, *Deutsche Volksmedizin*, 22–40.

45. Gerhard Wilke, "The Sins of the Father: Village Society and Social Control in the Weimar Republic," in Richard J. Evans and W. R. Lee, eds., *The German Peasantry: Conflict and Community in Rural Society from the Eighteenth to the Twentieth Centuries* (London: Croom Helm, 1986).

46. Gerhard Wilke, "Die Sünden der Väter: Bedeutung und Wandel von Gesundheit und Krankheit im Dorfalltag," in Alfons Labisch and Reinhard Spree, eds., *Medizinische Deutungsmacht im sozialen Wandel des 19. und frühen 20. Jahrhunderts* (Bonn: Psychiatrie-Verlag, 1989), 125, 131.

47. Gerhard Staack, "Die magische Krankheitsbehandlung in der Gegenwart in Mecklenburg" (PhD dissertation, Christian-Albrechts University, Kiel, 1930), 10–11.

48. StAM, Staatsanwaltschaften, 3178/4, p. 19, Karl Gröning manuscript, "Melker—Wachmann—Kohlentrinner: Beinahe ein alltäglicher Lebenslauf," dated February 16, 1951.

49. Jütte, *Geschichte der alternativen Medizin*, 90.

50. Michael Simon, *"Volksmedizin" im frühen 20. Jahrhundert: Zum Quellenwert des Atlas der deutschen Volkskunde* (Mainz: Gesellschaft f. Volkskunde in Rheinland-Pfalz, 2003), 175.

51. Simon, *"Volksmedizin,"* 171–72.

52. Beate Schubert and Günter Wiegelmann, "Regionale Unterschiede beim

Besprechen von Krankheiten im frühen 20. Jahrhundert," in *Volksmedizin in Nordwestdeutschland: Heilmagnetismus—"Besprechen"—Erfahrungsheilkunde* (Münster: Waxmann, 1994), 178–86.

53. KAH, S 10/270, "Wunderheiler" Bruno Gröning (Akten des Hauptamtes, 1949–1950), pp. 51–52. Graphologisches Gutachten, May 27, 1949.

54. KAH, S 10/270, "Wunderheiler" Bruno Gröning (Akten des Hauptamtes, 1949–1950), p. 235. Letter from Europäische Missions-Gesellschaft, August 24, 1949.

55. KAH, S 10/270, "Wunderheiler" Bruno Gröning (Akten des Hauptamtes, 1949–1950), 161–64 and 170. Letters from Kampfgruppe gegen Nihilismus dated June 26 and July 5, 1949.

56. KAH, S 10/270, "Wunderheiler" Bruno Gröning (Akten des Hauptamtes, 1949–1950), p. 25. Letter from Gronau, May 19, 1949.

57. KAH, S 10/270, "Wunderheiler" Bruno Gröning (Akten des Hauptamtes, 1949–1950), p. 85. Letter from Werries, June 7, 1949.

58. KAH, S 10/270, "Wunderheiler" Bruno Gröning (Akten des Hauptamtes, 1949–1950), p. 197. Letter from Miesbach, July 20, 1949.

59. "Das Leben Bruno Gröning," *Revue*, Nr. 30, September 4, 1949, 11. Clipping in IGPP Busam Sammlung.

60. KAH, S 32/7, Medizinalpolizei/Heilkunde, 1945–54. Erklärung, Oberstadtdirektor Herford, June 14, 1949.

61. KAH, S 32/7, Medizinalpolizei/Heilkunde, 1945–54. Oberstadtdirektor to Bruno Gröning, June 11, 1949.

62. "Der Wundertäter von Herford," *Badisches Tagblatt*, 72, June 23, 1949. Clipping in IGPP/123/100.

63. KAH, S 32/7, Medizinalpolizei/Heilkunde, 1945–54. An den Herrn Regierungspräsident in Detmold von dem Oberstadtdirektor Herford, June 16, 1949. "Der Wundertäter von Herford," *Badisches Tagblatt*, Nr. 72, June 23, 1949. Clipping in IGPP/123/100.

64. "Der Fall Gröning kommt vor die Landesregierung," *Freie Presse*, Nr. 71, June 18, 1949. Clipping in KAH, S Slg. E/E60.

65. "Der Wundertäter von Herford," *Badisches Tagblatt*, Nr. 72, June 23, 1949. Clipping in IGPP/123/100.

66. "Mich sendet Gott," *Stern*, No. 22, ca. mid-May, 1949. Clipping in IGPP Busam Sammlung, PA 259.

67. "Grönings Grenzen: 'Geheilte' werden wieder krank," *Freie Presse*, Nr. 66, 1949 (either June 5 or 6). Clipping in KAH, S Slg. E/E60.

68. "Das Wunder von Herford," *Der Hausfreund*, Nr. 23, June 4, 1949, p. 3.

69. KAH, S 32/7, Medizinalpolizei/Heilkunde, 1945–54. An den Herrn Regierungspräsident in Detmold von dem Oberstadtdirektor Herford, June 16, 1949.

70. StAM, Gesundheitsämter, 4256. Clipping from *Münchner Merkur*, "Tausende im Banne des Herforder 'Wunderdoktors,'" June 24, 1949.

71. "Der Wundertäter von Herford," *Badisches Tagblatt*, Nr. 72, June 23, 1949. Clipping in IGPP/123/100.

72. "Rätsel um den Wunderdoktor," *Quick*, June 5, 1949.

73. "Grönings Grenzen: 'Geheilte' werden wieder krank," *Freie Presse*, Nr. 66, 1949 (June 5 or 6). Clipping in KAH, S Slg. E/E60.

74. KAH, S 32/7, Medizinalpolizei/Heilkunde, 1945–54. St. Marien-Hospital II, Hamm-Westfalen, betr. G. Köster, June 21, 1949.

75. KAH, S 32/7 Medizinalpolizei/Heilkunde, 1945–54. Sozialminister des Landes Nordrhein-Westfalen an den Herrn Regierungspräsident in Detmold, June 26, 1949. See also StAM, BezA/LRA 57182, p. 19.

76. KAH, S 32/7, Medizinalpolizei/Heilkunde, 1945–54. Hans Vogt und Kurt Viering to Herrn Regierungspräsident in Detmold, June 28, 1949.

77. "Keine Arbeitserlaubnis für Gröning," *Die Welt* (Hamburg), Nr. 76, June 30, 1949; KAH, S 32/7, Medizinalpolizei/Heilkunde, 1945–54. Der Sozialminister des Landes Nordrhein-Westfalen an den Herrn Regierungspräsident in Detmold, June 26, 1949; StAM, BezA/LRA 57182, p. 19, Abschrift, SSD Fst. Herford Nr. 243 an Kripo Rosenheim, betr. Bruno Gröning, September 5, 1949.

78. "Die Ärzte werden sich wundern," *Die Welt* (Hamburg), Nr. 75, June 28, 1949.

79. A transcript of this press conference is printed in *Die Akte des Dr. rer. pol. Kurt Trampler und Bruno Gröning: Eine Dokumentation* (Berlin: Einhorn Presse, 2001), 46.

4. SOUL MEDICINE

1. See various letters in KAH, S 10/270, "Wunderheiler" Bruno Gröning (Akten des Hauptamtes, 1949–1950); here, p. 111, letter from R. Berger, Essen, an den Oberstadtdirektor, June 13, 1949.

2. Rp., "Der Wundertäter von Herford," *Badisches Tagblatt*, Nr. 72, June 23, 1949. Clipping in IGPP/123/100.

3. Poore, *Disability*, 169.

4. Jens Bergfeldt, *Herfords Wunderdoktor: Der Fall Gröning* (Wiedensahl und Minden: Heinz Schilling, ca. 1950), 2.

5. Schmidt, *Wunderheilungen*, 95–96.

6. StAM, Polizeidirektion München, 15558, p. 39. Durchschrift, September 12, 1949. Betr.: Bruno Gröning. Werner Bab, "Die Ursachen der Kriegsblindheit," *Berliner klinische Wochenschrift* 58:20 (May 16, 1921): 512–13.

7. Harrington, *The Cure Within*, 251.

8. Thomas Mann, *The Story of a Novel: The Genesis of Doktor Faustus*, trans. Richard Winston and Clara Winston (New York: Knopf, 1961), 76.

9. Sean A. Forner, *German Intellectuals and the Challenge of Democratic Renewal: Culture and Politics After 1945* (Cambridge: Cambridge University Press, 2014), 60.

10. Harrington, *The Cure Within*, 253–54.

11. Maurice Merleau-Ponty, *Phenomenology of Perception*, trans. Colin Smith (London: Routledge, 2010), 186.

12. "Wer ein Schnitzel findet, ist geheilt," *Der Spiegel* 28, July 7, 1949, p. 7.

13. Landesarchiv Baden-Württemberg, 466-5/7330, an den Herrn Sozialminister des Landes Nordrhein-Westfalen, August 1949, betr.: Ausübung der Heilkunde durch Bruno Gröning, Herford.

14. "Plan der Revue," *Revue*, Nr. 27, August 14, 1949, 8.

15. "Ich rieche Nazis," *Der Spiegel* 38, September 15, 1949, 14.

16. "Revolution in der Medizin?," *Revue*, Nr. 27, August 14, 1949, 1.

17. "Die Geschichte der Vorbereitung," *Revue*, Nr. 28, August 21, 1949, 8.

18. "Bruno Gröning: Phänomen eines Seelenarztes," *Revue*, Nr. 27, August 14, 1949, 8, 10–11, 18; "Bruno Gröning ein geborener Seelenarzt von großer Begabung," *Revue*, Nr. 28, August 21, 1949, 8, 10–11.

19. "Was Bruno Gröning in Heidelberg tut," *Stuttgarter Zeitung*, Nr. 139, August 13, 1949, 9. Clipping in Landesarchiv Baden-Württemberg, 466-5 /7330.

20. Fischer recommended Heidelberg: "Bruno Gröning ein geborener Seelenarzt von großer Begabung," *Revue*, Nr. 28, August 21, 1949, 9.

21. Of course the word "psychology" is also etymologically ambiguous. Its first use, in French, occurred in 1588 "in a book on ghosts and other miracles." Renaud Evrard, "The Orthodoxization of Psychology in France at the Turn of the Twentieth Century," in Lux and Paletschek, eds., *Okkultismus im Gehäuse*, 175.

22. "Briefe an Gröning—ein Alarmsignal!" *Revue*, Nr. 32, September 18, 1949, 10.

23. Gisela Bock, *Zwangssterilisation im Nationalsozialismus: Studien zur Rassenpolitik und Frauenpolitik* (Opladen: Westdeutscher Verlag, 1986), 8, 230–46; Hans-Walter Schmuhl, "Die Patientenmorde," in *Vernichten und Heilen: Der Nürnberger Ärzteprozeß und seine Folgen*, Angelika Ebbinghaus und Klaus Dörner, eds. (Berlin: Aufbau Verlag, 2001), 297.

24. Steven P. Remy, *The Heidelberg Myth: The Nazification and Denazification of a German University* (Cambridge: Harvard University Press, 2003), 130, 137.

25. Anne Harrington, *Reenchanted Science: Holism in German Culture from Wilhelm II to Hitler* (Princeton: Princeton University Press, 1996), 203.

26. Benno Müller-Hill, *Murderous Science: Elimination by Scientific Selection of Jews, Gypsies, and Others, Germany, 1933–1945*, trans. George R. Fraser (Oxford, UK: Oxford University Press, 1988), 92.

27. Harrington, *The Cure Within*, 81–82. See also Alexa Geisthövel and Bettina Hitzer, eds., *Auf der Suche nach einer anderen Medizin: Psychosomatik im 20. Jahrhundert* (Berlin: Suhrkamp, 2019).

28. Ralf Bröer and Wolfgang U. Eckart, "Schiffbruch und Rettung der modernen Medizin," *Ruperto Carola* 2 (1993): 4–9.

29. Harrington, *Reenchanted Science*, 202; Harrington, *The Cure Within*, 84–86; quote on 85.

30. "Bruno Gröning ein geborener Seelenarzt von großer Begabung," *Revue* Nr. 28, August 21, 1949, 10. The unspecified complaint is called an *Unterleibsleiden* in the text.

31. "Bruno Gröning ein geborener Seelenarzt von großer Begabung," *Revue*, Nr. 28, August 21, 1949, 9.

32. "Bruno Gröning ist kein Scharlatan," *Revue*, Nr. 29, August 28, 1949, 8.

33. "Gröning als Hellseher," *Revue*, Nr. 29, August 28, 1949, 18–19.

34. "Bruno Gröning: Phänomen eines Seelenarztes," *Revue*, Nr. 27, August 14, 1949, 10–11.

35. "Bruno Gröning: Phänomen eines Seelenarztes," *Revue*, 19.

36. "Bruno Gröning: Phänomen eines Seelenarztes," *Revue*, 9.

37. "Bruno Gröning ein geborener Seelenarzt von großer Begabung," *Revue*, 11.

38. "Briefe an Gröning—ein Alarmsignal!" *Revue*, Nr. 32, September 18, 1949, 10, 19. Details of various patients' lives also appear in other installments of the *Revue* series, especially August 14 and August 21, 1949.

39. Johannes Vossen, *Gesundheitsämter in Nationalsozialismus: Rassenhygiene und offene Gesundheitsfürsorge in Westfalen, 1900–1950* (Essen: Klartext, 2001), 285.

40. Norbert Sahrhage, *Diktatur und Demokratie*, 315.

41. "Briefe an Gröning—ein Alarmsignal!," *Revue*, 19.

42. "Herr Weiland sieht wieder gut," *Revue*, Nr. 32, September 18, 1949, 11.

43. Arthur Kleinman et al., "Pain as Human Experience: An Introduction," in Mary-Jo DelVecchio Good et al., eds., *Pain as Human Experience: An Anthropological Perspective* (Berkeley: University of California Press, 1992), 5–6.

44. Goltermann, *Die Gesellschaft der Überlebenden*, 165–216.

45. "Briefe an Gröning—ein Alarmsignal!," *Revue*, 10, 19.

46. Didier Fassin and Richard Rechtman, *The Empire of Trauma: An Inquiry*

into the Condition of Victimhood (Princeton: Princeton University Press, 2009).

47. "Briefe an Gröning—ein Alarmsignal!," *Revue,* Nr. 32, 10.

48. Robert G. Moeller, *War Stories: The Search for a Usable Past in the Federal Republic* (Berkeley: University of California Press, 2001), 3–4.

49. Grossmann, *Jews, Germans, and Allies,* 7.

50. As Michael Geyer writes, feelings of shame, mixed together with guilt about the Holocaust, produced not remorse but aggressive feelings of animus. See "The Place of the Second World War in German Memory and History," *New German Critique* 71 (Spring-Summer 1997): 5–40, here 17, 19.

51. "Briefe an Gröning—ein Alarmsignal!," *Revue,* Nr. 32, 10.

52. Geyer, "The Place of the Second World War," 18. Geyer observes that a "cold, apparently affectless confrontation with death was present" already in the late Weimar years, at least among intellectuals, and was part of the emotional heritage of the First World War. See also Geoffrey Campbell Cocks, *The State of Health: Illness in Nazi Germany* (New York: Oxford University Press, 2012), 1–3; Monica Black, *Death in Berlin: From Weimar to Divided Germany* (New York: Cambridge University Press, 2010), 102–8.

53. Michael H. Kater, "Die Medizin im nationalsozialistischen Deutschland und Erwin Liek," *Geschichte und Gesellschaft* 16:4 (1990): 442–43.

54. Goltermann, *Die Gesellschaft der Überlebenden,* 353.

55. Süss, *Death from the Skies,* 362–65.

5. MESSIAH IN MUNICH

1. Siegfried Sommer, "'Wunderdoktor' Gröning in München," *Süddeutsche Zeitung,* Nr. 98, August 20, 1949, 9.

2. "Fall Gröning weiter umstritten," *Die Welt,* Nr. 79, July 4, 1949.

3. Sommer, "'Wunderdoktor' Gröning in München," 9.

4. An example of how details of the *Revue* series were picked up by other news outlets: "'Wunderdoktor' Gröning—umworben und umstritten," *Münchner Allgemeine,* Nr. 35, 2. Jhg., August 28, 1949, 3. Clipping in Stadtarchiv Rosenheim.

5. StAM, Polizeidirektion 15558. Abschrift von Abdruck, Munich, August 24, 1949, lfd. Nr. 7. Bayer. Staatsmin. des Innern an die Regierung von Oberbayern. Betr.: Ausübung der Heilkunde durch Bruno Gröning, Herford.

6. "Bleibt Gröning in Bayern?" *Oberbayerische Volksblatt,* Nr. 102, August 30, 1949. Clipping in StAM, BezA/LRA 57182.

7. Thomas Großbölting, *Losing Heaven: Religion in Germany Since 1945,* trans. Alex Skinner (New York: Berghahn, 2017), 22–23.

8. See also "Großverdiener um Gröning, *Wort und Bild,* 4 Jhg., Nr. 39, September 25, 1949. Clipping in IGPP, Busam Sammlung, PA 172; "Schenk mir ein Pferdchen," *Der Spiegel* 40, September 29, 1949, p. 8, which describes Gröning's entourage. Sculptor: StAM, Staatsanwaltschaften 3178/2, p. 336, Vernehmungsniederschrift.

9. BAB, PK (ehem. BDC), Sig. PO 134, VBS 1/1160025110, Schmidt, Egon Arthur.

10. Schmidt, *Die Wunderheilungen,* 13.

11. BAB, R19, 2963, Schmidt, Egon Arthur.

12. *Stadtatlas München: Karten und Modelle von 1570 bis heute* (München: Technische Universität München, 1999), 60.

13. Joachim Slawik, "Steh auf und geh!" *Almfried,* Nr. 35, September 3, 1949, 2; Sommer, "'Wunderdoktor' Gröning in München," 9.

14. "Gröning und das Heilpraktikergesetz," *Süddeutsche Zeitung,* Nr. 100, August 25, 1949.

15. StAM, Polizeidirektion 15558, Stadtrat der Landeshauptstadt München, betr.: Menschensammlung durch Heilungssuchende, August 26, 1949, 10.

16. Josephson-Storm, *The Myth of Disenchantment,* 210–11; Kurlander, *Hitler's Monsters,* chapter 2.

17. Wolffram, *The Stepchildren of Science,* 131–89.

18. Victor Klemperer, *Munich 1919: Diary of a Revolution,* trans. Jessica Spengler (Cambridge: Polity Press, 2017).

19. "Ein Besuch beim Wunderdoktor," *Stuttgarter Zeitung,* Nr. 157, September 3, 1949, 4. Clipping in Landesarchiv Baden-Württemberg, 466-5 /7330, Gröning, Bruno.

20. "Großverdiener um Gröning, *Wort und Bild,* 4 Jhg., Nr. 39, September 25, 1949. Clipping in IGPP, Busam Sammlung, PA 172.

21. StAM, BezA/LRA 57182, Abschrift, Landpolizei Oberbayern, Kriminalaußenstelle Rosenheim, September 4, 1949. Betr.: Affäre Gröning.

22. Alfred Heueck, "Als Zaungast bei Bruno Gröning," *Schwäbische Landeszeitung,* Nr. 108, September 14, 1949. Clipping located in Stadtarchiv Rosenheim.

23. Heueck, "Als Zaungast bei Bruno Gröning."

24. Heueck, "Als Zaungast bei Bruno Gröning." Käsberger also related this episode.

25. StAM, BezA/LRA 57182, Abschrift, Landpolizei Oberbayern, Kriminalaußenstelle Rosenheim, September 4, 1949. Betr.: Affäre Gröning.

26. Heueck, "Als Zaungast bei Bruno Gröning."

27. StAM, BezA/LRA 57182, Abschrift, Landpolizei Oberbayern, Kriminalaußenstelle Rosenheim, September 4, 1949. Betr.: Affäre Gröning.

28. Anne Harrington, "Unmasking Suffering's Masks: Reflections on Old and New Memories of Nazi Medicine," in Arthur Kleinman, Veena Das, and Margaret M. Lock, eds., *Social Suffering* (Berkeley: University of California Press, 1997).

29. StAM, Staatsanwaltschaften 3178/4, pp. 708–13, Mitscherlich an das Schöffengericht, October 24, 1951.

30. StAM, Staatsanwaltschaften 3178/4, p. 715, Mitscherlich an das Schöffengericht, October 24, 1951.

31. These are themes that Mitscherlich would pursue in his breakthrough book, *Society Without the Father: A Contribution to Social Psychology*, trans. Eric Mosbacher (New York: Harcourt, Brace & World, 1969; orig. pub. 1963).

32. Nicolas Berg, *The Holocaust and the West German Historians: Historical Interpretation and Autobiographical Memory*, trans. Joel Golb (Madison, WI: University of Wisconsin Press, 2015), 23.

33. StAM, Staatsanwaltschaften 3178/4, p. 715, Mitscherlich an das Schöffengericht, October 24, 1951.

34. Alexander Mitscherlich and Margarete Mitscherlich, *Inability to Mourn: Principles of Collective Behavior* (New York: Grove Press, 1975), 26.

35. Horst Axtmann, "Gröning, ein Dokumentarfilm," *Illustrierte Filmwoche*, Ausgabe B, 4. Jhg., Nr. 43, October 29, 1949, 586.

36. Alfred Heueck, "Als Zaungast bei Bruno Gröning."

37. "Aufmarsch des Elends im Traberhof," *Badische Neueste Nachrichten*, Nr. 182, September 15, 1949, n.p. Clipping in Landesarchiv Baden-Württemberg, 466-5/7330, Gröning, Bruno.

38. Siegfried Sommer, "Glauben versetzt Berge," *Süddeutsche Zeitung*, August 30, 1949.

39. StAM, Polizei-Direktion 15558, 18. Überwachungsbericht, September 2, 1949.

40. "Die Nacht der großen Heilung," "Sonderausgabe über Grönings Erfolge," Nr. 1, Anfang September 1949. Clipping in IGPP, Busam Sammlung.

41. StAM, BezA/LRA 57182, an die Regierung von Oberbayern, September 7, 1949. Betr.: Ausübung der Heilkunde durch Bruno Gröning.

42. "Das Phänomen Bruno Gröning," *Neue Miesbacher Anzeiger*, September 10, 1949. Clipping in StAM, Gesundheitsämter 4256.

43. "Die Nacht der großen Heilung," "Sonderausgabe über Grönings Erfolge," IGPP.

44. Viktoria Rehn, "Ich kann nur gute Menschen heilen!" *Echo der Woche*, September 2, 1949. Clipping in Stadtarchiv Rosenheim.

45. "Ihren Stock brauchen Sie nicht mehr," *Münchner Allgemeine*, Nr. 36, September 4, 1949, n.p. Clipping in IGPP, Busam Pressesammlung.

46. StAM, BezA/LRA 57182, Landpolizei Oberbayern, Kriminalaußenstelle Rosenheim, Fernschreiben an das Präsidium der Landespolizei, September 10, 1949. The *Süddeutsche Zeitung* claimed there were 18,000 at the Traberhof: "Grönings Besuch im Polizeipräsidium," September 10, 1949. *Der Spiegel* referred to 15,000: "Schenk mir ein Pferdchen," 7.

47. "Aufmarsch des Elends im Traberhof," *Badische Neueste Nachrichten*.

48. StAM, Polizei-Direktion 15558, 39. Durchschrift, September 12, 1949. Betr.: Bruno Gröning; StAM, BezA/LRA 57182, betr.: Auftreten des "Wunderdoktors Brunno [*sic*] Gröning," September 6, 1949; Kurt Böhme, *Wunderheilungen: Lourdes—Gesundbeter—Gröning* (Berlin: Vlg. Psyche, 1950), 15.

49. BAB, "Welt im Film," 225, September 19, 1949. Accessed on June 1, 2017: https://www.filmothek.bundesarchiv.de/video/583657.

50. Kurt Trampler, *Die große Umkehr: Fragen um Bruno Gröning* (Seebruck am Chiemsee: Im Heering Vlg., 1950), 92.

51. "Ihren Stock brauchen Sie nicht mehr," *Münchner Allgemeine*.

52. "Aufmarsch des Elends im Traberhof," *Badische Neueste Nachrichten*.

53. Stadtarchiv Rosenheim, VI P O 1560, Bruno Gröning.

54. "Bavarian 'Healer' Attracts Germans," *New York Times*, September 8, 1949. Clark's title: *Die Protokolle des Bayerischen Ministerrats, 1945–62 On-Line*, "Einleitung," 35. Accessed September 7, 2018 http://www.bayerischer-ministerrat.de//index.php?vol=ehr21&doc=ehr21aENLT.

55. StAM, BezA/LRA 57182, 21. Betr.: Auftreten des 'Wunderdoktors' Brunno [*sic*] Gröning. September 6, 1949.

56. StAM, Polizei-Direktion 15558, 24. Betr.: Auftreten des Heilpraktikers Bruno Gröning, September 5, 1949. Also see "Gröning-Anhänger blockieren Verkehr," newspaper name unclear, September 9, 1949. Clipping in Stadtarchiv München, 167/14, Personen, Gröning, Bruno, Wunderdoktor.

57. StAM, Polizei-Direktion 15558, 18. Überwachungsbericht, September 2, 1949.

58. StAM, Polizei-Direktion 15558, 19. Überwachungsbericht, September 1, 1949.

59. StAM, Polizei-Direktion 15558, 23. Betr.: Menschenansammlung in der Lindwurmstraße, September 3, 1949.

60. "Mutter wollte ihr Kind opfern," *Hannoversche Presse*, 4. Jahrgang, Nr. 104, September 2, 1949. Clipping in IGPP.

61. Conrad Adlmaier, *Blick in die Zukunft* (Traunstein: Chiemgau Druck, 1950), 23.

62. Trampler, *Die große Umkehr*, 107.

63. "Gröning: Meine Kraft ist keine menschliche," n.p., September 3, 1949, 6. Clipping in Stadtarchiv Rosenheim.

64. "Gröning: Sender eines Strahlenfeldes?" *Revue*, Nr. 30, September 4, 1949, 10.

65. "Cosmic horizon" is Jacob Taubes's expression: *Occidental Eschatology*, trans. David Ratmoko (Stanford: Stanford University Press, 2009), 43.

66. "Lourdes and Traberhof," *Alpenbote Rosenheim*, Folge 1, September 1949. Clipping in Stadtarchiv München, 167/14, Personen: Gröning, Bruno, Wunderdoktor.

67. Rehn, "Ich kann nur gute Menschen heilen!"

68. "Gröning darf heilen," *Abendblatt*, September 7, 1949. Clipping in StAM, Staatsanwaltschaften 3178/5.

69. "Gröning darf heilen," *Abendblatt*.

70. "Erregte Debatte um Gröning," *Abendzeitung*, September 17, 1949. Clipping located in Stadtarchiv München, 167/14, Personen: Gröning, Bruno, Wunderdoktor.

71. "Auch der Stadtrat befasst sich mit dem 'Wunderdoktor,'" *Münchner Merkur*, September 7, 1949. Clipping located in Stadtarchiv München, 167/14, Personen: Gröning, Bruno, Wunderdoktor.

72. *Die Protokolle des Bayerischen Ministerrats 1945–62 On-Line*, Das Kabinett Ehard II, Nr. 78, Ministerratssitzung, September 9, 1949. Accessed September 7, 2018 http://www.bayerischer-ministerrat.de//index.php?vol=ehr21&doc=ehr21aENLT.

73. "Gröning darf heilen," *Abendblatt*; "Grönings Besuch im Polizeipräsidium," *Süddeutsche Zeitung*; "Gröning und das Innenministerium," *Münchner Allgemeine*, Nr. 36, 2. Jhg., September 4, 1949.

74. "Dr. Ehard über Gröning," *Die Abendzeitung*, September 6, 1949. Clipping in Stadtarchiv München, 167/14, Personen: Gröning, Bruno, Wunderdoktor.

75. Foil balls, black market: "Der Rosenheimer Landrat bei Gröning," *Oberbayerische Volksblatt*, Nr. 105, September 6, 1949, 8. Clipping in StAM, BezA/LRA 57182; address: "Hohlspiegel," *Der Spiegel* 38, September 15, 1949.

76. "Die Merkur-Reporter Unterwegs. Was sagt der Mann auf der Straße zu Gröning?" *Münchner Merkur*, September 7, 1949. Clipping in Stadtarchiv München, 167/14, Personen: Gröning, Bruno, Wunderdoktor.

77. For the weather, StAM, BezA/LRA 57182, Landpolizei Oberbayern, Kriminalaußenstelle Rosenheim, Fernschreiben an das Präsidium der LP, September 10, 1949. StAM, BezA/LRA 57182, "An die Regierung Oberbayerns, betr.: Ausübung der Heilkunde durch Bruno Gröning," September 7, 1949.

78. StAM, BezA/LRA 57182, Bayerisches Rotes Kreuz an Herrn Leo Hawart, September 13, 1949; "Gröning-Heilstätten im Landkreis Miesbach," *Miesbacher Zeitung*, September 14, 1949. Clipping in StAM, Gesundheitsämter 4256.

79. "Traberhof—öffentlicher Notstand," *Rosenheimer Tageblatt*, September 10, 1949. Clipping in StAM, BezA/LRA 57182; "Kann und darf Bruno Gröning heilen?" *Tagespost*, September 13, 1949. Clipping in IGPP, Busam Sammlung.

80. "Grönings Besuch im Polizeipräsidium," *Süddeutsche Zeitung*.

81. "Traberhof—öffentlicher Notstand," *Rosenheimer Tageblatt*, September 10, 1949. Clipping in StAM, BezA/LRA 57182.

82. StAM, BezA/LRA 57182, Abschrift, BLD-Kurzdienst, Blatt III, September 8, 1949.

83. StAM, BezA/LRA 57182, 26. Landpolizei Oberbayern, Kriminalaußenstelle Rosenheim, Abschrift, Fernschreiben an das Präs. d. LP v. Bay., betr.: Überwachung Traberhof, n.d., likely September 11, 1949.

84. "Gröning-Heilstätten im Landkreis Miesbach," *Miesbacher Anzeiger*, September 12, 1949. Clipping in StAM, Gesundheitsämter 4256. See also StAM, BezA/LRA/57182, 17. "Niederschrift aufgenommen 19. September 1949 zu Happing. Gegenstand der Beschlussfassung: Die Verhältnisse im Anwesen Traberhof," September 23, 1949.

85. StAM, Gesundheitsämter 4256, staatl. Gesundheitsamt Miesbach, September 12, 1949.

86. "Gröning braucht Ruhe," *Abendzeitung*, Nr. 233, September 15, 1949. Clipping in Stadtarchiv München, 167/14, Personen: Gröning, Bruno, Wunderdoktor.

87. "Gröning-Heilstätten im Landkreis Miesbach." See also StAM, BezA/LRA/57182, 17. "Niederschrift aufgenommen 19. September 1949 zu Happing. Gegenstand der Beschlussfassung: Die Verhältnisse im Anwesen Traberhof," September 23, 1949.

88. "Protest gegen die Zustände um den Traberhof," *Südost-Kurier*, September 17, 1949, reprinted in Ingrid Geupel, "Bruno Gröning: Das Phänomen eines Wunderheilers" (PhD dissertation, Fakultät f. Medizin, Technische Universität München, 1988), 61–62.

89. All clippings in IGPP Busam Sammlung, PA 048.

90. "Gröning und die Krise der Medizin," *Quick*, Jhg. 2, Nr. 39, September 25, 1949. Clipping in IGPP/E 123/100.

91. Rehn, "Ich kann nur gute Menschen heilen!"

92. "Gröning darf heilen," *Abendblatt*; "Schenk mir ein Pferdchen," *Der Spiegel*, 7.

93. See numerous clippings in Stadtarchiv München, ZA-P-489-16, Zoltikow. Also see "Graf Soltikow ans Telefon," *Die Zeit,* January 3, 1952.

94. "Extra-Blatt, Der 'Herforder Wunderdoktor,' Gröning entlarvt," September 27, 1949. Clipping located in IGPP, E 123/100.

95. "Schenk mir ein Pferdchen," *Der Spiegel,* pp. 7–8.

96. "Gröning stellt Strafantrag," *Münchner Merkur,* Nr. 121, September 29, 1949. StAM, Staatsanwaltschaften 3178/5.

97. "Glauben Sie an Bruno Gröning?" n.p., September 29, 1949. Clipping located in IGPP/Busam Sammlung, PA 209.

98. "Offener Brief an Bruno Gröning," *Revue,* Nr. 34, October 2, 1949. IGPP Busam Sammlung.

99. "Rätsel um Gröning," *Rheinischer Merkur,* October 1, 1949. Clipping located in Stadtarchiv München, 167/14, Personen: Gröning, Bruno, Wunderdoktor.

100. "Rolf-Engler Film antwortet," *Illustrierte Filmwoche,* Ausgabe B, 4. Jhg., Nr. 43, October 29, 1949, 586.

101. "Die Zeit ist aus den Fugen," *Oberbayerische Volksblatt,* "Rosenheimer Anzeiger," Nr. 126, October 25, 1949, Stadtarchiv Rosenheim VI P O 1560, Bruno Gröning.

102. "Giftmord an Gröning geplannt?" *Neuer Miesbacher,* October 8, 1949. StAM, BezA/LRA 219606.

103. "Grönings letzte Heilungen." Clipping from *Rosenheimer Tagblatt Wendelstein,* Nr. 8, October 18, 1949. Located in Stadtarchiv Rosenheim.

104. StAM, BezA/LRA 57182, Abschrift aus dem Bayerischen Landtagsdienst, 3. Jhg., Nr. 52, November 16, 1949.

105. Stadtarchiv Rosenheim VI P O, Bruno Gröning, letter from a mother in Hohenfichte, November 19, 1949.

106. Stadtarchiv Rosenheim VI P O, Bruno Gröning, letter from Husum, November 23, 1949.

107. "Ende des Gröning-Rummels," *8-Uhr-Blatt,* Nürnberg, December 17, 1949. Clipping located in StAM, Staatsanwaltschaften, 3178/5.

108. "Erste Gröning-Heilstätte in Mittenwald-Obb.," *Rosenheimer Tageblatt,* December 24, 1949. Clipping located in StAM, Staatsanwaltschaften, 3178/5.

109. "Grönings Patienten warten vergebens: Verlassen auf dem Traberhof," *Abendzeitung,* Nr. 311, September 29, 1949. Clipping located in Stadtarchiv München, 167/14, Personen: Gröning, Bruno, Wunderdoktor.

110. IGPP E 123/100. Letter to Herrn Dr. Wüst, Ludolf-Krehl-Klinik, Heidelberg, December 30, 1949.

6. IF EVIL IS THE ILLNESS, WHAT IS THE CURE?

1. StAM, Staatsanwaltschaften 3178/2, 355, Vernehmungsniederschrift, Sachgebiet Einsatz der Kriminalabteilung . . . der Landpolizei von Bayern, October 26, 1950; StAM, Staatsanwaltschaften 3178/3, Renée Meckelburg, "Tatsachenbericht," 477 (file page number), June 20–27, 1950; Opel P4: StAM, Staatsanwaltschften 3178/3, Heuner, "Tatsachenbericht," 443.

2. "Strahlen in den Polstern," *Der Spiegel* 36, September 6, 1950, p. 11.

3. StAM, Staatsanwaltschaften 3178/2, 375, Vernehmungsniederschrift, Sachgebiet Einsatz der Kriminalabteilung . . . der Landpolizei von Bayern, September 22, 1950; StAM, Staatsanwaltschaften 3178/2, 35, Staatliche Kriminalpolizei, Kriminalabt. Konstanz, May 17, 1950.

4. StAM, Staatsanwaltschaften 3178/3, Heuner, "Tatsachenbericht," 443.

5. StAM, Staatsanwaltschaften 3178/1, Pol. Bezirk Aurich to Pol. Präs. München, June 1, 1950; apartment: StAM, Staatsanwaltschaften 3178/3, Heuner, "Tatsachenbericht," 443, 453.

6. StAM, Staatsanwaltschaften 3178/3, Renée Meckelburg, "Tatsachenbericht," 477–79.

7. Frank Bajohr, *Parvenüs und Profiteure: Korruption in der NS-Zeit* (Frankfurt: Fischer, 2001), 189.

8. Peter Fritzsche and Jochen Hellbeck, "The New Man in Stalinist Russia and Nazi Germany," in Michael Geyer and Sheila Fitzpatrick, eds., *Beyond Totalitarianism: Stalinism and Nazism Compared* (Cambridge: Cambridge University Press, 2008), 302–42.

9. BAB, SS-Führerpersonalakten, Meckelburg, Otto, and BA-Berlin, RS (ehem. BDC), VBS 286/6035012513/Otto Meckelburg, Sig. D5418.

10. "Strahlen in den Polstern," *Der Spiegel*, 11; StAM, Staatsanwaltschaften 3178/2, 386, Vernehmungsniederschrift, Sachgebiet Einsatz der Kriminalabteilung . . . der Landpolizei von Bayern, October 11, 1950.

11. Biddiscombe, *The Denazification of Germany*, 40.

12. Ulrich Herbert, *Best: Biographische Studien über Radikalismus, Weltanschauung und Vernunft, 1903–1989* (Bonn: Dietz, 1996), 475.

13. StAM, Staatsanwaltschaften 3178/1, 20. No date, presumably March/April 1950.

14. StAM, Staatsanwaltschaften 3178/1, 104. Polizeibezirk Aurich, Wittmund, January 31, 1950.

15. StAM, Staatsanwaltschaften 3178/2, 383, Vernehmungsniederschrift, June 28, 1950; StAM, Staatsanwaltschaften 3178/1, 104. Polizeibezirk Aurich, Wittmund, January 31, 1950.

16. StAM, Staatsanwaltschaften 3178/2, 383, Vernehmungsniederschrift, June 28, 1950.

17. Norbert Frei, "Identitätswechsel: Die 'Illegalen' in der Nachkriegszeit," in Helmut König, Wolfgang Kuhlmann, and Klaus Schwabe, eds., *Vertuschte Vergangenheit: Der Fall Schwerte und die NS-Vergangenheit der deutschen Hochschulen* (Munich: C. H. Beck, 1997), 207, 216.

18. StAM, Staatsanwaltschaften 3178/1, 20–21, n.d., presumably 1950.

19. StAM, Staatsanwaltschaften 3178/2, 383, Vernehmungsniederschrift, Sachgebiet Einsatz der Kriminalabteilung . . . der Landpolizei von Bayern, June 28, 1950; StAM, Staatsanwaltschaften 3178/2, 384, Vernehmungsniederschrift, Sachgebiet Einsatz der Kriminalabteilung . . . der Landpolizei von Bayern, October 11, 1950; StAM, Staatsanwaltschaften 3178/1, Polizeibezirk Aurich, an das Polizeipräsidium in München, June 1, 1950.

20. Frei, "Identitätswechsel," 217–18.

21. Bettina Stangneth, *Eichmann Before Jerusalem: The Unexamined Life of a Mass Murderer*, trans. Ruth Martin (New York: Knopf, 2014), 62–63, 71–72.

22. StAM, Staatsanwaltschaften 3178/3, Renée Meckelburg, "Tatsachenbericht," 478–79.

23. StAM, Staatsanwaltschaften 3178/3, Renée Meckelburg, "Tatsachenbericht," 480.

24. StAM, Staatsanwaltschaften 3178/3, "Das war Bruno Gröning: Ein Tatsachenbericht von Ernst Heuner," n.d., presumably 1950, 441.

25. StAM, Staatsanwaltschaften 3178/3, Renée Meckelburg, "Tatsachenbericht," 480–84.

26. StAM, Staatsanwaltschaften 3178/3, Heuner, "Tatsachenbericht," 443.

27. StAM, Staatsanwaltschaften 3178/3, Renée Meckelburg, "Tatsachenbericht," 486, 497.

28. StAM, Staatsanwaltschaften 3178/3, Renée Meckelburg, "Tatsachenbericht," 497.

29. StAM, Staatsanwaltschaften 3178/3, Heuner, "Tatsachenbericht," 444; "Strahlen in den Polstern," *Der Spiegel,* 12.

30. StAM, Staatsanwaltschaften 3178/3, Renée Meckelburg, "Tatsachenbericht," 520.

31. StAM, BezA/LRA/57182, 19. Abschrift SSD Fst. Herford Nr. 243 an Kripo Rosenheim/Bayern, betr.: Bruno Gröning, September 4, 1949.

32. StAM, Staatsanwaltschaften 3178/3, Heuner, "Tatsachenbericht," 442. Fallen out: "Schenk mir ein Pferdchen," *Der Spiegel,* p. 8.

33. StAM, Staatsanwaltschaften 3178/3, Heuner, "Tatsachenbericht," 444.

34. StAM, Staatsanwaltschaften 3178/3, Renée Meckelburg, "Tatsachenbericht," 492.
35. StAM, Staatsanwaltschaften 3178/4, "Eingestellt in Richtung gegen Bruno Gröning et al.," January 18, 1951.
36. StAM, Staatsanwaltschaften 3178/3, Renée Meckelburg, "Tatsachenbericht," 499.
37. Stadtarchiv Rosenheim OAH 24, undated letter from Leo Hawart to Gemeinderat Happing, n.d. (presumably March/April 1950).
38. StAM, Staatsanwaltschaften 3178/3, Renée Meckelburg, "Tatsachenbericht," 526. Jungbauer, *Deutsche Volksmedizin*, 67.
39. StAM, Staatsanwaltschaften 3178/3, Renée Meckelburg, "Tatsachenbericht," 526.
40. StAM, Staatsanwaltschaften 3178/2, 365, Vernehmungsniederschrift, Helmut Hülsmann, July 20, 1950; Herford city director Fritz Meister reported something similar: KAH, S10/270, "Wunderheiler" Bruno Gröning (Akten des Hauptamtes, 1949–1950), 250, Oberstadtdirektor Meister an den Herrn Regierungspräsidenten Detmold, September 26, 1949.
41. StAM, Staatsanwaltschaften 3178/4, "Eingestellt in Richtung gegen Bruno Gröning et al.," January 18, 1951.
42. StAM, Staatsanwaltschaften 3178/3, Renée Meckelburg, "Tatsachenbericht," 504–5.
43. StAM, Staatsanwaltschaften 3178/3, Renée Meckelburg, "Tatsachenbericht," 489.
44. StAM, Staatsanwaltschaften 3178/1, 123. Vernehmungsniederschrift, June 27, 1950.
45. "Gröning in der Roxy-Bar," no newspaper, no date, presumably 1949–50. Clipping located in Stadtarchiv München, 167/14, Personen, Gröning, Bruno, Wunderdoktor.
46. StAM, Staatsanwaltschaften 3178/3, Renée Meckelburg, "Tatsachenbericht," 512, 515, 517–18.
47. StAM, Staatsanwaltschaften 3178/3, 439, Ernst Heuner, "Das war Bruno Gröning."
48. StAM, Polizeidirektion 15558, 54. Abschrift, Kriminalpolizei Herford an das Polizeipräs. München, betr.: Ermittlungen in Sachen Bruno Gröning, September 9, 1949.
49. "Schenk mir ein Pferdchen," *Der Spiegel*, 8.
50. StAM, Staatsanwaltschaften 3178/3, Renée Meckelburg, "Tatsachenbericht," 511.
51. StAM, Staatsanwaltschaften 3178/1, 123. Vernehmungsniederschrift, June 27, 1950.

52. StAM, Staatsanwaltschaften 3178/1, 123. Vernehmungsniederschrift, June 27, 1950; StAM, Staatsanwaltschaften 3178/2, 340, Vernehmungsniederschrift, Sachgebiet Einsatz der Kriminalabteilung beim Präsidium der Landpolizei von Bayern, October 10, 1950.

53. StAM, Staatsanwaltschaften 3178/1, 124. Vernehmungsniederschrift, June 27, 1950.

54. StAM, Staatsanwaltschaften 3178/3, Renée Meckelburg, "Tatsachenbericht," 494, 513.

55. StAM, Staatsanwaltschaften 3178/3, Renée Meckelburg, "Tatsachenbericht," 518.

56. StAM, Staatsanwaltschaften 3178/3, Heuner, "Tatsachenbericht," 439.

57. Schmidt, *Die Wunderheilungen*, 50, 57.

58. Rehn, "Ich kann nur gute Menschen heilen!"

59. A. Kaul, *Das Wunder von Herford: Die merkwürdige Heilerfolge des Bruno Gröning* (Laudenbach: Lauda Vlg., 1949), 13. Located in KAH, S Slg. E/E 348-02.

60. Böhme, *Wunderheilungen*, 14.

61. Trampler, *Die große Umkehr*, 75.

62. StAM, BezA/LRA 57182. Abschrift zur Kenntnisnahme an das Landrat Rosenheim, Evang.-Luth. Pfarramt to Evang.-Luth. Landeskirchenrat, September 10, 1949.

63. StAM, Gesundheitsämter, 4256. Clipping from *Münchner Merkur*, "Tausende im Banne des Herforder 'Wunderdoktors,'" June 24, 1949. See also Schmidt, *Wunderheilungen*, 49–50.

64. StAM, Staatsanwaltschaften 3178/3, Renée Meckelburg, "Tatsachenbericht," 482.

65. Amanda Porterfield, *Healing in the History of Christianity* (Oxford, UK: Oxford Universitiy Press, 2005), 22, 5.

66. "Scharfer ärztlicher Vorstoß gegen Gröning," *Stuttgarter Zeitung*, Nr. 169, September 17, 1949, 7. Clipping in Landesarchiv Baden-Württemberg, Best. 466-5/7330, Gröning, Bruno.

67. This is my riff on a challenging question my colleague Nikki Eggers puts to students in her Health and Healing in Africa course at the University of Tennessee, Knoxville: "If witchcraft is the illness, what is the cure?" Her inspiration, in turn, was Gwyn Prins's essay, "But What Was the Disease? The Present State of Health and Healing in African Studies," *Past & Present* 124 (August 1989). Various essays in Steve Feierman and John M. Janzen's *Social Basis of Health and Healing in Africa* (Berkeley: University of California Press, 1992) point in similar directions, as does Stacey Langwick's *Bodies, Politics, and African Healing: The Matter of Maladies in Tanzania* (Bloomington: Indiana University Press, 2011); and Eggers's

own "Mukombozi and the *Monganga:* The Violence of Healing in the 1944 Kitawalist Uprising," *Africa* 89:3 (2019).

68. Opel Olympia: StAM, Staatsanwaltschaften 3178/3, 444; Wangerooge: StAM, Staatsanwaltschaften 3178/3, Renée Meckelburg, "Tatsachenbericht," 520.

69. "Gröning verursacht Wintersaison," *Neue Presse* (Coberg), January 10, 1950. Clipping in StAM, Staatsanwaltschaften 3178/5.

70. Pastor Wilfried Voigt's "Bericht über eine 'Massenheilung' des 'Wunderdoktors' Gröning am 16./17. Januar 1950 im Hotel Hanken." IGPP, Busam Sammlung, PA 204.

71. "Strahlen in den Polstern," *Der Spiegel*, 12.

72. Pastor Wilfried Voigt's "Bericht über eine 'Massenheilung' des 'Wunderdoktors' Gröning am 16./17. Januar 1950 im Hotel Hanken." IGPP, Busam Sammlung, PA 204.

73. StAM, Staatsanwaltschaften 3178/3, Heuner, "Tatsachenbericht," 465.

74. Pastor Wilfried Voigt's "Bericht über eine 'Massenheilung' des 'Wunderdoktors' Gröning am 16./17. Januar 1950 im Hotel Hanken." IGPP, Busam Sammlung, PA 204.

75. StAM, Staatsanwaltschaften 3178/3, Heuner, "Tatsachenbericht," 465.

76. Pastor Wilfried Voigt's "Bericht über eine 'Massenheilung' des 'Wunderdoktors' Gröning am 16./17. Januar 1950 im Hotel Hanken." IGPP, Busam Sammlung, PA 204.

77. Quoted in Pastor Wilfried Voigt's "Bericht über eine 'Massenheilung' des 'Wunderdoktors' Gröning am 16./17. Januar 1950 im Hotel Hanken." IGPP, Busam Sammlung, PA 204.

78. StAM, Staatsanwaltschaften 3178/3, Heuner, "Tatsachenbericht," 465.

79. Pastor Wilfried Voigt's "Bericht über eine 'Massenheilung' des 'Wunderdoktors' Gröning am 16./17. Januar 1950 im Hotel Hanken." IGPP, Busam Sammlung, PA 204.

80. StAM, Staatsanwaltschaften 3178/3, Renée Meckelburg, "Tatsachenbericht," 520; StAM, Staatsanwaltschaften 3178/3, Akte d. Schöffengerichts, 3.

81. "Gröning in Oldenburg . . . der rege und bewege sich!" No paper given, February 7, 1950. Clipping located in IGPP, Busam Slg., PA 200.

82. StAM, Staatsanwaltschaften 3178/1. Abschrift von Dr. med. Julius Ahlhorn, "Erfahrungsbericht über die 'Massenheilung' Grönings vom 9.–10. Februar 1950 i.d. Astoria (Oldenburg)."

83. "Gröning in Oldenburg . . . der rege und bewege sich!" No paper given, February 7, 1950. Clipping located in IGPP, Busam Slg., PA 200.

84. StAM, Staatsanwaltschaften 3178/3, Renée Meckelburg, "Tatsachenbericht," 520.

85. "Gröning in Oldenburg . . . der rege und bewege sich!" No paper given, Feburary 7, 1950. Clipping located in IGPP, Busam Slg., PA 200. Prices from Statistisches Bundesamt/Wiesbaden, ed., *Statistisches Jahrbuch f. die Bundesrepublik Deutschland* (Stuttgart-Cologne: W. Kohlhammer, 1954), 472–75.

86. StAM, Staatsanwaltschaften 3178/3, Renée Meckelburg, "Tatsachenbericht," 528.

87. StAM, Staatsanwaltschaften 3178/1, Abschrift von Dr. med. Julius Ahlhorn, "Erfahrungsbericht über die 'Massenheilung' Grönings vom 9.–10. Februar 1950 i.d. Astoria (Oldenburg)."

88. StAM, Staatsanwaltschaften 3178/1, Abschrift von Dr. med. Julius Ahlhorn, "Erfahrungsbericht über die 'Massenheilung' Grönings vom 9.–10. Februar 1950 i.d. Astoria (Oldenburg)."

89. "Das Phänomen Bruno Gröning," *Neue Miesbacher Anzeiger,* September 10, 1949; "Tausende im Banne des Herforder Wunderdoktors," *Münchner Merkur,* June 24, 1949. Both clippings in StAM, Gesundheitsämter 4256.

90. StAM, Staatsanwaltschaften 3178/1. Abschrift von Dr. med. Julius Ahlhorn, "Erfahrungsbericht über die 'Massenheilung' Grönings vom 9.–10. Februar 1950 i.d. Astoria (Oldenburg)."

91. StAM, Staatsanwaltschaften 3178/3, Renée Meckelburg, "Tatsachenbericht," 532. First healings carried out in early March, according to StAM, Staatsanwaltschaften 3178/3, Akte d. Schöffengerichts, p. 3; "glorious view": StAM, Staatsanwaltschaften 3178/3, Heuner, "Tatsachenbericht," 458.

92. StAM, 3178/3, Abschrift of Urteil, May 27, 1952.

93. "Strahlen in den Polstern," *Der Spiegel,* 11, 13.

94. StAM, Staatsanwaltschaften 3178/3, Renée Meckelburg, "Tatsachenbericht," 533–34.

95. "Gröning Heilstätte bei Behörden unbekannt," *Hochland Bote* (Garmisch), January 13, 1950; and "Gröning Heilstätte wird vorbereitet," *Straubinger Tagblatt,* January 13, 1950. Clippings in StAM München/Staatsanwaltschaften 3178/5.

96. "Sogar Grönings Badewasser wird noch verlangt," *Fränkische Presse* (Bayreuth), March 21, 1950. Clipping located in StAM, Staatsanwaltschaften 3178/5.

97. StAM, Staatsanwaltschaften 3178/3, Renée Meckelburg, "Tatsachenbericht," 522.

98. StAM, Staatsanwaltschaften 3178/3, Renée Meckelburg, "Tatsachenbericht," 536.

99. StAM, Staatsanwaltschaften 3178/3, Heuner, "Tatsachenbericht," 472.

100. "Herr Gröning ist wieder im Lande," *Süddeutsche Zeitung,* Nr. 77, April 1–2, 1950, p. 4. Clipping located in StAM, Staatsanwaltschaften 3178/5.

101. StAM, Staatsanwaltschaften 3178/1, Pol. Bezirk Aurich to Pol. Präs. München, betr. Meckelburg, June 1, 1950.

102. StAM, Staatsanwaltschaften 3178/2, 360, Vernehmungsniederschrift, Anneliese Hülsmann, July 20, 1950.

103. StAM, Staatsanwaltschaften 3178/1, 205, Polizeibezirk Aurich, January 31, 1950.

104. "Herr Gröning ist wieder im Lande," *Süddeutsche Zeitung*, Nr. 77, April 1–2, 1950, 4. Clipping located in StAM, Staatsanwaltschaften 3178/5.

105. "Zwecks Heilung vorsprechen," *Der Spiegel* 23, June 6, 1951, 7.

106. "Herr Gröning ist wieder im Lande," *Süddeutsche Zeitung*, Nr. 77, April 1–2, 1950, 4. Clipping located in StAM, Staatsanwaltschaften 3178/5.

107. "Gröning außer Verfolgung," *8-Uhr-Blatt* (Nuremberg), April 14, 1950. Clipping in StAM 3178/5.

108. "Gröning-Heilstätten vor der Entscheidung," *Hochland Merkur* (Garmisch-Partenkirchen), May 10, 1950. Clipping located in StAM, Staatsanwaltschaften 3178/5.

109. StAM, Staatsanwaltschaften 3178/1, Vernehmungsniederschrift, June 27, 1950.

110. StAM, Staatsanwaltschaften 3178/1, 118–19, Rechtsanwältin Fr. Vögel-König zur Staatsanwaltschaften beim Landgericht München II, June 26, 1950.

111. StAM, Staatsanwaltschaften 3178/6, Oberstaatsanwalt München II an Herrn Generalstaatsanwalt beim Oberlandesgericht, betr.: Ermittlungsverfahren, July 17, 1950.

112. StAM, Staatsanwaltschaften 3178/3, Renée Meckelburg, "Tatsachenbericht," 541, 526.

113. StAM, Staatsanwaltschaften 3178/1, p. 128. Vernehmungsniederschrift, June 27, 1950.

114. "Gröning mit 3 hochblonden Damen," *8-Uhr-Blatt* (Nuremberg), June 10, 1950. Clipping located in StAM, Staatsanwaltschaften 3178/5; "Heilen Sie auch Krebs?" *Der Spiegel* 29, July 14, 1954, pp. 12–15.

7. SICKNESS THAT COMES FROM SIN

1. "A Visit to Germany: From a Medical Correspondent," *The Lancet*, December 16, 1950, p. 817.

2. Monique Scheer, *Rosenkranz und Kriegsvisionen: Marienerscheinungen im 20. Jahrhundert* (Tübingen: Tübinger Vereinigung f. Volkskunde 2006), 171.

3. Cornelia Göksu, *Heroldsbach: Eine verbotene Wallfahrt* (Würzburg: Echter Vlg., 1991), 13–21.

4. Michael E. O'Sullivan, "West German Miracles: Catholic Mystics, Church Hierarchy, and Postwar Popular Culture," *Zeithistorische Forschungen/Studies in Contemporary History*, Online-Ausgabe 6:1 (2009), 11–34, accessed at: http://www.zeithistorische-forschungen.de/1-2009 /id=4628 (accessed on May 1, 2015). Monique Scheer, *Rosenkranz und Kriegsvisionen*, 169. More broadly on postwar Catholic miracles, see also Michael O'Sullivan, *Disruptive Power: Catholic Women, Miracles, and Politics in Modern Germany, 1918–1965* (Toronto: University of Toronto Press, 2018); and Yuliya Komska, *The Icon Curtain: The Cold War's Quiet Border* (Chicago: University of Chicago Press, 2015).

5. Johannes B. Walz, *Die Protokolle von Augenzeugen zu den "Muttergottes-Erscheinungen" von Heroldsbach-Thurn*, vol. III (1958), 99–102.

6. Rudolf Kriß, "Heroldsbach: Eine verbotene Wallfahrt der Gegenwart," in Leopold Schmidt, ed., *Kultur und Volk: Beiträge zur Volkskunde aus Österreich, Bayern und der Schweiz* (Vienna: Selbstverlag des Österreichischen Museums f. Volkskunde, 1954), 210.

7. Göksu, *Heroldsbach*, 49.

8. For an example, see the testimony of Frau K., in Walz, *Die Protokolle*, vol. III, 99–102. See also "Heller Schein im gelben Laub," *Der Spiegel*, 27 October 1949, p. 32.

9. Göksu, *Heroldsbach*, 42–48.

10. Rudolf Kriß, "Heroldsbach in volkskundlicher Sicht: Zum Wallfahrtswesen der Gegenwart," *Österreichische Zeitschrift f. Volkskunde*, Bd. 6, Heft 3–4 (1952), 120.

11. Kriß, "Heroldsbach: Eine verbotene Wallfahrt," 210. On the Sator formula, see Herbert Freudenthal, *Das Feuer im deutschen Brauch und Glauben* (Berlin: De Gruyter, 1931), 420.

12. Kriß, "Heroldsbach: Eine Verbotene Wallfahrt," 211, 214; O'Sullivan, "Miracles," 23.

13. Göksu, *Heroldsbach*, 47, 51.

14. Göksu, *Heroldsbach*, 41.

15. Kriß, "Heroldsbach in volkskundlicher Sicht," 110.

16. Göksu, *Heroldsbach*, 77–83, 88; O'Sullivan, "West German Miracles," 16.

17. O'Sullivan, "West German Miracles," 16, 18, 25.

18. Brian P. Levack, *The Devil Within: Possession and Exorcism in the Christian West* (New Haven: Yale University Press, 2013), 82–93.

19. StAM, Polizeidirektion München 11301, Überwachungsbericht, November 28, 1951.

20. StAM, Polizeidirektion München 11301, Abschrift, Strafanzeige, November 29, 1951; on Bavaria's antichicanery (anti-*Gaukelei*) law, see Schäfer, *Der Okkulttäter*, 6. The law was changed in 1954.

21. StAM, Polizeidirektion München 11301, Abschrift of statement given by Marianne D., November 16, 1951.
22. StAM, Polizeidirektion München 11301, Abschrift, Ev.-Luth. Dekanat an das Pol. Präs. München, November 17 and 23, 1951.
23. StAM, Polizeidirektion München 11301, Statement of Kirmayer, Antonius, December 18, 1951.
24. "Gröning darf wieder heilen," *Der Hausfreund*, September 24, 1949, 12.
25. StAM, Polizeidirektion München 11301, statement of Kirmayer, Antonius, November 26, 1951; statement of Köhler, Fritz, November 27, 1951.
26. StAM, Polizeidirektion München 11301, Statement of Köhler, Fritz, November 27, 1951.
27. StAM, Polizeidirektion München 11301, Statement of Kirmayer, Antonius, November 26, 1951.
28. StAM, Polizeidirektion München 11301, Schlussbericht, January 15, 1952.
29. Information about Espenlaub comes from personal correspondence with Rainer Gabriel, who is conducting oral-history research into Espenlaub's life; and from Böhme, *Wunderheilungen*, 9–11.
30. Paul Gerhardt Voigt, *Gesundheit und Heil* (Hannover: Lutherhaus-Vlg., 1959), 19–20.
31. Böhme, *Wunderheilungen*, 9–10; KAH, S10/270, an die Stadtverwaltung Herford from Richard Wenz, June 23, 1949.
32. Böhme, *Wunderheilungen*, 9–10.
33. Hermann Zaiss, *Gottes Imperativ: Sei Gesund!* (Marburg/Lahn: Verlagsbuchhandlung Hermann Rathmann, 1958), 10–13, 42–44.
34. Voigt, *Gesundheit*, 20.
35. Zaiss, *Sei gesund!* 5.
36. Tim Linder, *Hermann Zaiss: Einblicke in sein Leben* (Wuppertal: R. Brockhaus, 2000), 88.
37. "Bruno Gröning heilt in München," *Mittelbayerische Zeitung* (Regensburg), August 30, 1950. Clipping in StAM, Staatsanwaltschaften 3178/5. Monocle: StAM, Polizeidirektion München 15558, Nr. 100, betr.: Bruno Gröning, unerlaubter Ausübung der Heilkunde, October 23, 1950.
38. StAM, Polizeidirektion München 15558, Nr. 76–77, betr.: Bruno Gröning, October 24, 1950; StAM, Polizeidirektion München 15558, Nr. 94, Stadtrat der Landeshauptstadt München, betr.: Bruno Gröning, October 30, 1950.
39. StAM, Polizeidirektion München 15558, Nr. 99, betr.: Bruno Gröning, unerlaubte Ausübung der Heilkunde, October 23, 1950.
40. StAM, Polizeidirektion München 15558, Nr. 75, betr.: Bruno Gröning, October 17, 1950.

41. StAM, Staatsanwaltschaften 3178/5, Landespolizei-Oberbayern, Kriminalaußenstelle an die Bezirksinspektion der Landpolizei, München-Pasing, October 21, 1950 (Meier) and Abschrift, Staatl. Gesundheitsamt München-Land an Bay. Staatsmin. d.I., Gesundheitsabt., betr.: Auftreten des Bruno Gröning, October 23, 1950 (Bachmann).

42. Vortrag, Bruno Gröning, Krailling, October 5, 1950, p. 4. https://www .bruno-groening-stiftung.org/images/stories/bgs-media/pdf/vortraege /bruno-groening_1950-10-05_vortrag_krailling_ich-habe-heute.pdf.

43. Abschrift des stenographischen Protokolls eines Vortrags Bruno Grönings vom 12.10.1950, Wagnerbräu, Lilienstr., München, https://www.bruno -groening-stiftung.org/images/stories/bgs-media/pdf/vortraege/EN/EN _bruno-groening_1950-10-12_talk_it-is-difficult-to-accomplish-the-purpose _2-col.pdf.

44. Pastor Wilfried Voigt's "Bericht über eine 'Massenheilung' des 'Wunderdoktors' Gröning am 16./17. Januar 1950 im Hotel Hanken." IGPP, Busam Sammlung, PA 204.

45. Bruno Gröning, *Reden,* Bd. II (Berlin: Edition Busam, 1999), 68–69.

46. Goltermann, *Die Gesellschaft der Überlebenden*, 122–23.

47. Dornheim, *Kranksein im dörflichen Alltag*, 243–45.

48. Siegfried Sommer, "Glauben versetzt Berge," *Süddeutsche Zeitung*, August 30, 1949.

49. BAK, B 142/3930/267–288, Kurzprotokoll der 10. Sitzung des Ausschusses f. Fragen des Gesundheitswesens, July 12, 1950. On Hammer: Albrecht Kirchner, "Abschlussbericht der Arbeitsgruppe zur Vorstudie 'NS-Vergangenheit ehemaliger hessischer Landtagsabgeordneter' der Kommission des Hessischen Landtags für das Forschungsvorhaben 'Politische und parlamentarische Geschichte des Landes Hessen'" (Wiesbaden, 2013).

50. BAK, B 142/3930/448, Bayer. Staatsmin. des Innern an das Bundesministerium des Innern, March 16, 1950; BAK, B 142/3929, "Stellungnahme der ärztlichen Berufsvertretungen zu den Änderung des Heilpraktikergesetzes vom 17.2.1939," n.d. (presumably 1950); BAK, B 141/6908/71-2, Anlage zum Protokoll Nr. 24 (Sitzung vom 13. Juli 1955) des Ausschusses f. Fragen des Gesundheitswesens.

51. Geoffrey Cocks, *Psychotherapy in the Third Reich: The Göring Institute*, 2nd ed. (New Brunswick, NJ: Transaction, 1997).

52. BAK, B 142/3930/290-296, Kurzprotokoll der 12. Sitzung des Ausschusses f. Fragen des Gesundheitswesens, September 14, 1950.

53. Wolf von Siebenthal, *Krankheit als Folge der Sünde: Eine Medizinhistorische Untersuchung* (Hannover: Schmorl & von Seefeld Nachf., 1950), 7.

54. Von Siebenthal, *Krankheit als Folge*, 89–90, 93–95.

55. StAM, Staatsanwaltschaften 3178/3, Renée Meckelburg, "Tatsachen-bericht," 541–42.

56. James Shapiro, *Oberammergau: The Troubling Story of the World's Most Famous Passion Play* (New York: Vintage, 2001), 142, 153; Helena Waddy, *Oberammergau in the Nazi Era: The Fate of a Catholic Village in Hitler's Germany* (Oxford, UK: Oxford University Press, 2010), 250–51.

57. Waddy, *Oberammergau*, 249–51.

58. Waddy, *Oberammergau*, 190.

59. Waddy, *Oberammergau*, 245.

60. Shapiro, *Oberammergau*, 142; Waddy, *Oberammergau*, 250–51.

61. Amos Elon, *Journey Through a Haunted Land: The New Germany* (New York: Holt, Rinehart and Winston, 1967), 13–14.

62. Rudy J. Koshar, *Germany's Transient Pasts: Preservation and National Memory in the Twentieth Century* (Chapel Hill, NC: University of North Carolina Press, 1998), 234–35.

63. Michael Meng, *Shattered Spaces: Encountering Jewish Ruins in Postwar Germany and Poland* (Cambridge: Harvard University Press, 2011), 113–29.

64. Jan T. Gross, *Neighbors: The Destruction of the Jewish Community in Jedwabne, Poland* (New York: Penguin, 2002), 112–13.

8. ARE THERE WITCHES AMONG US?

1. Landesarchiv Schleswig-Holstein (hereafter: LSH), Abt 352, Itzehoe, Nr. 413, pp. 25–26, April 8, 1954. The identities of individuals who surface in German archival documents are protected up to ninety years after their birth. Because I did not always know when each of the subjects of this chapter was born, I have generally chosen to use only the first or last name of those individuals involved in the episode the chapter describes.

2. LSH, Abt 352, Itzehoe, Nr. 413, pp. 25–26, April 8, 1954. Detail about the two groups living across the street from the same file, p. 20.

3. LSH, Abt 352, Itzehoe, Nr. 413, pp. 25–26, April 8, 1954.

4. LSH, Abt 352, Itzehoe, Nr. 413, pp. 39–40, April 26, 1954.

5. LSH, Abt 352, Itzehoe, Nr. 413, p. 3, March 3, 1954.

6. LSH, Abt 352, Itzehoe, Nr. 413, p. 17, April 8, 1954.

7. LSH, Abt 352, Itzehoe, Nr. 413, p. 70, June 16, 1954.

8. "Hexen-Aberglaube im Zeitalter der Wasserstoffbombe," *Volkszeitung Kiel*, Nr. 75, March 30, 1954. Clipping located in LSH, Abt. 352, Itzehoe, Nr. 413.

9. LSH, Abt 352, Itzehoe, Nr. 413, p. 3, March 3, 1954.

10. LSH, Abt. 352, Itzehoe, Nr. 413, p. 199.

11. LSH, Abt 352, Itzehoe, Nr. 413, p. 24, April 8, 1954, and p. 28, April 10, 1954; LSH, Abt 352, Itzehoe, Nr. 413, Vermerk, April 10, 1954.

12. LSH, Abt 352, Itzehoe, Nr. 413, p. 7, n.d.

13. "Hexen-Aberglaube im Zeitalter der Wasserstoffbombe," *Volkszeitung Kiel*, Nr. 75, March 30, 1954. Clipping located in LSH, Abt. 352, Itzehoe, Nr. 413.

14. LSH, Abt. 352, Itzehoe, Nr. 413, p. 7, n.d.

15. LSH, Abt. 352, Itzehoe Nr. 413, p. 237, "Im Namen des Volkes," June 9, 1955.

16. LSH, Abt. 352, Itzehoe, Nr. 413, p. 18, n.d.

17. LSH, Abt 352, Itzehoe, Nr. 413, p. 21, April 9, 1954.

18. LSH, Abt 352, Itzehoe, Nr. 413, pp. 40–42, April 26, 1954.

19. LSH, Abt 352, Itzehoe, Nr. 413, pp. 40–42, April 26, 1954.

20. Albert Hellwig, *Verbrechen und Aberglaube* (Leipzig: Teubner, 1908), 13.

21. Rudolf Olden, *Propheten in deutscher Krise: Das Wunderbare oder die Verzauberten* (Berlin: Rowohlt, 1932), 19–20, quoting the "letzten Jahresbericht der evangelischen-lutherischen Kirche in Hamburg."

22. Eduard Juhl, "Aberglaube und Zauberei: Wahn oder Wirklichkeit?" 5. Heft der Volksmission (Schleswig-Holstein: Selbstverlag der Bekennenden ev. luth. Kirche, 1935), 3–4, 6. Pamphlet located in Evangelisches Zentralarchiv Berlin (hereafter: EZA) 180/44.

23. Joachim Friedrich Baumhauer, *Johann Kruse und der 'neuzeitliche Hexenwahn': Zur Situation eines norddeutschen Aufklärers und einer Glaubensvorstellung im 20. Jahrhundert untersucht anhand von Vorgängen in Dithmarschen* (Neumünster: Karl Wachholtz Vlg., 1984), 101; Owen Davies, *Grimoires: A History of Magic Books* (Oxford, UK: Oxford University Press, 2009), 345, n. 104.

24. Schäfer, *Der Okkulttäter*, x.

25. Baumhauer, *Johann Kruse*, 72, n. 244, quoting "Hexengläubige im Bodenseegebiet," *Badisches Tagblatt*, Baden-Baden, August 8, 1957.

26. Karl-Heinz Christiansen, "Hexenspuk im Heidedorf," no newspaper given, April 18, 1951, clipping in HH, ZGS 2.2, Nr. 247.

27. Hans J. Mesterharm, "Attacke gegen Hexenwahn," no newspaper given, November 25, 1953. Clipping in HH, ZGS 2.2, Nr. 247.

28. Reiner Schulze, "Verfolgt als Hexe," *Welt am Sonntag*, Nr. 34, August 21, 1955, p. 2. Clipping located in HH, Nds. 401, Acc 112/83, Nr. 564.

29. LSH, Abt 352, Itzehoe, Nr. 413, pp. 25–26, April 8, 1954.

30. LSH, Abt 352, Itzehoe, Nr. 413, p. 21, April 9, 1954.

31. LSH, Abt. 352, Itzehoe, Nr. 418, Gutachte, p. 76, March 21, 1955.

32. Schäfer, *Der Okkulttäter*, x–xi.

33. David W. Kriebel, *Powwowing Amongst the Pennsylvania Dutch: Traditional Medical Practice in the Modern World* (University Park, PA: Pennsylvania State University Press, 2007), 117. Cited in Davies, *Grimoires,* 209–10.

34. Behringer, *Witches and Witch-Hunts,* 2.

35. Generally, see Willem de Blécourt, "The Witch, Her Victim, the Unwitcher, and the Researcher: The Continued Existence of Traditional Witchcraft," in Bengt Ankarloo and Stuart Clark, eds., *Witchcraft and Magic in Europe: The Twentieth Century* (Philadelphia: University of Pennsylvania Press, 1999). On Denmark: Gustav Henningsen, "Witch Persecution After the Era of the Witch Trials: A Contribution to Danish Ethnohistory," *Scandinavian Yearbook of Folklore* 44 (1988): 103–53. England: Owen Davies, "Healing Charms in Use in England and Wales, 1700–1950," *Folklore* 107 (1996): 19–32. Finland: Laura Stark-Arola, *Magic, Body and Social Order: The Contribution of Gender Through Women's Private Rituals in Traditional Finland* (Helsinki: Finnish Literature Society, 1998). France: Jeanne Favret-Saada, *Les Mots, la mort, les sorts: La sorcellerie dans le Bocage* (Paris: Gallimard, 1977), translated into English as *Deadly Words: Witchcraft in the Bocage* (Cambridge, UK: Cambridge University Press, 1981), trans. Catherine Cullen. Italy: Thomas Hauschild, *Macht und Magie in Italien: Über Frauenzauber, Kirche und Politik* (Gifkendorf: Merlin Verlag, 2002). Poland: Aldona Christina Schiffmann, "The Witch and Crime: The Persecution of Witches in Twentieth-Century Poland," *Scandinavian Yearbook of Folklore* 43 (1987): 147–64. West Germany: Baumhauer, *Johann Kruse,* and Inge Schöck, *Hexenglaube in der Gegenwart: Empirische Untersuchungen in Südwestdeutschland* (Tübingen: Tübinger Vereinigung f. Volkskunde, 1978).

36. Peter Geschiere, *Witchcraft, Intimacy, and Trust: Africa in Comparison* (Chicago: University of Chicago Press, 2013), xv; Michael D. Bailey, "Provincializing European Witchcraft: Thoughts on Peter Geschiere's Latest Synthesis," *Magic, Ritual, and Witchcraft* (Summer 2015): 86–87; Robin Briggs, *Witches and Neighbors: The Social and Cultural Context of European Witchcraft* (New York: Penguin, 1996).

37. Leopold Schmidt, *Volksglaube u. Volksgut* (1966), 282. Cited in Baumhauer, *Johann Kruse,* 205.

38. Lattimore, Bertram Gresh, Jr., *The Assimilation of German Expellees into the West German Polity and Society Since 1945: A Case Study of Eutin, Schleswig-Holstein* (The Hague: Martinus Nijhof, 1974), 5; George Gerolimatos, "Structural Change and Democratization of Schleswig-Holstein's Agriculture, 1945–1973" (PhD diss., History, UNC-Chapel Hill, 2014), 111–13; Jürgens, "Entnazifizierungspraxis in Schleswig-Holstein," 54; Baumhauer, *Johann Kruse,* 205.

39. Baumhauer, *Johann Kruse*, 269–70.

40. Koshar, *Germany's Transient Pasts*, 238.

41. Alexander Otto-Morris, *Rebellion in the Province: The* Landvolkbewegung *and the Rise of National Socialism in Schleswig-Holstein* (Frankfurt a.M.: Peter Lang, 2013), 19, 335.

42. Uwe Danker and Astrid Schwabe, *Schleswig-Holstein und der Nationalsozialismus*, 2nd ed. (Neumünster: Wachholtz Vlg., 2006), 40.

43. Allan Borup, *Demokratisierungsprozesse in der Nachkriegszeit: Die CDU in Schleswig-Holstein und die Integration demokratieskeptischer Wähler* (Bielefeld: Vlg. f. Regionalgeschichte, 2010), 132.

44. LSH, Abt. 352, Itzehoe, Nr. 418, Nervenärztliches Gutachten, March 21, 1955, pp. 33–34.

45. LSH, Abt 352, Itzehoe, Nr. 413, p. 33, April 22, 1954.

46. LSH, Abt. 352, Itzehoe, Nr. 418, Nervenärztliches Gutachten, March 21, 1955, pp. 35–36.

47. LSH, Abt. 352, Itzehoe, Nr. 418, Nervenärztliches Gutachten, March 21, 1955, p. 34.

48. LSH, Abt. 352, Itzehoe, Nr. 418, Nervenärztliches Gutachten, March 21, 1955, pp. 38–39.

49. LSH, Abt 352, Itzehoe, Nr. 413, pp. 33–34, April 22, 1954; LSH, Abt. 352, Itzehoe, Nr. 418, Nervenärztliches Gutachten, March 21, 1955, p. 49.

50. LSH, Abt 352, Itzehoe, Nr. 413, p. 33, April 22, 1954.

51. LSH, Abt. 352, Itzehoe, Nr. 413, Gutachte, Aktenauszug, March 21, 1955, pp. 30–33.

52. LSH, Abt. 352, Itzehoe, Nr. 418, Nervenärztliches Gutachten, March 21, 1955, pp. 46–47, 73.

53. LSH, Abt. 352, Itzehoe, Nr. 418, Nervenärztliches Gutachten, March 21, 1955, pp. 34, 36.

54. LSH, Abt 352, Itzehoe, Nr. 413, p. 35, April 22, 1954.

55. LSH, Abt. 460.16, Nr. 219; LSH, Abt 352, Itzehoe, Nr. 413, p. 17, April 8, 1954.

56. LSH, Abt. 352, Itzehoe, Nr. 414, statement by Walter, October 19, 1954.

57. LSH, Abt. 351, Nr. 1130, p. 26, Abschrift, November 11, 1954.

58. LSH, Abt. 352, Nr. 414, statement by Käthe, October 19, 1954.

59. Jeanne Favret-Saada, *Deadly Words*, 63, 169; *Anti-Witch*, introduction, x.

60. Danker and Schwabe, *Schleswig-Holstein und der Nationalsozialismus*, 176, 183.

61. Gerolimatos, "Structural Change and Democratization," 111; Jessica Jürgens, "Entnazifizierungspraxis in Schleswig-Holstein: Eine Fallstudie f. den

Kreis Rendsburg, 1946–49," *Zeitschrift der Gesellschaft f. Schleswig-Holsteinische Geschichte*, Band 125 (Neumünster, 2000), 150–51.

62. Gerolimatos, "Structural Change and Democratization," 111.

63. Gerolimatos, "Structural Change and Democratization," 111–13; Jürgens, "Entnazifizierungspraxis in Schleswig-Holstein," 169.

64. Jürgens, "Entnazifizierungspraxis in Schleswig-Holstein," 169–71.

65. Hans Fallada, *Nightmare in Berlin,* trans. Allen Blunden (Melbourne: Scribe, 2016), 69.

66. Baumhauer, *Johann Kruse,* 265, 269.

67. Michel de Certeau, *The Possession at Loudun,* trans. Michael B. Smith (Chicago: University of Chicago Press, 1996), 27–28.

68. LSH, Abt. 352, Itzehoe, Nr. 413, Gutachte, Aktenauszug, p. 2.

69. LSH, Abt 352, Itzehoe, Nr. 413, p. 62, June 12, 1954.

70. As numerous clippings in LSH, Abt. 352, Itzehoe, Nr. 416 attest.

71. "Der Hexer von Sarzbüttel," *Hamburger Abendblatt,* Nr. 235, Jahrgang 7, October 9–10, 1954, p. 16.

72. LSH, Abt. 352, Itzehoe, Nr. 419, p. 23, Landgericht in Itzehoe from Pinneberg, Holstein, October 10, 1954.

73. LSH, Abt. 352, Itzehoe, Nr. 419, n.p., letter from Grünenthal, October 11, 1954.

74. LSH, Abt. 352, Itzehoe, Nr. 419, n.p., letter from Uelzen, October 21, 1954.

75. "Der Hexer von Sarzbüttel," *Hamburger Abendblatt,* Nr. 235, Jahrgang 7, October 9–10, 1954.

76. LSH, Abt. 352, Itzehoe, Nr. 418, Gutachte, March 21, 1955, pp. 28–29.

77. LSH, Abt. 352, Itzehoe, Nr. 418, Psychiatrische und Nervenklinik der Universität Kiel, nervenärztliches Gutachten, March 21, 1955, p. 73.

78. LSH, Abt. 352, Itzehoe, Nr. 418, Gutachte, Aktenauszug, March 21, 1955, p. 62. Dr. Völkel's "Spezialforschungsgebiet" according to later court documents, was superstition. See LSH, Abt. 352, Itzehoe, Nr. 413, p. 373, "Im Namen des Volkes," May 23, 1956.

79. LSH, Abt. 352, Itzehoe, Nr. 418, Psychiatrische und Nervenklinik der Universität Kiel, nervenärztliches Gutachten, March 21, 1955, pp. 66, 74.

80. LSH, Abt. 352, Itzehoe, Nr. 418, Gutachte, Aktenauszug, March 21, 1955, pp. 67, 69, 70.

81. LSH, Abt. 352, Itzehoe, Nr. 418, Gutachte, March 21, 1955, pp. 60–62, 66, 69, 70, 72, 78.

82. LSH, Abt. 352, Itzehoe, Nr. 418, Gutachte, March 21, 1955, pp. 51–53.

83. Baumhauer, *Johann Kruse,* 250.

84. LSH, Abt. 352, Itzehoe, Nr. 418, Gutachte, March 21, 1955, pp. 53–55.

85. LSH, Abt. 352, Itzehoe, Nr. 418, Gutachte, March 21, 1955, pp. 62, 71.

86. LSH, Abt. 352, Itzehoe, Nr. 418, Gutachte, March 21, 1955, p. 75.

87. LSH, Abt. 352, Itzehoe, Nr. 418, Gutachte, March 21, 1955, p. 80.

88. G. E. Störring, *Besinnung und Bewusstsein: Persönlichkeitsaufbau und Persönlichkeitszerfall aus psychologisch-pädagogischer, soziologischer und psychiatrischer Sicht* (Stuttgart: Georg Thieme Vlg., 1953), 91–94.

89. Störring, *Besinnung*, 97, 99, 100.

90. Störring, *Besinnung*, 102.

91. LSH, Abt. 352, Itzehoe, Nr. 418, Gutachte, March 21, 1955, p. 66.

92. LSH, Abt. 352, Itzehoe, Nr. 418, Gutachte, March 21, 1955, pp. 28–29, 74, 76.

93. LSH, Abt. 352, Itzehoe, Nr. 418, Gutachte, March 21, 1955, pp. 81–82, 84.

94. "'Satan' kam in Ochsenkarren," *Bersenbrücker Kreisblatt*, date stamped June 1, 1955. Clipping located in HH, Zgs. 2.1.

95. LSH, Abt. 351, Nr. 1130, Clippings from *Schleswig-Holstein Volkszeitung*, May 10–June 1, 1955.

96. "'Satan' kam in Ochsenkarren," *Bersenbrücker Kreisblatt*.

97. Oma C.: clippings from *Schleswig-Holstein Tagespost*, May 25, 1955, and *Südschleswigischen Heimatzeitung*, May 26, 1955; both in LSH, Abt. 351, Nr. 1130.

98. LSH, Abt. 352, Itzehoe Nr. 413, p. 232, "Im Namen des Volkes," June 9, 1955.

99. LSH, Abt. 352, Itzehoe Nr. 413, p. 236, "Im Namen des Volkes."

100. LSH, Abt. 352, Itzehoe Nr. 413, pp. 241–42, 249, 252, "Im Namen des Volkes."

101. LSH, Abt. 352, Itzehoe Nr. 413, pp. 247, 252, "Im Namen des Volkes."

102. LSH, Abt. 352, Itzehoe Nr. 413, pp. 248, 255, 256, "Im Namen des Volkes."

103. LSH, Abt. 352, Itzehoe Nr. 413, pp. 257, 259–60, 263, 265, "Im Namen des Volkes."

104. LSH, Abt. 352, Itzehoe Nr. 419, p. 89, Frau Arma H. to Herrn E., June 1, 1955.

105. LSH, Abt. 352, Itzehoe, Nr. 419, p. 109. Letter from Ehrenberg, October 21, 1955.

106. LSH, Abt. 352, Itzehoe Nr. 419, p. 87, Herr E. to Herrn Landgerichtsdirektor Rostock, June 2, 1955.

107. LSH, Abt. 352, Itzehoe, Nr. 413, pp. 279, 281–82, 284–85, Kremendahl, Revision.

108. BAK, B 142/3930/66–71. "Im Namen des Volkes," November 1, 1955.

109. LSH, Abt. 351, Nr. 1130, p. 41. Oberstaatsanwalt to Herrn Justizminister des Landes Schleswig-Holstein, April 28, 1956.

110. LSH, Abt. 352, Itzehoe, Nr. 413, p. 373, "Im Namen des Volkes," May 23, 1956.

111. Baumhauer, *Johann Kruse,* 222.

112. LSH, Abt. 352, Itzehoe, Nr. 418, p. 76, Gutachte, March 21, 1955.

113. LSH, Abt. 352, Itzehoe, Nr. 413, p. 373, "Im Namen des Volkes," May 23, 1956.

9. KRUSE'S CRUSADE

1. "Bis das Blut kommt," *Der Spiegel* 14, April 4, 1951, p. 10.

2. HH, Nds. 401, Acc. 112/83, Nr. 564, p. 8. An den Herrn Kulturminister in Niedersachsen, September 12, 1955.

3. Karl-Heinz Christiansen, "Hexenspuk in Heidedorf," no newspaper given, April 18, 1951, clipping in HH, ZGS 2.2, Nr. 247.

4. Baumhauer, *Johann Kruse,* 214–15.

5. LSH, Abt. 351, Nr. 1130, clipping from *Schleswig–Holstein Volkszeitung,* December 1, 1955.

6. "Eberling antwortet Kruse: Mich haben die Menschen gerufen!" *Schleswig–Holstein Volkszeitung,* December 8, 1955. Clipping located in LSH, Abt. 351, Nr. 1130.

7. Karin Lieven, "Die Hexen sind unter uns," [Münchner] *Merkur am Sonntag,* February 16–17, 1963. Clipping in EZA 180/44; Thomas Hauschild, "Hexen in Deutschland," in *Der Wissenschaftler und das Irrationale,* Band 1, Hans P. Duerr, ed. (Frankfurt: Syndikat, 1982), 556.

8. Otto-Morris, *Rebellion in the Province,* 19.

9. Joachim Whaley, *Religious Toleration and Social Change in Hamburg, 1529–1819* (London: Cambridge University Press, 1985), 146.

10. Baumhauer, *Johann Kruse,* 47–48, 63.

11. Baumhauer, *Johann Kruse,* 61.

12. Baumhauer, *Johann Kruse,* 25.

13. Bettina Goldberg, *Abseits der Metropolen: Die jüdische Minderheit in Schleswig-Holstein* (Neumünster: Wachholtz Vlg., 2011), notes that only around 2,000 Jews lived in Schleswig-Holstein before 1933, most in the larger cities of Kiel and Lübeck. Ulrich Lange, ed., *Geschichte Schleswig-Holsteins: Von den Anfängen bis zur Gegenwart* (Neumünster: Wachholtz, 1996), 549, cites a larger figure: 4,152. The discrepancy may possibly be accounted for in that Lange includes Hamburg-Altona, which was part of Schleswig-Holstein until 1937.

14. Kruse, *Hexenwahn in der Gegenwart* (Leipzig, 1923), 43. Cited in Christoph Daxelmüller, "Vorwort," in *Handwörterbuch des deutschen Aberglaubens* (hereafter: *HDA*), ed. Hanns-Bächtold-Stäubli (Berlin: De Gruyter, 2000), 25.

15. Cited in Daxelmüller, "Vorwort," 25.

16. Baumhauer, *Johann Kruse*, 71–72.

17. HH, Nds. 401, Acc. 112/83, Nr. 564, Johann Kruse an das Niedersächsische Kultusministerium, May 26, 1952; Hans J. Mesterharm, "Attacke gegen Hexenwahn," no newspaper given, November 25, 1953. Clipping in HH, ZGS 2.2, Nr. 247.

18. "Bis das Blut kommt," *Der Spiegel* 14, April 4, 1951, p. 10.

19. HH, Nds. 401, Acc. 112/83, Nr. 564, Johann Kruse an das Niedersächsische Kultusministerium, May 26, 1952.

20. HH, Nds. 401, Acc. 112/83, Nr. 564, Johann Kruse an das Niedersächsische Kultusministerium, May 26, 1952.

21. HH, Nds. 401, Acc. 112/83, Nr. 564, letter to Johann Kruse from Niedersächsische Kultusministerium, June 26, 1952.

22. Johann Kruse, *Hexen unter uns? Magie und Zauberglauben in unserer Zeit* (Hamburg: Verlag Hamburgische Bücherei, 1951), 141.

23. HH, Nds. 401, Acc. 112/83, Nr. 564, letter to Johann Kruse from Niedersächsische Kultusministerium, June 26, 1952; HH, Nds. 401, Acc. 112/83, Nr. 564, an Herrn J. Kruse, September 15, 1952.

24. HH, Nds. 401, Acc. 112/83, Nr. 564, letter to Johann Kruse from Niedersächsische Kultusministerium, June 26, 1952.

25. Kruse, *Hexen unter uns?*, 7–8.

26. HH, Nds. 401, Acc. 112/83, Nr. 564, J. Kruse to Niedersächsische Kultusministerium, July 24, 1952.

27. Hans J. Mesterharm, "Attacke gegen Hexenwahn," no newspaper given, November 25, 1953. Clipping in HH, ZGS 2.2, Nr. 247.

28. "Hexenverfolgung 'nach Vorschrift,'" *Die Ansage*, Nr. 216, February 16, 1955. Clipping in LSH, Abt. 352, Itzehoe, Nr. 419.

29. Martin Schneider, "Soldaten der Aufklärung," in *Okkultismus*, Lux and Palatschek, eds., 283, n. 29.

30. "Witchcraft in Germany," *Western Folklore* 15:1 (January 1956): 66, cites Reuters story in *Los Angeles Times*, July 31, 1955. Cited in Davies, *Grimoires*, 345–46, n. 104.

31. "Hexenverfolgung 'nach Vorschrift,'" *Die Ansage*, Nr. 216, February 16, 1955. Quote in "Hexenwahn in Schleswig-Holstein," *Südschleswigische Heimatzeitung*, January 26, 1955. Both clippings in LSH, Abt. 352, Itzehoe, Nr. 419.

32. *Neue Deutsche Wochenschau* for May 4, 1956, accessed on October 15, 2018 at https://www.filmothek.bundesarchiv.de/video/586223.

33. HH, Nds. 100, Acc 47/94, Nr. 63, Kruse to Niedersächsisches Ministerium des Innern, Hannover, December 29, 1955.

34. HH, Nds. 401, Acc 112/83, Nr. 564, Niedersächsisches Minister des Innern to Nieders. Kultusminister, Hannover, January 18, 1956.

35. HH, Nds. 100, Acc 47/94, Nr. 63. Landeskriminalamt Niedersachsen to Herrn Niedersächsischen Minister des Innern, January 28, 1956.

36. HH, Nds. 100, Acc. 47/94, Nr. 63, pp. 12–13, Landeskriminalpolizeiamt Niedersachsen to Niedersachsen Min. des Innern, March 16, 1956.

37. HH, Nds. 120, Lün. Acc. 108/84, Nr. 10, Abschrift, Bericht, n.d., presumably May 1956.

38. HH, Nds. 410, Acc. 112/83, Nr. 564, p. 33, Niedersächsische Minister des Innern an den Herrn Innenminister des Landes Schleswig-Holstein, October 23, 1956.

39. HH, Nds. 100, Acc. 47/94, Nr. 63, p. 19, Niedersächsische Sozialminister an die Herren Regierungspräsidenten, April 27, 1956. "Kampf gegen Aberglauben und Hexenwahn," *Osterholzer Kreisblatt*, May 12, 1956. Clipping in HH, VVP 17, Nr. 3558.

40. HH, Nds 100, Acc. 47/94, Nr. 63, p. 29, an Frau Ministerialrätin Mosolf, October 29, 1956; HH, Nds 401, Acc 112/83, Nr. 564, p. 32, Mosolf to Grabenhorst, November 6, 1956.

41. HH, Nds.100, Acc. 47/94, Nr. 63, pp. 31–32. Auszugsweise Abschrift aus dem Protokoll, October 30–31, 1956.

42. HH, Nds.100, Acc. 47/94, Nr. 63, pp. 31–32. Auszugsweise Abschrift aus dem Protokoll, October 30–31, 1956.

43. HH, Nds. 401, Acc. 112/83, Nr. 564, p. 30. Betr.: Hexenwahn heute noch und Kurpfuscherei aus Aberglauben, October 29, 1956.

44. HH, Nds.100, Acc. 47/94, Nr. 63, pp. 31–32. Auszugsweise Abschrift aus dem Protokoll, October 30–31, 1956.

45. "Die Hexenmeister sind unter uns," *Allgemeine Zeitung,* April 28–29, 1956, n.p. Clipping in HH, VVP 17, Nr. 3558; Rainer Schulze, "Verfolgt als Hexe!" *Welt am Sonntag*, Nr. 34, p. 2, August 21, 1955. Clipping in HH, Nds. 401, Acc 112/83, Nr. 564; Baumhauer, *Johann Kruse,* 85–86.

46. HH, Nds. 401, Acc 112/83, Nr. 564, p. 3, J. Kruse to Niedersächsische Kultusministerium, May 26, 1952; Hans J. Messerharm, "Attacke gegen Hexenwahn," no newspaper given, November 25, 1953. Clipping in HH, ZGS 2.2, Nr. 247; Rainer Schulze, "Verfolgt als Hexe!" *Welt am Sonntag*, Nr. 34, p. 2, August 21, 1955. Clipping in HH, Nds. 401, Acc 112/83, Nr. 564.

47. HH, Nds. 401, Acc 112/83, Nr. 564, J. Kruse to Ministerium des Innern, Hannover, August 31, 1954.

48. Rainer Schulze, "Verfolgt als Hexe!" *Welt am Sonntag*, Nr. 34, p. 2, August 21, 1955. Clipping in HH, Nds. 401, Acc 112/83, Nr. 564.

49. "Ermittlungsverfahren gegen Planet-Verlag," *Offenburger Tageblatt*, January 28, 1956. Clipping located in HH, Nds. 401, Acc 112/83, Nr.

564, p. 15; LSH, Abt. 352, Itzehoe, Nr. 418, Amtsgericht Braunschweig an Staatsanwaltschaften Itzehoe, October 15, 1956; Baumhauer, *Johann Kruse*, 85–87.

50. Davies, *Grimoires*, especially chapter 1.

51. Stephen Bachter, "Anleitung zum Aberglauben: Zauberbücher und die Verbreitung magischen 'Wissens' seit dem 18. Jahrhundert" (PhD diss., Universität Hamburg, 2005), 95–96.

52. Adolf Spamer, "Zauberbuch und Zauberspruch," *Deutsches Jahrbuch f. Volkskunde* 1 (1955): 117; Hauschild, "Hexen in Deutschland," 537; Bachter, "Anleitung zum Aberglauben," 112–13.

53. Davies, *Grimoires*, 248.

54. Kurlander, *Hitler's Monsters*, 110–14; Davies, *Grimoires*, 249–50.

55. As a search on the German antiquarian bookseller website ZVAB.de reveals.

56. *Das sechste und siebente Buch Moses*, F. H. Masuch, ed. (Braunschweig: Planet, 1950), 16–17.

57. Davies, *Grimoires*, 254; Bachter, "Anleitung zum Aberglauben," 136–37; Karl-Peter Wanderer, "Gedruckter Aberglaube: Studien zur volktümlichen Beschwörungsliteratur" (PhD diss., Frankfurt am Main, 1976), 27.

58. Philipp Schmidt, "Skandal in der Geschichte der deutschen Rechtsprechung," July 17, 1960, n.p. Clipping in HH, Nds. 401, Acc. 112/83, Nr. 564, 47.

59. Spamer, "Zauberbuch und Zauberspruch," 113.

60. A colleague who grew up in the Rhineland in the 1950s related this to me.

61. Schäfer, *Der Okkulttäter*, 106.

62. Claus Philip, "Gröning gegen Gröning," *Abendzeitung*, May 8, 1953. Clipping in IGPP, Busam Slg.

63. Schöck, *Hexenglaube in der Gegenwart*, 183.

64. LSH, Abt. 352, Itzehoe, Nr. 419, n.p., letter dated October 9, 1954.

65. Baumhauer, *Johann Kruse*, 232–33.

66. LSH, Abt. 352, Itzehoe, Nr. 413, Gutachte, March 21, 1955, p. 49.

67. LSH, Abt. 352, Itzehoe, Nr. 413, Gutachte, Aktenauszug, p. 30.

68. "Jude/Jüdin," *HDA*, 811–12, 815.

69. Kriß, "Heroldsbach: Eine verbotene Wallfahrt," 210.

70. Rudolf Kriß, "Heroldsbach, Statistiken und jüngste Entwicklung," *Bayerisches Jahrbuch für Volkskunde 1955* (Regensburg: Vlg. Josef Habbel, 1955), 111. The pamphlet was titled "The Salvation of Mankind, the Mystery of Franconia."

71. A. Jacoby, "Mosis, das sechste und siebente Buch," *HDA*, Band 6, 587.

72. Davies, *Grimoires*, 253.

73. Susan Neiman, *Slow Fire: Jewish Notes from Berlin* (New York: Schocken, 1992), 39–40.

74. Ra'anan Boustan and Joseph E. Sanzo, "Christian Magicians, Jewish Magical Idioms, and the Shared Magical Culture of Late Antiquity," *Harvard Theological Review* 110:2 (2017): 221.

75. Boustan and Sanzo, "Christian Magicians," 221.

76. Bronislaw Malinowski, *Coral Gardens and Their Magic: A Study of the Methods of Tilling the Soil and of Agricultural Rites in the Trobriand Islands*, vol. II (Allen & Unwin, 1935), 214, 218.

77. Davies, *Grimoires*, 30–31, 74–5. The meaning for the Nazis of Jewish culture's originary status is the theme of Confino, *A World Without Jews*.

78. Court documents of the Moses books trials appear no longer to exist. What can be known of the proceedings must be pieced together from the press and contemporary accounts, including those penned by Will-Erich Peuckert and Otto Prokop. See Peuckert, *Verborgenes Niedersachsen: Untersuchungen zur Niedersächsischen Volkssage und zum Volksbuch* (Göttingen: Vlg. Otto Schwartz, 1960); and A. Eigner and O. Prokop, "Das sechste und siebente Buch Moses: Zur Frage der Kriminogenität von Büchern und besonders laienmedizinischen Schundliteratur," in *Medizinischer Okkultismus: Paramedizin* (Stuttgart: Gustav Fischer Vlg., 1964).

79. Baumhauer, *Johann Kruse*, 88, 91; Schäfer, *Der Okkulttäter*, 55.

80. Peuckert, *Verborgenes Niedersachsen*, 124.

81. Johanna Micaela Jacobsen, "Boundary Breaking and Compliance: Will-Erich Peuckert and Twentieth-Century German *Volkskunde*" (PhD diss., Folklore and Folklife, University of Pennsylvania, 2007), 3; the entry was one of 110 Peuckert published in the *HDA*.

82. "Jude/Jüdin," *HDA*, 817.

83. Thomas Hauschild, "Hexen in Deutschland," in *Der Wissenschaftler und das Irrationale,* vol. 1 (1981), 559.

84. Jacobsen, "Boundary Breaking," 48.

85. Jacobsen, "Boundary Breaking," 57–58, 61, 89.

86. Daxelmüller, "Vorwort," 41–42.

87. LSH, Abt. 605, Nr. 537, Innenmin. des Landes Schleswig-Holstein an die Landeskanzlei, May 14, 1957.

88. Baumhauer, *Johann Kruse*, 88.

89. "Hexenspuk in der Heide," *Grafschafter Nachrichten*, December 22, 1956, n.p. Clipping in HH, VVP 17, Nr. 3558.

90. HH, Nds. 100, Acc. 47/94, Nr. 63, p. 34, Niedersächsische Sozialminister an Herrn J. Kruse, March 7, 1957.

91. Rolf Seufert, "Geschäft mit dem Aberglauben," newspaper not given, May 20, 1957. Clipping in HH, ZGS 2.2, Nr. 247.

92. LSH, Abt. 605, Nr. 537, Innenminister des Landes Schleswig-Holstein an

den Herrn Justizminister, Kiel, betr.: Bekämpfung der neuzeitlichen Hexen-wahns, December 12, 1957.

93. LSH, Abt. 605, Nr. 537, Vermerk, November 29, 1957.

94. Mark Benecke, *Seziert: Das Leben von Otto Prokop* (Berlin: Das Neue Berlin, 2013).

95. Baumhauer, *Johann Kruse*, 89–90.

96. Baumhauer, *Johann Kruse*, 90, 93.

97. Peuckert makes these insinuations in *Verborgenes Niedersachsen*. See also HH, Nds. 401, Acc. 112/83, Nr. 564, 50. Vermerk, November 4, 1960.

98. HH, Nds. 401, Acc. 112/83, Nr. 564, 50. Vermerk, November 4, 1960.

99. HH, Nds. 401, Acc. 112/83, Nr. 564, 45, Kruse an das Niedersächsische Kultusministerium, September 26, 1960; and HH, Nds. 401, Acc. 112/83, Nr. 564, 51, an Herrn Johann Kruse, December 5, 1960.

100. HH, Nds. 401, Acc. 112/83, Nr. 564, 45. Kruse to Niedersächsisches Kultusministerium, September 26, 1960.

101. HH, Nds. 401, Acc. 112/83, Nr. 564, 51, an Herrn Johann Kruse, December 5, 1960.

10. DAWN OF THE NEW AGE

1. Uta G. Poiger, *Jazz, Rock, and Rebels: Cold War Politics and American Culture in a Divided Germany* (Berkeley: University of California Press, 2000).

2. Wolfgang Benz, "Postwar Society and National Socialism: Remembrance, Amnesia, Rejection," in *Tel Aviver Jahrbuch f. deutsche Geschichte* 19 (1990), 8.

3. Julius P. F. Hütt, "Auf der Anklagebank: Bruno Gröning," *Kriminal Illustrierte*, May 15, 1957; "War es fahrlässige Tötung?" *Gong*, March 16, 1957. Clippings in IGPP.

4. "Gröning, Die Karriere eines Scharlatans," *7 Tage*, n.d. (presumably July 1957), clipping in IGPP (no further information given on document); "Grönings Weg zum Wunderheiler," *7 Tage*, (day illegible) July 1957, clipping in IGPP, PA 031a.

5. StAM, Staatsanwaltschaften 3178/4, p. 724, Otto Meckelburg, June 1951; StAM, Staatsanwaltschaften 3178/4, p. 719, Otto Meckelburg, betr.: Eidestattliche Erklärung, June 3, 1951. Mildenberger, "Heilstrom," n. 88 suggests that Enderlin "surprised" police with news about Ruth, citing StAM 3178/1, Vernehmung, Eugen Enderlin, June 23, 1953. But Meckelburg seems to have informed them earlier.

6. "Zwecks Heilung vorsprechen," *Der Spiegel 23*, June 6, 1951, p. 7.

7. StAM, Staatsanwaltschaften 3178a/1, p. 142, Landespolizei Säckingen/ Baden, Ersuchen der Krim. Außenstelle Fürstenfeldbruck, October 19, 1954.

8. StAM, Staatsanwaltschaften 3178a/1, p. 144, Staatliches Gesundheitsamt Säckingen an die Landespolizei Säckingen, November 5, 1954; StAM, Staatsanwaltschaften 3178a/3, p. 437, Protokoll, August 1, 1957.

9. StAM, Staatsanwaltschaften 3178a/3, pp. 437–38, Protokoll, August 1, 1957.

10. StAM, Staatsanwaltschaften 3178a/1, p. 144, Staatliches Gesundheitsamt Säckingen an die Landespolizei Säckingen, November 5, 1954; StAM, Staatsanwaltschaften 3178a/3, p. 437, Protokoll, August 1, 1957.

11. StAM, Staatsanwaltschaften 3178a/1, pp. 144–45, Staatliches Gesundheitsamt Säckingen an die Landespol. Säckingen, betr. B. Gröning wegen Verdachts der fahrl. Tötung, November 5, 1954.

12. StAM, Staatsanwaltschaften 3178a/3, pp. 431, 433, Protokoll, August 1, 1957.

13. StAM, Staatsanwaltschaften 3178a/3, 435, Protokoll, July–August 1957.

14. StAM, Staatsanwaltschaften 3178/1/145a, Gemeinschaft zur Erforschung und Unterstützung Grön'scher an Herrn K., February 12, 1950.

15. StAM, Staatsanwaltschaften 3178a/1, pp. 144–45, Staatliches Gesundheitsamt Säckingen an die Landespol. Säckingen, betr. B. Gröning wegen Verdachts der fahrl. Tötung, November 5, 1954.

16. StAM, Staatsanwaltschaften 3178/1/145h, K. to Meckelburg, March 28, 1950.

17. StAM, Staatsanwaltschaften 3178a/2, p. 10, K. to Meckelburg, May 6, 1950.

18. StAM, Staatsanwaltschaften 3178a/2, p. 12, K. to Gröning, May 15, 1950.

19. StAM, Staatsanwaltschaften 3178a/2, p. 15, K. to Meckelburg, June 17, 1950.

20. StAM, Staatsanwaltschaften 3178a/3, pp. 431–32, Protokoll, August 1, 1957.

21. StAM, Staatsanwaltschaften 3178a/2, Ruth K's letters to Gröning, May–June 1950.

22. StAM, Staatsanwaltschaften 3178a/2, p. 15, K. to Gröning, June 17, 1950.

23. StAM, Staatsanwaltschaften 3178a/2, p. 23, K. to Gröning, October 4, 1950.

24. StAM, Staatsanwaltschaften 3178a/2, p. 25, K. to Enderlin, October 11, 1950.

25. StAM, Staatsanwaltschafen 3178a/3, p. 425, Protokoll, August 1, 1957.

26. StAM, Staatsanwaltschaften 3178a/2, p. 26, K. to Gröning, November 1, 1950.

27. StAM, Staatsanwaltschaften 3178a/2, p. 30, K. to Enderlin, December 5, 1950.

28. StAM, Staatsanwaltschaften 3178a/2, p. 32, K. to Enderlin, December 18, 1950.

29. StAM, Staatsanwaltschaften 3178a/2, p. 141, K. to Gröning, January 7, 1951.

30. "Die Wunderkur brachte ihr den Tod," *Süddeutsche Zeitung*, Nr. 172, July 19, 1957. Clipping in IGPP. One paper said Herr K. died of an embolism: "Ein Mädchen zerbricht an Gröning," *Abendzeitung*, Nr. 92, April 26, 1955, p. 3, clipping in IGPP, Busam Slg.

31. StAM, Staatsanwaltschaften 3178a/1, p. 136, Bay. Landespolizei, Vernehmungsniederschrift von Enderlin, August 18, 1954.

32. StAM 3178/4, Oberstaatsanwalt Munich II, January 18, 1951.

33. StAM, Staatsanwaltschaften 3178a/2, p. 173, Anklageschrift, March 7, 1955.

34. StAM, Staatsanwaltschaften 3178a/1, Landratsamt Starnberg, Abt. II, Vermerkung, November 22, 1952.

35. StAM, Staatsanwaltschaften 3178a/1, Bayerische Landpolizei, Kriminalaußenstelle Fürstenfeldbruck, March 1, 1953.

36. StAM, Staatsanwaltschaften 3178a/1, pp. 46–47, Landeskriminalpolizei, Außenstelle Hameln, August 5, 1953; StAM, Staatsanwaltschaften 3178a/1, p. 53, Staatl. Gesundheitsamt an die Stadtverwaltung Hameln, September 15, 1953.

37. StAM, Staatsanwaltschaften 3178a/1, p. 95, Niederschrift, Michelson, October 23, 1953.

38. "Herr Gröning und seine Grönium," *Süddeutsche Zeitung*, Nr. 113, May 19, 1951. Clipping in StAM, Polizeidirektion 15558, p. 162. StAM, Polizeidirektion München, 15558, p. 168, betr.: Verhandlung gegen Bruno Gröning [und] Mitangeklagten, March 19, 1952; StAM, Staatsanwaltschaften 3178/3, Begläubigte Abschrift, Urteil, May 27, 1952. StAM, Polizeidirektion München, 15558, pp. 171, 173, clippings from *Münchner Merkur* (No. 144) and *Abendzeitung* (No. 155), both dated July 9, 1952. In January 1952, Gröning also stood trial for fraud, extortion, and violating a law concerning public gatherings in the southern Bavarian locale of Garmisch-Partenkirchen. StAM, Staatsanwaltschaften 3178/6, "Eingestellt in Richtung gegen Bruno Gröning," January 21, 1952.

39. StAM, Staatsanwaltschaften 3178a/1, Baerische [*sic*] Landpolizei, Landpolizei Station Moorenweis, Vernehmungsniederschrift, March 5, 1953.

40. StAM, Staatsanwaltschaften 3178a/3, Anwalt Reuss to Bruno Gröning, April 10, 1952.

41. "Legal illegality": "Was macht Gröning heute?" *Grüne Blatt,* Jhg. 6, Nr. 5, February 1, 1953. Clipping in IGPP E 123/100.

42. "Gröning Anhänger weinen," *Abendzeitung,* November 23, 1953. Clipping located in IGPP/Busam Sammlung, PA 214.

43. Friedrich Retlow, *Bruno Gröning's Heilstrom: Seine Natur und seine Wirkung* (n.p., n.d., ca. 1953), 3.

44. "Geht der Rummel wieder los?" n.p., n.d. (presumably 1953). Clipping in IGPP, PA 012.

45. StAM, Staatsanwaltschaften 3178a/1, Bayerische Landpolizei, Kriminal-außenstelle Fürstenfeldbruck, an die Staatsanwaltschaften beim Landgericht München I, March 1, 1953. StAM, Staatsanwaltschaften 3178a/1, Krim. Pol. Stuttgart, statement from Privatgelehrter Bruno Gröning, January 31, 1955.

46. StAM, Staatsanwaltschaften 3178a/1, pp. 159–60, Krim. Pol. Stuttgart, statement from . . . Privatgelehrter Bruno Gröning, January 31, 1955.

47. StAM, Staatsanwaltschaften 3178a, p. 144. Staatliches Gesundheitsamt Saeckingen an die Landespol. Saeckingen, betr. Bruno Gröning wegen Verdachts der fahrl. Tötung, November 5, 1954.

48. StAM, Staatsanwaltschaften 3178a/1, pp. 159–60. Krim. Pol. Stuttgart, statement, Privatgelehrter Bruno Gröning, January 31, 1955.

49. StAM, Staatsanwaltschaften 3178a/3, pp. 367–69, Landespolizei Nürtingen, betr.: Ermittlungsverfahren gegen B. Gröning, June 25, 1956; Erwin Gamber, *Luzifers Griff nach der Lebenden* (Bietingheim: Turm Vlg., ca. 1954), 56, 63, 64.

50. StAM, Staatsanwaltschaften 3178a/3, 429, Protokoll, July 30–August 1, 1957.

51. StAM, Staatsanwaltschaften 3178a/2, Erfolgsberichte, n.d., presumably recorded in 1957.

52. Anna Lux, "Passing Through the Needle's Eye: Dimensionen der universitären Integration der Parapsychologie in Deutschland und den USA," in Lux and Palatschek, eds., *Okkultismus.*

53. Inge Strauch, "Die 'geistigen' Heilungen von Dr. rer. Pol. Trampler," in Wilhelm Bitter, ed., *Magie und Wunder in der Heilkunde: Ein Tagungsbericht* (Stuttgart: Ernst Klett Vlg., 1959), 125–29.

54. A. Jores, "Magie und Zauber in der modernen Medizin," *Deutsche medizinische Wochenschrift,* 80. Jhg., Nr. 24, June 17, 1955.

55. Harrington, *Reenchanted Science;* Mitchell G. Ash, *Gestalt Psychology in German Culture, 1890–1967: Holism and the Quest for Objectivity*

(Cambridge, UK: Cambridge University Press, 1995); Christopher Lawrence and George Weisz, eds., *Greater Than the Parts: Holism in Biomedicine, 1920–1950* (Oxford, UK: Oxford University Press, 1998).

56. Erwin Liek, *Das Wunder in der Heilkunde* (Munich: Lehmanns Vlg., 1930), 175–76. See also Michael Hau, *The Cult of Health and Beauty in Germany: A Social History, 1890–1930* (Chicago: University of Chicago Press, 2005); and Susanne Michl, "'Gehe hin, dein Glaube hat dir geholfen': Kriegswunder und Heilsversprechen in der Medizin des 20. Jahrhunderts," in Geppert and Kössler, eds., *Wunder*, 211–36.

57. Paul Mevissen, "Der Mann mit dem Zeichen Rasputins," *Frankfurter Nachtausgabe*, April 22, 1955, p. 4. Clipping in Stadtarchiv Rosenheim.

58. "Gröning: 'Dieser Prozeß ist f. mich eine Erholung,'" *Abendpost*, August 1, 1957, clipping in IGPP, PA 029; "Gröning sagt: Ich kann gar nicht heilen!" *Münchner Merkur*, July 31, 1957, clipping in Stadtarchiv München, 167/14, Personen, Gröning, Bruno, Wunderdoktor; "Gröning verurteilt und freigesprochen," *Münchner Merkur*, August 2, 1957, p. 4, clipping in IGPP, PA 026.

59. "Gröning geht vor Gericht!" *Revue*, Nr. 31, August 3, 1957, p. 9. Clipping in IGPP (no further information given on document).

60. "Der Dämon ist entzaubert," *Bild*, 6. Jhg., Nr. 176, August 1, 1957, p. 18. Clipping in IGPP/E 123/100.

61. "Gröning sagt: ich kann gar nicht heilen!" *Münchner Merkur*, July 31, 1957. Clipping in Stadtarchiv München, 167/14, Personen, Gröning, Bruno, Wunderdoktor.

62. StAM, Staatsanwaltschaften 3178a/3, pp. 419–22, Protokoll, August 1, 1957.

63. StAM, Staatsanwaltschaften 3178a/3, pp. 423, 424–25, Protokoll, August 1, 1957.

64. StAM, Staatsanwaltschaften 3178a/2, p. 296. Psychiatrische und Nervenklinik . . . der Universität Freiburg, an dem Schöffengericht München-Land, February 9, 1957.

65. StAM, Staatsanwaltschaften 3178a/3, pp. 423–24, Protokoll, August 1, 1957.

66. StAM, Staatsanwaltschaften 3178a/3, pp. 425–26, Protokoll, August 1, 1957.

67. StAM, Staatsanwaltschaften 3178a/3, pp. 426–27, 429, Protokoll, August 1, 1957.

68. StAM, Staatsanwaltschaften 3178a/3, p. 432, Protokoll, August 1, 1957. Sunglasses: "Bittere Anklage einer Mutter gegen Gröning," *Bild*, 6. Jhg., Nr. 176, August 1, 1957, p. 1. Clipping in IGPP/E 123/100.

69. "Heilen Sie auch Krebs?" *Der Spiegel* 29, July 14, 1954, pp. 12–15.

70. StAM, Staatsanwaltschaften 3178a/3, pp. 434, 435, 437–38, Protokoll, August 1, 1957.

71. StAM, Staatsanwaltschaften 3178a/3, p. 441, Protokoll, August 1, 1957.

72. "Der Fall Bruno Gröning," *Welt am Sonntag*, August 4, 1957. Clipping in IGPP (no further information on document).

73. StAM, Staatsanwaltschaften 3178a/3, p. 446, Urteil, August 1, 1957.

74. Dirk Blasius, "Tuberkulose: Signalkrankheit deutscher Geschichte," *Geschichte in Wissenschaft und Unterricht* 1 (1996): 329–30.

75. Winfried Süss, *Der "Volkskörper" im Krieg: Gesundheitspolitik, Gesundheitsverhältnisse und Krankenmord im nationalsozialistischen Deutschland* (Munich: Oldenbourg Vlg., 2003), 138, 319–22, 254.

76. StAM, Staatsanwaltschaften 3178a/3, p. 449, Urteil, August 1, 1957.

77. StAM, Staatsanwaltschaften 3178a/2, pp. 277, 282. Jung an das Schöffengericht, February 9, 1957.

78. StAM, Staatsanwaltschaften 3178a/2, pp. 292, 293–94. Psychiatrische und Nervenklinik . . . der Universität Freiburg, an dem Schöffengericht München-Land, February 9, 1957.

79. StAM, Staatsanwaltschaften 3178a/2, pp. 293–94.

80. StAM, Staatsanwaltschaften 3178a/2, pp. 297–303.

81. StAM, Staatsanwaltschaften 3178a/3, Urteil, January 14–16, 1958.

82. StAM, Staatsanwaltschaften 3178a/3, letters from Böttcher, Liebner, Zimmermann, and Bundesführer der Partei der guten Deutschen, dated January 15–21, 1958. On Unger: "Die guten Deutschen von Plaidt," *Die Zeit*, Nr. 35, August 29, 1957.

83. StAM, Staatsanwaltschaften 3178a/3, 496–97, Revisionsbegründung, March 28, 1958.

84. StAM, Staatsanwaltschaften 3178a/3, p. 544, begl. Anschrift, betr. Bruno Gröning wegen fhl. Tötung, February 21, 1959.

85. "Nachruf: Bruno Gröning," *Der Spiegel* 6, February 4, 1959, p. 62.

CONCLUSION

1. "Der Hexenspuk in Mailach," *Süddeutsche Zeitung*, June 6, 1962; Hans Morper, "Die 'Hexe' sollte in ihrem Haus verbrennen," *Stuttgarter Zeitung,* June 7, 1962. Clippings in EZA 180/44.

2. LSH, Abt. 605, Nr. 537, Innenmin. des Landes Schleswig-Holstein an den Herrn Ministerpräsidenten, May 19, 1961.

3. LSH, Abt. 605, Nr. 537, Vermerk, June 8, 1961.

4. Leopold Schmidt, "Die Wiederkehr des Volksglaubens: Versuch einer Umschau nach dem Zweiten Weltkrieg," in Leopold Schmidt, ed.,

Volksglaube und Volksbrauch: Gestalten, Gebilde, Gebärden (Berlin: E. Schmidt Vlg., 1966).

5. Karl-Heinz Kallenbach, "Ist die Welle des 'Hexenwahns' vorbei?" *Frank-furter Rundschau*, August 28, 1965, p. 68. Clipping in EZA 180/44.

6. Kallenbach, "Ist die Welle des 'Hexenwahns' vorbei?"

7. "Rätsel um den Tod Grönings," *7 Tage*, February 14, 1959. Clipping in KAH, S Slg. E/E60.

8. "Viele Fragen nach Grönings Grab," *Bild*, date unclear, presumably 1960. Clipping in KAH, S Slg. E/E60.

9. Paul Mevissen and Werner Schmidt, "Mein Leben mit Bruno Gröning," *Neue Illustrierte*, June 20, 1965, p. 65. Clipping in KAH, S Slg. E/E60.

10. Colin Dickey, "The Suburban Horror of the Indian Burial Ground," *The New Republic*, October 19, 2019.

11. Monica Black, "The Supernatural and the Poetics of History," *Hedgehog Review* 13:3 (Fall 2011): 72–81.

12. Avery F. Gordon, *Ghostly Matters: Haunting and the Sociological Imagi-nation* (Minneapolis: University of Minnesota Press, 2008), 98.

ACKNOWLEDGMENTS

It is my privilege to have this chance to thank all the people and institutions without whose help I could not have researched and written *A Demon-Haunted Land*.

The University of Tennessee, Knoxville, gave me the time and some of the funding required to complete the book. Humanities education at public universities is increasingly endangered in the United States today, but UTK continues to work for the common good by providing faculty with the resources necessary to conduct inquiries into the human experience. The work our state universities do, often under great pressure—ideological, financial, and otherwise—should never be forgotten or overlooked.

My home department, the history department, is a tremendously stimulating place in which to teach and think. Chad Black, Ernie Freeberg, Luke Harlow, Vejas Liulevicius, Tore Olsson, Victor Petrov, Denise Philips, and Shellen Wu, as well as historian members of the Medical Humanities research seminar sponsored by UTK's Humanities Center—Kristen Block, Nikki Eggers, and Sara Ritchey—and my (now former) UTK colleagues, Jay Rubenstein and Tom Burman, were especially supportive.

At a variety of archives and libraries, I was assisted by accomplished professionals who made my work better and easier. In particular, I would like to thank Christoph Laue at the Kommunalarchiv Herford; Elisabeth Angermair and Anton Löffelmeier, Stadtarchiv München; Dr. Robert Bierscheider, Staatsarchiv München; Sven Schön at the Landesarchiv Schleswig-Holstein; and Eberhard Bauer and Uwe Schellinger at the Institut für Grenzgebiete der Psychologie und Psychohygiene in Freiburg. Ruth Pabst at the Evangelisches Zentralarchiv in Berlin has now helped me with not one but two book projects. The interlibrary services staff at Hodges Library at UTK may have despaired about whether I would ever return a loan on time, even once. I thank them for their hard work on my behalf and for long years of forbearance. I thank Herr Hanken of Wangerooge for sharing his personal Bruno Gröning collection with me one lovely day.

Sharing my work at various stages helped me understand what kind of book I was trying to write. I am grateful to all of the following institutions for offering me that chance: the Institute for Advanced Studies in Culture at the University of Virginia; the Shelby Cullom Davis Center at Princeton University; the Max Planck Institute for Human Development, Berlin; the Brian Bertoti graduate student conference at Virginia Tech; the Dorothy Lambert Whisnant Lecture on Women's History, Clemson University; St. Anthony's College, University of Oxford; the German Studies Association; the American Academy in Berlin; the University of Heidelberg's Heidelberg Center for American Studies; the XXIII Bath House Readings at Memorial International Society in Moscow; the Modern Europe Colloquium at Yale University; the Selma Stern Zentrum für Jüdische Studien Berlin-Brandenburg at the Humboldt University in Berlin; the Max Kade Center for European Studies at Vanderbilt University; the European History Colloquium at Indiana University; and the Religious Studies department at Williams College. My personal thanks go to

Dan Rodgers, Yair Mintzker, Joachim Häberlen, Michael Meng, Paul Betts, Steve Smith, Irina Prokhorova, Adam Tooze, Stefanie Schüler-Springorum, Stefanie Fischer, Joy Calico, Michelle Moyd, Mark Roseman, Jason Ā. Josephson-Storm, and Grant Shoffstall.

I benefited greatly from fellowships from the American Council of Learned Societies and the American Academy in Berlin. This would not have been the same book if I had not had the chance, at the very beginning, to work among the extraordinary fellows at the AAB. Talking each day not only with brilliant and accomplished scholars but also artists and writers taught me more than many a faculty colloquium has. Thanks to the wonderful AAB staff, and all the fall 2014 fellows—Beatriz Colomina, Dan Eisenberg, Myles Jackson, Anthony McCall, Mark Meadow, Dan Rosenberg, Adam Ross, Hillel Schwartz, Louise Walker, and Marjorie Woods—and their delightful partners and families. My friend, novelist and editor Adam Ross, also did me the great honor of publishing a piece of what became this book in the *Sewanee Review*.

Three fantastic historians I am lucky enough to call my friends read the whole manuscript and offered extensive comments: Ellen Boucher, Alon Confino, and Eric Kurlander. I cannot thank them enough for the gift of their time, comradeship, insight, and care.

Many friends answered writing questions, helped with research puzzles, gave advice about publishing, and provided moral support and hours of conversation both serious and delightful over the years: David Bernardy, Paul Betts, Dorothee Brantz, Alon Confino, Winson Chu, Jen Evans, Michael Geyer, Svenja Goltermann, Yuliya Komska, Molly Loberg, Michael Meng, Erik Midelfort, Michelle Moyd, Till van Rahden, Mark Roseman, Catherine and Garriy Shteynberg, Nick Stargardt, and Joni Tevis. Thanks, my friends!

Teaching is one of the best ways to work out research ideas, and students in my fall 2016 Medicine in the Third Reich course gave me some space to experiment. Tremendous thanks to Jasmine, Jamie, Alex, Jordan, Michael, Sydni, Spencer, Caitlin, Kaitlyn, Madeline, Elizabeth, Tory, Heather, Kristi, Jeremy, Meg, and Maggie.

My agent, Deborah Grosvenor, deserves more than thanks. She deserves a medal. She worked with me for years on a book proposal and then introduced me to the extraordinary Sara Bershtel. Working with a publisher of Sara's reputation, rigor, and brilliance has been an honor. Great thanks to Sara and to her team at Metropolitan, especially the wonderful Grigory Tovbis.

One person makes life and everything in it more interesting and conspiratorial, in the best possible way, every day. Matthew Gillis is the cosmic center, for me, of everything.

INDEX

ABOUT THE AUTHOR

MONICA BLACK is a professor of history at the University of Tennessee and the author of *Death in Berlin: From Weimar to Divided Germany*, which won the prestigious Fraenkel Prize, among other awards. She lives in Knoxville.